To Howard

D0661014

Blessings on your

Labors for Christ

here @ Ambrose — th

is a mighty good work

work for Christ!!

THE END OF EVANGELICALISM?
DISCERNING A NEW FAITHFULNESS FOR MISSION

THEOPOLITICAL VISIONS

SERIES EDITORS:

Thomas Heilke
D. Stephen Long
and C. C. Pecknold

Theopolitical Visions seeks to open up new vistas on public life, hosting fresh conversations between theology and political theory. This series assembles writers who wish to revive theopolitical imagination for the sake of our common good.

Theopolitical Visions hopes to re-source modern imaginations with those ancient traditions in which political theorists were often also theologians. Whether it was Jeremiah's prophetic vision of exiles "seeking the peace of the city," Plato's illuminations on piety and the civic virtues in the Republic, St. Paul's call to "a common life worthy of the Gospel," St. Augustine's beatific vision of the City of God, or the gothic heights of medieval political theology, much of Western thought has found it necessary to think theologically about politics, and to think politically about theology. This series is founded in the hope that the renewal of such mutual illumination might make a genuine contribution to the peace of our cities.

FORTHCOMING VOLUMES:

Mark Ryan
The Politics of Practical Reason: The Church at the Margin of Moral Theory

Michael L. Budde
The Borders of Baptism: Identities, Allegiances, and the Church

John C. Nugent
The Politics of YHWH: John Howard Yoder, the Old Testament, and Social Ethics

Peter J. Leithart
Empire: A Biblical and Augustinian Analysis

The End of
EVANGELICALISM?
Discerning a New Faithfulness for Mission

Towards an Evangelical

Political Theology

DAVID E. FITCH

 CASCADE *Books* · Eugene, Oregon

THE END OF EVANGELICALISM? DISCERNING A NEW FAITHFULNESS
FOR MISSION
Towards an Evangelical Political Theology

Theopolitical Visions 8

Copyright © 2011 David E. Fitch. All rights reserved. Except for brief quotations in
critical publications or reviews, no part of this book may be reproduced in any manner
without prior written permission from the publisher. Write: Permissions, Wipf and
Stock Publishers, 199 W. 8th Ave., Suite 3, Eugene, OR 97401.

Cascade Books
An Imprint of Wipf and Stock Publishers
199 W. 8th Ave., Suite 3
Eugene, OR 97401

www.wipfandstock.com

Revised Standard Version of the Bible, copyright 1952 [2nd edition, 1971] by the
Division of Christian Education of the National Council of the Churches of Christ in
the United States of America. Used by permission. All rights reserved.

All scripture quotations, unless otherwise indicated, are taken from the Holy Bible,
New International Version®, NIV®. Copyright ©1973, 1978, 1984 by Biblica, Inc.™ Used
by permission of Zondervan. All rights reserved worldwide. www.zondervan.com

Scripture quotations taken from the New American Standard Bible®, Copyright
© 1960, 1962, 1963, 1968, 1971, 1972, 1973, 1975, 1977, 1995 by The Lockman
Foundation. Used by permission. (www.Lockman.org)

ISBN 13: 978-1-60608-684-1

Cataloging-in-Publication data:

Fitch, David E., 1956–

The end of evangelicalism? discerning a new faithfulness for mission : towards an
evangelical political theology / David E. Fitch.

xxvi + 226 p. ; 23 cm. — Includes bibliographical references and index.

Theopolitical Visions 8

ISBN 13: 978-1-60608-684-1

1. Evangelicalism—United States. 2. Mission of the church—United States. I. Title. II.
Series.

BR1642.U5 F55 2011

Manufactured in the U.S.A.

To Rae Ann and Max

For the ways you have supported me and made possible the joining

of our lives together into His Mission.

Contents

Acknowledgments

This is a book I had no business writing. It combines a difficult and eccentric political philosopher with the political fate of evangelicalism. Combining the two almost guarantees that few will read it. After all, few evangelicals have ventured to read political cultural philosopher Slavoj Žižek and, if they have, they most likely have found him to be so troubled that he is not worth the effort it will take to understand him. Likewise, most avid readers of Žižek, continental philosophy, and the challenge of dialectical materialism will have long written off evangelicalism as important except as a cultural curiosity. Nonetheless, as I read Žižek, I stubbornly thought he might be the key to unlocking much of what has gone wrong for evangelicalism as a political presence in North America. So I wrote this book anyway. But I could not have got such a book published without a lot of help, encouragement, critical engagement, and just plain "egging on" from friends along the way. Allow me, if you will, to thank a few of them.

Thanks to Gordon Hackman, Michael Moore, J. R. Rozko, and Matt Tebbe for reading parts of the manuscript and giving helpful suggestions. Thanks to John Franke, Donald Dayton, Craig Van Gelder, Kevin Vanhoozer, and Scot McKnight for giving this a read and some helpful feedback. Thanks especially to Geoff Holsclaw who co-pastors with me and provoked me to read Žižek. He gave this book many helpful suggestions and helped refine the analysis. Special thanks to Jonathan Foiles who was my acting Teaching Assistant in the class I taught on missional theology at Northern Seminary in the winter of 2010 where many of these ideas were fleshed out. He helped me with the glossary and also gave the manuscript a helpful editing. Thanks to that entire missional theology class at Northern Seminary. That was a rich and generative time together that made this book possible. And thanks to Bob Hosack and Steve Ayers of Baker Publishing who helped shaped this book in its earlier stages (even though I published it elsewhere).

Special thanks to Steve Long who invited me to present some of these ideas to the gathering of the Christian Theological Research Fellowship at the annual meeting of the AAR in Chicago 2008. That provided the occasion for me to get going on these thoughts. Thanks to Jamie K. A. Smith and Bruce Benson who responded to my presentation at that time and offered some helpful suggestions. I owe Steve a debt of thanks for inviting me to publish this study in the Theopolitical Visions Series of Cascade Books.

Thanks to Charlie Collier, who shepherded the editing process of this book at Cascade.

Thanks as well to Northern Seminary who granted me a sabbatical when the whole world including the seminary was under financial strain. The administration could have easily opted out. This book is one the fruits of that time away from teaching and administration.

I should also like to mention "the breakfast club" at the neighborhood McDonald's. These guys, led by "the Mayor" (Bob Hughes) and "Tommie" Maloney have been a force for prodding me on. As I daily worked out of my "other office" these guys made sure I kept my nose to the grindstone. Thanks guys!

Lastly, I say a heartfelt thank you to my wife Rae Ann for all the times she has sustained me, supported me, and held down the fort at home while I was away writing, making presentations, or otherwise involved in the ministry of church leadership. Thanks to my son Elmer "Max" for his forbearance when "dad" was pre-occupied with this book. Together, they made this book possible. To them I dedicate this book. They are witnesses to the hope for the world in God's mission. They give me added motivation to pursue God's faithfulness in our times.

Introduction: Towards an Evangelical Missional Political Theology

"Order your common life in a manner worthy of the gospel of Christ . . ."
—Philippians 1:27[1]

Six years ago my wife and I moved into a new neighborhood. In a short time, we found ourselves sitting around an outdoor fire pit chatting with our new neighbors. Eventually they discovered that I was a pastor and launched into a series of questions about our church. We tried to answer our neighbors as best we could, but then came the question that caught us off guard. "Are you an evangelical like president Bush is an evangelical?" An arctic-like chill settled over the conversation. Though they tried to hide it, our neighbors' disdain towards this image of Christianity was palpable. Fortunately I was able to convince them that we were different than the image they held. Since then we have gained many good friends on that block. Nonetheless it was clear to us that, at the height of the Bush years in the presidency, evangelicals had become branded as a certain kind of arrogant, dispassionate people, and we were bearing the brunt of that.

With the ending of the Bush administration, one might suspect this phenomenon has passed. Since that incident, however, many friends and acquaintances have recounted similar experiences to me. When they too were exposed as evangelicals, they were also asked questions like "Do you think I am going to hell if I don't agree with you?" or "are

1. Translated by Fowl, *Philippians*, 63.

xi

you one of those kind of evangelicals?" Situations like these, I suggest, illustrate the enduring "image problem" we evangelicals are facing in many parts of North America. Whether because of our own actions or because of "guilt by association," we carry the burden of being perceived negatively as a certain "kind of people," and it is hindering our public witness.

THE CRISIS IN EVANGELICALISM AND WHAT IT REVEALS

There is of course much debate as to what the current state of evangelicalism is. What cannot be denied, however, is the negative trajectory of both the influence and perception of evangelicals in North American culture as a whole. The rise of the Evangelical Right in the first decade of the new millennium is now largely behind us. In its aftermath there was a severe backlash against evangelicals from various media and cultural influences in the following years.[2] As evangelicals we still live within that negative shadow. In 2008, our once dominant electoral influence disappeared as Barack Obama was elected president. Two years later, even with the setback to the Obama administration in the 2010 elections and the rise of the "Tea Party" movement, we have yet to recover our once-dominant political power. Organizations like Focus on the Family and the National Association of Evangelicals were virtually absent in the various 2010 campaigns. From all appearances, our cultural and political witness as evangelicals appears to be on the wane.

Surrounding the time of the Obama election many pronounced a "coming collapse" for evangelicalism, an "end" to evangelicalism, or even the beginning of a "post-evangelical" era in North America. Michael Spencer, for instance, in January of 2009, wrote of "The Coming Collapse of Evangelicalism." Spencer, a well-known blogger under the name of Internet Monk (who sadly has since passed away) looked at various statistics (including the ARIS survey) and concluded that traditional evangelicalism was declining precipitously.[3] He projected a much

---

2. I survey some of this data in the first chapter of this book.

3. The ARIS numbers came from the American Religious Identification Survey conducted by Trinity College Hartford Connecticut 2008 found at http://www.americanreligionsurvey-aris.org/. One can locate Spencer's four-part article series on "the collapse" online at http://www.internetmonk.com/archive/my-prediction-the-coming-evangelical-collapse-1.

smaller and less influential church within ten to twenty years. His blog post received a flurry of attention from both evangelicals and the secular media. The article produced a minor media sensation being either reprinted or responded to by *The Christian Science Monitor*, hundreds of blogs, and the evangelical standard-bearer magazine *Christianity Today*. Spencer's analysis of the statistics was and continues to be hotly debated. Nonetheless, the ensuing media sensation proved telling. It bore witness to the growing awareness that the sustainability of evangelicalism as a social presence is in serious trouble.

Around the same time, Jon Meacham wrote a headline article for *Newsweek* entitled "The End of Christian America" which made a case similar to Spencer's for the slow death of the "conservative" (i.e., evangelical) Christian political movement in North America.[4] A bit earlier, entering the 2008 election, progressive-evangelical activist Jim Wallis wrote *The Great Awakening: Reviving Faith and Politics in a Post-Religious Right America*, announcing, in effect, the same thing: that the political presence of the evangelical right was no longer viable in North America.[5] Whether one agrees with these authors or not, each of these publications caused a notable stir among the secular media as they took note of the decline of evangelicalism in one area or another. Their works bore witness to the public perception that evangelicalism had pushed too far in its political agendas. Its approach to cultural engagement was sorely lacking and now there was a backlash. Rarely had one group ascended so fast to power and influence only to meet with an equally precipitous decline.

Perhaps the icing on the cake was a report put out in 2007 by David Kinnaman, a social scientist/administrator for the evangelical-friendly Barna research and marketing firm. He, along with co-author Gabe Lyons, published a book entitled *UnChristian*, where he offered a compelling survey of "what a New Generation really thinks about Christianity." He documented how average young Americans see evangelical Christians as arrogant, judgmental, duplicitous, and dispassionate.[6] This book generated huge sales for a book of this kind. Today its

4. Jon Meacham, "The End of Christian America."

5. Wallis, *Great Awakening*. Dave Tomlinson a few years before had written a widely read book from England announcing the coming of a post-evangelicalism entitled *Post-Evangelical*.

6. Kinnaman and Lyons, *UnChristian*, 26–30.

statistics are some of the most quoted within evangelicalism. Alongside Kinnaman's findings, the so-called "post-evangelical" movement emerged, composed mostly of former evangelicals chastising evangelicals for their arrogant, judgmental, and even dispassionate ways. The publishing success of Brian McLaren, an evangelical leader in this critique, is just one example of the heightened activity within this realm of Christian publishing driven by this critique of evangelicalism.[7] It all gives more evidence to the perceived crisis of character in evangelicalism at the end of this current decade.

To reiterate, many of these statistics concerning evangelicalism's demise are greatly in dispute. Indeed, several books and articles have been published in recent days defending evangelicals both in terms of our numbers "holding our own" and the kinds of people we actually are.[8] Despite the ambiguity of the evidence, however, few would deny that there is a crisis in perception of evangelicals in North America. Indeed, the fact that books/articles are being published defending evangelicals is testimony in itself to the negative broad perception of evangelicals in North America. The decline of both the public's perception of us as people as well as our political influence is therefore a reality we cannot escape. It raises the question: is our way of life failing to make the gospel compelling amidst the society in which we live? Misperception or reality, something has gone wrong with our witness and the situation demands our attention.

7. Brian McLaren's books beginning with *A New Kind of Christian* up to his present day *A New Kind of Christianity* reflect a critique, albeit irenic, of this kind of evangelicalism. Their immense popularity attests to the reality of this backlash against this kind of evangelical. See further in this regard McKnight, "Ironic Faith of Emergents." See also in this regard Tomlinson, *Post-Evangelical*.

8. For instance, George Barna of the statistical research firm The George Barna Group published a much-derided article in his *Barna Report* entitled "Surprisingly Few Adults Outside Christianity Have Positive Views of Christians." Barna asked non-U.S. Christians about their attitudes towards Christians. Only 44 percent had a positive view of Christian clergy. Just 32 percent had a positive view of born-again Christians. And a mere 22 percent had a positive view of evangelicals. This was later quoted as authentic by Sider, *Scandal*, 28. John Stackhouse, however, questioned these statistics in his "What Scandal? Whose Conscience?" The continuing merit of these statistical reports on the evangelical demise has been in much debate in the last few years. See B. R. E. Wright, *Christians are Hate-Filled Hypocrites*. In addition, see Thorsen and Wilkens, *Everything You Know about Evangelicals*, where they argue against most of the perceptions the general public has of evangelicals.

WHY EVANGELICALS NEED POLITICAL THEOLOGY

How did evangelicalism arrive at this place? How did evangelicals come to be perceived as "these kinds of people"? Granted, we do not know whether we actually are "these kinds of people" or whether the media has just produced this image of us. Whatever the case, however, we should respond by investigating whether our cultural accusers have something upon which to base their opinions. We need to examine whether our belief and practice have indeed produced this arrogant, exclusivist, judgmental, and dispassionate people that the American media says we are.

By putting things in this way, I am putting forth a core assumption of this book: that belief plus the practice of that belief shapes a community's disposition in the world. "Belief plus practice" not only shapes our way of life together, it shapes the "kinds of people" we become. This is neither controversial nor especially new,[9] and I hope to defend this assumption in the chapters that lie ahead. For now, however, if we can accept this assumption, should we not as evangelicals be asking if our belief and practice shape our communal life in such a way that it embodies the gospel? If we discover it does not, should we not then ask why? At the present time, there are reasons to suspect that our social presence as evangelicals has become inhospitable to the world and God's mission in it. It only makes sense, then, that we do some social (psycho)analysis on ourselves and ask what's going on with our belief and practice that could possibly shape our lives as a community in this way.

This is the kind of work political theology can do. It asks how what we believe about God (theology) orders our life together in the world

---

9. The idea that beliefs together with practices shape a people's social character is another way to say that belief and practice produce culture. Cultural theorists have affirmed this for years. Some cultural theorists might label "beliefs" by different words like values, webs of significance, or cognitive functions. Some cultural theorists also might label "practices" with words like rituals, means of socialization, or behavior patterned relationships. On this, see Dyrness, *Earth is God's*, ch. 3 for a concise survey of the history of the study of culture. The idea that the two work together to shape a culture is un-controversial. Likewise, the statement that culture exists to pass on patterns of behavior and socialize people into certain expectations and ways of life is also equally non-controversial and is as old as the field of anthropology itself. One can see this as early as Kluckhohn's classic essay "Concept of Culture."

(politics). This book asks this question of evangelicalism. I am seeking to connect the beliefs (and practices) of evangelicals to the shape that our political presence takes in the world for the gospel. By "political presence," however, I am not primarily referring to evangelicalism's various alliances with either the conservative right or the progressive left in U.S. national politics. I am talking about our corporate disposition in society, i.e., what kinds of people we have become in the world. As a short form, I will constantly refer to this political presence as our "politic" in the world: i.e., our way of life together unified and formed into an organic whole by our beliefs and practices of those beliefs.[10] In this book, I am asking how does what we believe shape our "politic" in the world?

It seems axiomatic that our "politic" as evangelicals should give witness to what we believe. Who we are as a people should reflect the gospel we preach. This seems obvious, yet it is what we are assessing in this book concerning evangelicalism's own politic in North America. As we examine the history and recent culture of evangelicalism, I develop the thesis that evangelicalism has become an "empty politic" driven by what we are against instead of what we are for. As a result, we find ourselves often in subtle enjoyments that are perverse. They take the form of "You see we were right!" or "I'm glad we're not them." As a result, our beliefs have somehow shaped us into something incongruent with the very affirmations we gather to proclaim. Putting all other opinions of us aside, I suggest that our belief and practice have somehow shaped us as a people inhospitable to God's mission.

This antagonistic aspect of our corporate existence is a sign of what I'll call in the book an "empty politic." Using some political theory borrowed from cultural theorist Slavoj Žižek, I show how this antagonism works and is evidence that we have lost the core of our life together. With the help of theologian John Milbank and others, I then describe an alternative form of politics: "a politic of fullness" that participates in the life of the Incarnate Christ as a work of the Father, extended

10. I use the word "politic" as a play on the phrase "body politic," which emphasizes the idea that a society's government and its people function together as a living organic whole. In the case of this book, I use the term "politic" to emphasize how a group of people coming together under common belief and practice produces a way of life that is organic and takes on a corporate disposition in the world. This social collective life, bred in a people by its belief and practice, I refer to as its "politic."

through the Spirit into the world. Using this distinction between "an empty politic" versus "a politic of fullness," I describe how a way of life together is birthed in the fullness of Christ as opposed to one birthed out of antagonism. I propose that we evangelicals leave behind the life of the latter politic for the life together in Christ for God's mission in the world.

Doing a political theology like this puts our corporate witness as evangelicals front and center. It affirms that if our witness is to impact our culture, then our corporate way of life must be congruent with the beliefs we proclaim. It asks us to examine our way of life together as His community and to see it as indispensible for the church's witness. Such a political theology assumes that if we desire to participate in God's mission, we must inhabit the world communally with the very disposition of Christ Himself. For all these reasons, and given the current state of evangelicalism, doing a political theology along these lines seems very much in order.

CAN EVANGELICALS BE MISSIONAL?

If I may put even more of my cards on the table, the expanded thesis of this book is that three "cardinal" beliefs of evangelicalism have shaped us (in recent history) as evangelicals into an inhospitable politic to the world and God's mission in it. These beliefs are a) the inerrant Bible; b) the decision for Christ; and c) the Christian nation. In the three middle chapters of this book, I describe how these beliefs developed over the last century so as to shape us as a people prone to an arrogant, duplicitous, and dispassionate posture in the world.

My objective, however, is *not* to dismantle or bring an "end" to this version of evangelicalism. Rather, I seek to provide an opening for evangelicalism to be renewed and to flourish into the missional calling that lies before us in the new post-Christendom West. I do not discredit the value that lies behind these three evangelical historical commitments. Some may find these traditional evangelical beliefs archaic. I am not so sure. I suggest that the commitments to the authority of Scripture, a conversionist salvation, and an activist evangelistic stance of the church in the world, which these beliefs attest to, are essential to a vibrant Christian faith in North America. In the last chapter of this book, therefore, I seek to rearticulate the ways we speak about and practice these beliefs so that we may be shaped as a politic consistent with the gospel and with God's mission in the world. As opposed to the way the public has caricatured us, I show how these beliefs can and should shape our lives communally for incarnational presence, authentic witness, hospitable engagement, and the daily inhabitation of God's mission (*missio Dei*) in the world. This is what an evangelical political theology should do: orient our lives into God's mission.

This language of "the mission of God" (*missio Dei*), "incarnational" presence, and "authentic witness" is common today among the missional church movement in North America. In the last decade, leaders, authors, and theologians of this movement have emptied many a pen to call the church into God's mission.[11] In so doing, this movement has gained national prominence among evangelical churches. Nonetheless, as I see it, a love-hate relationship exists between evangelicals and this burgeoning missional movement. Generally speaking, evangelicals have either a) looked upon "missional church" with suspicion because of its liberal social-gospel overtones; or b) tried to co-opt it in order to grow more of their church's "pragmatized" programs. On either basis, it is open to question whether evangelicalism can be "missional."

I contend that a missional theology that is grounded in political theology can help diagnose both of these issues and make way for a new "missional" evangelicalism. Regarding the first issue, missional theologians have often played into the evangelical antipathy towards the social gospel by starting their theologies with the doctrine of *missio Dei* and then fleshing out the rest of their theological commitments from this starting point.[12] Many evangelicals have resisted this starting point dating back to the modern origins of *missio Dei* theology in

---

11. Included among these leaders would be foundational authors such as Lesslie Newbigin and David Bosch, who were followed by the Gospel and Our Culture Network authors Darrell Guder, George Hunsberger, Craig Van Gelder, and Al Roxburgh. A whole new set of authors too numerous to mention followed in their footsteps including Alan Hirsch and Michael Frost.

12. This starting point is most succinctly stated in the following famous quote from David Bosch, "Mission [is] understood as being derived from the very nature of God. It is thus put in the context of the doctrine of the Trinity, not of ecclesiology or soteriology. The classical doctrine of the *missio Dei* as God the Father and the Son sending the Spirit [is] expanded to include yet another 'movement': Father, Son, and Holy Spirit sending the church into the world." Bosch, *Transforming Mission*, 390.

the post-WWII mission conferences of the World Council of Churches (known as the International Missionary Council [IMC] meetings). These conferences affirmed the *missio Dei* as the theme for missions in the twentieth century. They acclaimed that God is active in the world via the *missio Dei* outside of and apart from the church. As Jürgen Moltmann famously stated, "it is not the church that has a mission of salvation to fulfill in the world; it is the mission of the Son and the Spirit through the Father that includes the church."[13] The 1952 IMC meeting in particular challenged Protestants of all kinds to work for social justice, leaving behind the more traditional work of the church in evangelism and discipleship.[14] For evangelicals, this version of the doctrine of *missio Dei* was unfortunate because it downplayed "humanity's need for reconciliation with God" and de-centered the missional work of God away from the church.[15]

Similar concerns about *missio Dei* bother some evangelicals today about the current missional movement. They ask what form does the church take in the missional church movement? They complain that too often the church gets so dispersed in missional efforts that little recognizable or viable remains of the church.[16] They ask about salvation and why so few conversions are reported in the missional church?[17]

13. Moltmann, *Church in the Power*, 64.

14. The history of the evangelical suspicion of *missio Dei* theology is recounted by Bosch, *Transforming Mission*, ch. 12.

15. See McIntosh, "Missio Dei," for a brief recounting of these historical developments around the term *missio Dei* and evangelicalism. Thanks to the missiologist Ed Stetzer and his blog for this reference. For a fuller account, see Flett, *Witness of God*, ch. 4.

16. Frost and Hirsch, for example, argue that the church is a centered set as opposed to a bounded set with no clear line of distinction between who is in and out of Christian faith. This has led to some evangelical angst about a defined church practice. *Shaping of Things to Come*, 50. Likewise, Alan Hirsch famously argues that ecclesiology comes "out the back" of missiology. See *Forgotten Ways*, 143–44. Its form takes shape after mission has progressed within a context. This has led to similar issues for evangelicals. Michael Frost recounts a typical cautious evangelical response to missional church in his book *Exiles*, where he says, "Whenever I have spoken to mainstream church leaders and clergy about 'communitas' (*the concept of community at liminal edges of institutional church*), I have sensed resistance, sometimes an out and out rejection of what I'm saying." *Exiles*, 13; italics mine.

17. Again, this discussion has been widely dispersed over the internet. High-profile pastors such as James McDonald of Moody Radio (WMBI Chicago) and megachurch Harvest Bible Chapel, Rolling Meadows, IL, and Mark Driscoll of Mars Hill Church

These same evangelicals wonder where orthodoxy and Scripture factor in to the missional church. The fact that preaching is often minimized in these churches does not help matters. These evangelicals ask about how we guard the faith from being syncretized into a total contextualization without a high view and practice of Scripture?

The political theology that I am proposing in this book directly addresses these issues. It starts with these three beliefs—Scripture, conversionist salvation, and an active evangelistic church in the world—and asks how they shape a people concretely for participation in the *missio Dei*. It thereby avoids taking the concept of the *missio Dei* and extracting it from its concrete life in the church from which it then gets applied as an intellectual principle over all things. Instead, it hones in on how our evangelical commitments shape us (or do not shape us) for participating in the *missio Dei*. It makes explicit the concrete political implications of these central evangelical doctrines for mission.

On the other hand, this kind of political theology also addresses the evangelical tendencies to turn everything "missional" into another pragmatic tool. The complaint of many missional authors is that megachurches use "missional" as another technique to drive numerical success and make evangelicalism more appealing to its already existing constituents.[18] As "social justice" has become more attractive and consumerism less so, megachurches have turned towards marketing "missional." Meanwhile, they accommodate an ongoing separation of church from an actual way of life in and among society. The political theology that I am proposing in this book resists conceptualizing "missional" into such a program by insisting that the gospel is a way of being as a people in the world. It forces the church to assess the way its belief and practice shape a way of life together in the world for God's mission. It makes it impossible to avoid the realities of the ways our be-

---

in Seattle, a conservative megachurch, blasts the missional church for lack of converts. See online: http://blog.harvestbiblefellowship.org/?p=1466 and http://blog.christianitytoday.com/outofur/archives/2008/06/do_missional_ch.html.

18. For instance, missional author Alan Hirsch, says "The word 'missional' over the years has tended to become very fluid and as it was quickly co-opted by those wishing to find new and trendy tags for what they themselves were doing, be they missional or not . . ." as quoted online at http://www.friendofmissional.org/, lines 28–32. See Rick Meigs' dialogue with Alan Hirsch on this same subject and the ensuing nation wide "synchro-blog" on the issue in the summer of 2008 online at http://blindbeggar.org/?p=606.

lief and practice can be used to foster complicity in the world. It forces us to ask how our everyday way of life, our disposition as a people (i.e., our politic), engages the world as the embodiment of Christ and his mission in the world.

In essence, then, this book is doing missional theology in its purest form. It is a reshaping of evangelicalism's belief and practice for "political" participation in God's mission in the world. We are examining the entire evangelical project from the point of view of political formation and God's mission. The result is an evangelical missional political theology.

EVANGELICALISM AND THE CAFFEINE-FREE DIET COKE

A key actor in this book is the political and cultural theorist Slavoj Žižek. Žižek can be obscure, profound, entertaining, and bizarre, often all at the same time. He has strengths to lend to this project as well as weaknesses. He will guide the first half of this book's political analysis of evangelicalism.

One of Žižek's more famous cultural analyses surrounds his illustration of the Caffeine-Free Diet Coke. In his book *The Fragile Absolute* he narrates how Coca-Cola was originally concocted as a medicine (originally known as a nerve tonic, stimulant, and headache remedy).[19] It was eventually sweetened, and its strange taste was made more palatable. Soon it became a popular drink during Prohibition that still possessed medicinal qualities (it was deemed "refreshing" as well as the perfect "temperance drink"). Over time, however, its sugar was replaced with sweetener and its caffeine was extracted, and so today we are left with Caffeine-Free Diet Coke: a drink that does not fulfill any of the concrete needs of a drink. The two reasons why anyone would drink anything—it quenches thirst/provides nutrition and it tastes good—have, in Žižek's words, "been suspended."

Today, Coke has become a drink that does not quench thirst, does not provide a stimulant, and whose strange taste is not particularly satisfying. Nonetheless, it is the most consumed beverage in the world. It plays on the mysterious enjoyment we get out of consuming it as something to enjoy in surplus after we have already quenched our thirst.

19. Žižek, *Fragile Absolute*, 22.

We drink Coke because "Coke is 'it,'" not because it satisfies anything material. In essence, all that remains of what was once Coke is a pure semblance, an artificial promise of a substance which never material- izes. In Žižek's words, we "drink nothing in the guise of something . . ." It is "in effect merely an envelope of a void."[20]

Žižek uses Caffeine-Free Diet Coke as an illustration of how capitalism works. Taking some liberties with Žižek and his excellent illustration, I believe the Coke metaphor also works for understanding evangelicalism in its present period in history. Many of evangelicalism's beliefs and practices have become separated from the concrete reality around which they first came into being. In its beginnings, especially as evangelicalism was shaped by the fundamentalist-modernist contro- versies of the 1920s, "the inerrant Bible," "the decision for Christ," and the idea of "the Christian Nation" articulated beliefs for evangelicals that helped connect them to the realities of our life in Christ in the face of several cultural challenges. For fifty to seventy-five years, these articulations served us well but also evolved and became hardened. As American society advanced and our lives became busier and ordered towards American affluence, we practice these same beliefs, but they have become disconnected from what they meant several generations ago. As a result, the inerrant Bible, the decision for Christ, and the Christian Nation mean very little for how we live our day-to-day lives as evangelical Christians. They are ideological banners to which we as- sent. They are tied to behavioral practices that we engage in but they bear little or no connection to our lives in Christ together for God's mission in the world. Just as our society drinks Coke as an "it," as some- thing that makes us feel good but has little substantial value as a drink, so we practice these beliefs as something we add on to our lives. It is something we do as an extra to our already busy lives that makes us feel better. Evangelical church, as symbolized in many ways by the large consumer megachurches, has become an "add-on," "a semblance" of something which once meant something real. It is a surplus enjoyment we enjoy after we have secured all of our immediate needs.

Surely there are many evangelical churches of all sizes which do not fit this description, and God's work continues among us despite our fallenness. Yet, as is typical of Žižek, his Coke illustration provokes

20. Ibid., 23.

us to ask questions about the things that drive us to come together. He describes in multiple ways what a politic looks like, when, like a Caffeine-Free Diet Coke, it is "empty" at its core, driven by forces other than what we accept as real. Žižek, of course, sees all social reality as 'empty,' driven by antagonisms and contradictions as opposed to something real to which we aspire. What I wish to explore, with Žižek's help, is how evangelicalism in particular has become this kind of "empty politic," driven by other things than our life together in Christ for the world. In the face of its failings, there is hope for an alternative politic for evangelicalism, "a politic of fullness," where our everyday way of life is centered (by these beliefs) into a participation in the Incarnate Christ and the life we have with the triune God in the world in and through him. Although challenging, I contend Žižek provides the basis for a fresh look at evangelicalism along these lines that leads us to somewhere else in the midst of our political malaise.

This Book Is Not for Everybody But I Can Still Try

The flow of this book proceeds as follows. The first chapter begins with the question "is evangelicalism at an end?" It outlines the case for evangelicalism being in a crisis of sorts that at the very least deserves our attention. I then propose a way for diagnosing the crisis that leads us to the political theories of Slavoj Žižek. Chapter 2 outlines the specific parts of Žižek's work that I make regular use of in the three chapters that follow it. Chapters 3, 4, and 5 are the meat of the book. In each of the three chapters, I dissect the origins of one of the three main beliefs of evangelicalism, the inerrant Bible, the decision for Christ, and the Christian nation. I analyze how these beliefs have shaped us into a kind of people that is threatening the viability of evangelicalism as a way of life in North America. I use episodes from the public lives of evangelicals, our institutions, and the media perception of us that reveal some of our more extreme excesses. I show how these episodes illustrate the drives behind why we believe what we do. I show how these caricatures make sense given the way the basic evangelical beliefs function within our way of life. I try to show how evangelicalism, unbeknownst to many of us who live inside it, has become a politic "empty" of the life we have in Christ. Tragically, it has shaped us more often than not into a way of life that is antagonistic to the gospel we seek to share in the world.

After completing the work of the first five chapters, I take the sixth chapter to outline a direction to recover the core of our life together in Christ as evangelicals. I show how each of the three main beliefs of evangelicals can be rearticulated and the practices reoriented so as to draw us into a participation in Christ himself and the life with the triune God and his mission. I close the book with an epilogue offering some comments on the post-evangelical emerging church and missional church movements in North America. I do so because the enduring question of this book is, What does a new faithfulness look like "politically" for evangelicals given our current situation and the changing cultural realities of North America? I offer some optimistic appraisals of these movements as well as some cautions inherent in them for those who wish to fulfill the promise of birthing a new, post-evangelical faithfulness for our time.

This book, however, is probably not an easy read for the average reader. It finds itself (happily) in an academic book series and it engages the often elusive work of political and cultural theorist Slavoj Žižek. It relies on the reader's ability to labor through some description of Žižek's political and cultural theory. The book also engages many key theological figures of the twentieth century and so it relies on the reader having some familiarity with the current theological landscape.

For those who may wish to bypass some of the academic heavy lifting in this book, I recommend the following shortcut. Chapter 2 is a readable survey of Žižek's early political theory upon which I base much of the cultural analysis in this book. For those who find it laborious, however, I urge you to skip chapter 2 entirely and go right to chapters 3, 4, and 5, relying on the glossary provided at the back of the book. Read these chapters by referring to and returning often to this glossary. The concepts should become clearer as you read along. Much of the Žižek I am using is intuitive enough that the reader can glean the best of the cultural analysis on evangelicalism in those chapters by doing just that. I think you will to be able to glean from these pages alone what I mean when, playing off Žižek, I suggest that evangelicalism has become an "empty" politic.

It will also help the reader to note that whenever I capitalize and put in quotations "the Inerrant Bible," "the Decision for Christ" or "the

Christian Nation" I am referring to these beliefs as they function ideo-
logically as master-signifiers within the political life of evangelicalism.
As I explain in chapter 2 and in the glossary, when a belief becomes a
master-signifier it in essence acts as an object to which people pledge
their allegiance. It functions to organize diverse people into a common
assent. The reader should note that when I capitalize these terms and
put them in quotes I am no longer speaking about what they actually
refer to, i.e., the Scriptures, salvation in Christ, or the church's activity
in the world. I am speaking about them in terms of the way they function as ideological objects for evangelicals.

I want to be clear that I have no intention in this book of denying
the authority of Scripture, the substitutionary theory of the atonement,
or the evangelistic calling of the church in the world. That simply is not
my purpose in this book. The critique of evangelicalism and the three
terms "the Inerrant Bible," "the Decision for Christ," or "the Christian
Nation," is an ideological critique. In other words, I am critiquing the
way these terms have evolved so as to function as political objects
within the culture of evangelicalism.

There will be times when I speak about public figures, many of
them self-identified evangelicals. In Žižekian fashion, I am using them
as illustrations of the larger political dynamic going on within the evangelical culture we are examining. The reader should note here that I
have no intent to disparage the personal character of any of these people. As with Žižek, I contend that their media/cultural material reflects
back upon us more about who we are as evangelicals than anything
about them personally.

Lastly, the reader should notice that throughout the book I use
the words "the Incarnate Christ" to refer to Jesus Christ. I do so to
underscore the Trinitarian implications of Christians participating in
the person and work of Jesus Christ. When speaking of "the Incarnate
Christ" I am focusing on the entire reality of God the Father sending
the Son to take on incarnate flesh. This reality includes not only God
sending his Son to be born in human flesh in and among humanity but
also the extension of this work incarnationally by the ongoing work
of the Spirit proceeding from the Father and the Son into the world
through his church and beyond. Central within this movement is the
redemptive work of Christ's life, death, resurrection, and ascension to
the right hand as Lord. To participate, then, in "the Incarnate Christ" as

both an individual and as a social body implies much more than what many might mean when we refer to the second person as Jesus or Jesus Christ. I wish to include the entire dynamic movement of the triune history in our relationship with God through Jesus Christ because this is what allows for our continued participation in God's mission in the world. I wish to avoid any misunderstanding that would suggest that a political presence can be formed in the world *solely* around a personal belief in and a patterning of one's life after the person and work of Jesus.

Towards a Missional Evangelical Political Theology

According to New Testament theologian Stephen Fowl, the apostle Paul challenges the church in Phil 1:27 to order its "common life" together for a pattern of life that yields "the disposition" of Christ in the world.[21] In the same way, missional theologian Darrell Guder claims that the Pauline letters focus on the formation of Christian communities "to lead a life worthy of the calling to which they have been called" (Eph 4:1).[22] The underlying suspicion of this book is that we evangelicals have been failing at this task. We have not articulated what we believe and then practiced it in such as way as to shape communities that incarnate Christ's character in the world for his mission. Instead, it is frightening how it seems our public persona has become caricatured as exactly the opposite. The task that lies ahead in this brief book is to analyze what happened here and then to reorient evangelical belief and practice for the political task of shaping communities into God's mission in the world. This is the challenge, as I see it, of a political theology that is uniquely evangelical and by definition missional. To this task we now turn.

---

21. Fowl, *Philippians*, 63.
22. Guder, *Continuing Conversion*, 58.

CHAPTER 1

The End of Evangelicalism?

"Most people I meet assume that Christian means very conservative, entrenched in their thinking, anti-gay, anti-choice, angry, violent, illogical, empire builders, they want to convert everyone, and they generally cannot live peacefully with anyone who does not believe what they believe."

—David Kinnaman, President of Barna Group[1]

There is never a shortage of soothsayers willing to call for the "end of" something. The current times are no exception. In the recent past, we have been told that we have arrived at the "the end of history" (Fukuyama), "the end of modernity" (Fatima), and even more famously, the "end of metaphysics" (Heidegger). We are living in a whole series of post-worlds including the post-Enlightenment, post-modern, post-Christendom, and even "post-American" worlds.[2] We are asking what comes after Christendom, after modernity, or after metaphysics. All of these phrases refer to an ending of sorts to a previous era's undergirding structures of thought, politics, or economic life. Seeing that evangelicalism in North America is closely aligned with many of these same structures, is it not also time to ask about "the end of Evangelicalism"? Should we be asking what comes after evangelicalism in America?

1. Kinnaman and Lyons, *UnChristian*, 26.

2. Fareed Zakaria, most notably, proposed that we are now entering a post-American world in a book with that title.

There are signs within the American culture that evangelicalism—the movement—is arriving at an "ending" of sorts. Evangelicalism's influence within American society is painfully on the wane. As recent as just this past decade, evangelicalism had carried a significant amount of political influence within American society and seemed confident of its identity as a church in America. Today, many evangelicals seem confused as to what the label "evangelical" might even mean. There are indications that evangelicalism as a social entity has passed a "tipping point" concerning its own place in North American society and culture. We can observe this taking place in several different ways.

Most obviously, evangelicalism's presence in American politics has declined precipitously. As a group, we once carried enormous influence on American political elections—particularly in 2000 and 2004. Today that influence has diminished. Evangelicals became the single biggest voting block in getting George Bush elected to the presidency in 2000 and 2004.[3] Yet in the 2008 political campaigns, evangelicals disappeared almost entirely from the political arena as Barack Obama ran for the presidency. Obama then entered office with a stratospheric 78 percent approval rating.[4] Evangelicals by and large did not approve and were strangely silent. For those evangelicals who did join in the Obama campaigns, such as social activist Jim Wallis of Sojourners, they exerted a new kind of evangelical influence that was small and inclusivist. For Wallis, leader of the progressive evangelicals, it was the beginning of "a Post-Religious Right America."[5] Whatever one might think of the progressive evangelicals and their aid in getting the new president elected, it is remarkable how little influence and role any evangelical people (including progressive ones) played in the 2008 election compared to the prior elections of George W. Bush.

Likewise, evangelicalism's place of cultural influence in both the American economy and Hollywood, once strong, has fallen on hard times. Just a few years ago, James Dobson's *Focus on The Family*, as well as other evangelical-based groups, led surprisingly successful boycotts

---

3. Gushee and Phillips, "Moral Formation and the Evangelical Voter," 25.

4. *New York Times*, January 18, 2009. Online http://www.nytimes.com/2009/01/18/us/politics/18poll.html?_r=1.

5. Wallis, *Great Awakening*. Brian McLaren and other so-called progressive evangelicals ran ads and helped support Obama during the 2008 presidential campaign.

against Fortune 500 companies, changing their corporate behavior.[6] Evangelicals influenced directly the marketing of films in Hollywood as several evangelical megachurches became the focal point for marketing Mel Gibson's *The Passion of the Christ*, making it a huge blockbuster hit in 2004. Many more films followed.[7] Riding the crest of the Bush presidency, evangelicals exerted unprecedented influence in abortion and stem cell research policy-making of Washington. In the aftermath of a failed Bush presidency, however, along with a broken economy and a culture hostile to evangelicals, these once courageous voices of evangelicalism sit strangely mute.

Perhaps the most disturbing "tipping point" of all for evangelicals, though, is the manner in which the perception of evangelicals in American culture at large has turned for the worse. American media had generally showed courteous appreciation for evangelicals since WWII. Billy Graham was regularly listed among the most admired men in America, and this was no surprise. Beginning with the second term of the Bush administration, however, a stream of *NY Times* best-seller books negative towards evangelicals started to flow through American media.[8] Aimed squarely at the evangelical "religious right," these books painted conservative Christians with a broad stroke, characterizing them as angry, intolerant, hateful, fascists, religious profiteers, hypocrites, sexually duplicitous, and worshipers "on the altar of

---

6. An example of this kind of influence is Focus of the Family's boycott, along with the American Family Association, of Proctor and Gamble in 2004–2005 because of their support of gay marriage legislation in their home state and their supporting of gay-affirming television programming through the purchase of advertising. Procter and Gamble ceased advertising on those shows in April of 2005.

7. In 2004, the mammoth Willow Creek Community Church along with a few other strategic churches were marketing venues for the pre-screening of *The Passion* complete with a live interview with Mel Gibson. This enabled Mel Gibson to promote a film Hollywood was not willing to promote. This led to a coalition of megachurches, which became the setting for pre-screenings and/or distribution of promotional materials for Christian-friendly Hollywood films. Later, a marketing organization for Christian-friendly films among these places of evangelical influence emerged called "Willow Creek Marketing." It is not known whether there was any connection between this marketing organization and Willow Creek Community Church of S. Barrington, IL.

8. A list of these *NY Times* best-seller books include: White, *Religion Gone Bad*, Hedges, *American Fascists*, Gilgoff, *Jesus Machine*, Harris, *Letters to a Christian Nation*, Lanham, *Sinner's Guide to the Evangelical Right*, Balmer, *Thy Kingdom Come*, Hitchens, *God is Not Great*.

free enterprise." The American culture industry supported these images by producing unflattering images of evangelicals via the cinema, such as the judgmental zealot Hilary (played by Mandy Moore) in the 2004 movie *Saved* or the constant caricatures of evangelicals put forth by Bill Maher on his own HBO talk show. Scandals involving some of evangelicalism's most visible cultural figures only served to reinforce these cultural stereotypes. When NAE president Ted Haggard confessed his sexual impropriety, or evangelical broadcaster Pat Robertson unleashed his condemnation upon New Orleans during its most vulnerable time, evangelicals could only cringe. We could no longer easily dismiss the cultural caricatures drawn of us as just another piece of disingenuous secularist diatribe put forth by the "liberal media." In the latter half of the Bush presidency, despite some counter-balancing efforts in the media,[9] evangelicalism's cultural credibility passed a "tipping point" and began to turn sour.

For most evangelicals, our worst suspicions proved true in the survey work compiled by David Kinnaman, president of the George Barna research firm, in his 2007 book *UnChristian*. In an infamous quotation, Kinnaman relayed the opinions of the typical non-Christian about Christians in American society: "Most people I meet assume that Christian means very conservative, entrenched in their think-ing, antigay, anti-choice, angry, violent, illogical, empire builders, they want to convert everyone, and they generally cannot live peacefully with anyone who does not believe what they believe."[10] Kinnaman then proceeds to outline statistical evidence showing how specifically evan-gelical Christians are perceived by the public at large as being negative, hypocritical, too focused on people as targets for their conversion, anti-homosexual, sheltered, too political, and judgmental.[11] No doubt, these statistics, and others like them, can be debated as to whether they have been exaggerated.[12] Nonetheless, they have received so much attention

9. Writers such as Jeffery Sheler and Andrew Greeley have made efforts to combat negative stereotypes of evangelicals. See Sheler, *Believers* and Greeley and Hout, *Truth About Conservative Christians*. Likewise, Matt Groenig, some suggest, has honored evangelicals in his character Ned Flanders on *The Simpsons*. See Pinsky, "Blessed Ned."

10. Kinnaman and Lyons, *UnChristian*, 26.

11. Ibid., 28–30. As already referred to in the Introduction, n. 2, George Barna has reported many additional statistics. Ron Sider as well has summarized many of these statistics in *Scandal*, 28.

12. For a critique of these statistics read Stackhouse, "What Scandal?" and B. R. E.

among the American public that it is now almost a moot point as to whether they are reliable or not. They have become ensconced as part of the popular culture. They are a sign of the decline of evangelicalism's cultural presence in America.

During this same time period, many new church movements rose to criticize evangelicalism. Most of the ones doing the criticizing were former evangelicals. The emerging church, for example, led by figures such as Brian McLaren, the former Plymouth Brethren evangelical, arose to protest evangelicalism's narrow gospel and lack of a compassionate social presence. Likewise, evangelical leaders among the missional church movement engaged what they saw was a socially walled-off evangelicalism that had become incapable of reaching an increasingly post-Christendom society.[13] Neo-monastic expressions of church, led by Shane Claiborne—who had attended evangelical stronghold Wheaton College and worked at the proto-type evangelical megachurch Willowcreek—came alongside the missional movement to emphasize community and a just social presence over against the individualism of American evangelicalism. Liturgical renewal movements, and movements calling for a revival of Christian spiritual disciplines, were led by evangelicals Robert Webber and Dallas Willard as well as several emerging church authors. They pushed for a renewal of spiritual formation practices to replace the lifeless legalistic versions of evangelical discipleship. All of these movements represent a disenchantment that was rising from within evangelicalism. They could be read as a further sign of deterioration within traditional forms of evangelicalism.

This decade-long list of observations portrays a movement in upheaval. It only makes sense then to inquire whether evangelicalism has entered a crisis.[14] As we observe a large majority of our youth not returning to our churches after college,[15] we rightfully ask whether

---

Wright, *Christians are Hate-Filled Hypocrites*.

13. Though the missional movement was birthed early on within the mainline Protestant churches, in the last ten years leaders have arisen with decidedly evangelical-like doctrine and backgrounds. I speak here of leaders/authors like Alan Hirsch, Michael Frost, Alan Roxburgh, Reggie McNeal, Eddie Gibbs, and Ed Stetzer.

14. See Michael Spencer on the burgeoning evangelical crisis: "The Coming Evangelical Collapse." There were numerous blog and printed media responses to Spencer's contention that evangelicalism was on the verge of collapse, including Galli's "On the Lasting Evangelical Survival" from *Christianity Today*.

15. As reported in *New York Times* by Goodstein and elsewhere, various evan-

evangelicalism has a future, indeed whether it is imploding as a viable cultural force. Given the cultural signs, evangelicalism looks like a church groping for a place to stand. It appears to lack confidence in its own understanding of its mission amidst the new hostilities of post-Christendom America. How should evangelicals respond?

EVANGELICALISM AS A POLITICAL IDEOLOGY IN CRISIS

Many evangelicals have already responded to this gathering malaise. Some, for example, have challenged evangelicalism to return to a purer Protestant orthodoxy. David Wells, a prime spokesman in this regard, decries the "market-driven" assumptions of American evangelicals showing how they undercut the doctrinal foundations of evangelicalism in North America. He criticizes evangelicals for their loss of a sense of absolute biblical truth associating them with the emerging church and other movements that engage postmodern issues as part of their church strategy. The answer for Wells is for evangelicals to have the "courage to be Protestant."[16] Similarly, The Gospel Coalition organization, headed by professor Don Carson of Trinity Evangelical Divinity School—along with prominent reformed evangelicals John Piper and Tim Keller, has coalesced a gathering of evangelicals for the purpose of renewing a more balanced Protestant orthodoxy among evangelical churches and their church plants.[17] They prescribe a more holistic gospel under the Reformed banner.

---

gelicals are asserting the figure that only 4 percent of teenagers raised in evangelical churches and leaving home for college ever return to evangelical church after college. This prompted the National Association of Evangelicals to pass a resolution in 2006 deploring "the epidemic of young people leaving the evangelical church." "Evangelicals Fear the Loss of Their Teenagers." In addition, see the litany of statistics reported by S. Wright and Graves, *ReThink*. Of course, once again these statistics have been in much dispute as well. See again Bradley Wright's *Christians are Hate-Filled Hypocrites*.

16. Most notably in Wells, *Courage to Be Protestant*.

17. Once can read The Gospel Coalition's main documents on www.thegospelcoalition.org. Presaging the development of "the Gospel Coalition" was Albert Mohler's provocations. Mohler, president of Southern Baptist Theological Seminary, talked explicitly about the evangelical identity crisis in 2004. He asserted that evangelicalism was going through a "megashift" that "looks remarkably like the liberal theology evangelicals once rejected. Central doctrines such as Christ's substitutionary atonement, verbal inspiration, the exclusivity of the gospel, the reality of hell, and justification by faith alone are rejected in favor of a new evangelical paradigm." "Evangelical

Others have responded in the opposite direction addressing evangelicalism's exclusivist and closed-off version of Christianity. The British Anglican Dave Tomlinson, for example, has asserted that evangelicalism is overly pragmatic, control oriented, and suffocating to discipleship. He proposes a "post-evangelicalism" that is more open, confident in its stories, and engaging with surrounding culture.[18] Several "emerging church" and "missional church" authors push similar concerns. In addition, evangelical social activists Jim Wallis and Ron Sider have pushed for a more socially just evangelicalism.[19] They decry the alignment of evangelicalism with conservative Republican political agendas. In so doing, they suggest, evangelicals have lost the distinctive message of the gospel that brings justice and redemption to all.

Various other groups of evangelicals have composed "manifestos" calling for similar changes in evangelicalism. In 2006, a study group of various members of holiness evangelical denominations assembled at evangelical college Azusa Pacific University in California to write the Holiness Manifesto. Like David Wells and The Gospel Coalition, this group decried the pragmatism and consumerism of the North American evangelical church. Unlike Wells, they called for evangelicals to preach a holistic justice-oriented gospel that would work for the transformation of the world. In 2006, evangelical Robert Webber put forth his Ancient Evangelical Future Call. It brought together over three hundred prominent evangelical leaders and theologians to contribute to and endorse this document. It also decried the pragmatism and consumerism of American evangelicals and called for a return to the full narrative of the gospel as worked out in history in the worship, justice, and salvation of the church.[20] Several prominent evangelical leaders in 2008 once again published a document entitled "the Evangelical Manifesto." They called for the re-defining of evangelicalism via a more

---

Identity Crisis," on www.AlbertMohler.com. In response, Mohler, Wells, and The Gospel Coalition pushed for a return to classic Protestant orthodoxy as they viewed it. In recent years there is a growing number of young Neo-Reformed church leaders who follow them in their conviction that a purer, if not more missional, vision of Reformed theology will lead evangelicalism out of its malaise. On this, see Hansen, *Young, Restless, Reformed.*

18. Tomlinson, *Post-Evangelical.*

19. Sider, *Scandal*; Wallis, *God's Politics*; Wallis, *Great Awakening.*

20. For a full account of the AEF Call, see David Neff, "Together in the Jesus Story."

holistic theology and a more inclusive evangelicalism.[21] All of these efforts decried a failure in evangelicalism's narrow, individualist, overly pragmatic theology and practice.

Over against these approaches, I want to propose a different response. I suggest we examine evangelicalism's failure as a way of life in North America. Let us not separate evangelical doctrine unto itself and examine it for its (Protestant) orthodoxy. Let us not do the same for evangelical practice and examine it for its social effectiveness. Instead, let us examine the way our doctrine and practice function to bind a social body together for witness in the world. Let us examine evangelicalism as "a politic."[22]

One way to do this is by looking at evangelicalism as a political ideology. An ideology is a set of beliefs and practices that bind a people together into a functioning community or—using another word—a politic. In Marxist terms, ideology is that naïve or "false consciousness" which constructs social reality for people. It is what people assume about the way things are and how those assumptions are maintained in order to live together. The study of ideology examines the ways such a belief system sustains a way of life that orders a people towards certain kinds of compliance and motivation. Moving beyond its Marxist origins, the study of ideology can explore the ways belief systems shape individuals into a certain kind of people with certain ways of life. An ideology can enter a crisis when the objects/ideas around which its people gather cease to fund a sustainable way of life. Presented with new challenges from a given situation, such an ideology can lose its power to hold together subjects into a socially cohesive group. It becomes an ideology in crisis. I suggest, in light of the current upheaval, we examine evangelicalism as such an ideology in crisis.

Doing this, I suggest, offers several advantages. For example, this kind of approach joins the study of theology with the ways of life it

---

21. See the manifesto at www.anevangelicalmanifesto.com.

22. Again, to remind the reader, I use the word "politic" to describe our way of life together unified and formed into an organic whole by our beliefs and practices of those beliefs. It is a play on the phrase "body politic" which emphasizes the idea that a society's government and its people function together as a living organic whole. I use the term "politic" then to emphasize how a group of people coming together under a common belief and practice produce a way of life that is organic and living and takes on a corporate disposition in the world. This social collective life bred in a people by its belief and practice, I refer to as its "politic."

forms in a people. We are forced to examine front and center how our beliefs and practices shape us as a people into certain ways of life. We are forced to ask what kinds of people we become in the process. By looking at evangelicalism as an ideology, we can ask about the kind of people evangelicalism produces and whether such people are congruent with the mission of God we seek to participate in. In the end, we also end up examining the evangelical politic (our way of life together) for its ability to provide the basis for our survival amidst the cultural challenges we face: in this case, the challenges presented by the new cultures of post-Christendom.

No doubt this way of approaching evangelicalism will be foreign to many. It might even suggest that we view evangelicalism's theological affirmations as pure ideology. But this is not the case. For as I hope to make clear, I affirm what we evangelicals believe about God, the Bible, Jesus Christ, and salvation. Yet, given all of what we have observed in the opening pages of this chapter, we need to scrutinize the way evangelicals articulate these beliefs and practice them for the "kind of people" they make us into. If we discover that the kind of people we have become is at odds with the gospel we proclaim, we then need to discern the source of this disconnect. Looking at how evangelicalism functions as a political ideology enables us to get at the heart of these issues in ways that other modes of questioning simply cannot.

EVANGELICALS IN NEED OF A POLITICAL THEOLOGY

As evangelicals, we have rarely evaluated our way of life together. Traditionally we have been more focused on the rightness of our theology or, even more so, on the pragmatics of getting individuals "saved." Meanwhile, the evidence piles up of the cultural disfavor we evangelicals have accrued in North America. Our social presence (or lack of one) has impaired our witness for the gospel. In response to this bad news, however, we have often responded by either defending our beliefs apologetically or decrying more loudly the cultural decline around us while taking on a martyr complex. In some cases we have simply tossed up our hands and considered our recent ostracism within America to be the cost of "standing for truth." These have been our preferred modes of political engagement. In the process, we have avoided addressing the bleak reality that (in post-Christendom parts of North America) evangelicalism is failing badly at being a compelling social presence for the gospel. Many of us therefore, who love evangelicalism and call it our church, assert that it is time to put aside our fixation with national politics, the culture wars, and defending our beliefs apologetically. Instead, we need to account for our own communal life as an embodiment of the gospel in our society. We need to ask how we became these kinds of people.

Until recently, evangelicals have been able to ignore the issue of our social presence in society because we were living in a Christendom setting where this was rarely important to our mission. We were comfortably part of a larger pre-existing Christianized social order. Today however, bereft of broad cultural support for Christianity in general, we struggle for moorings in the waters of post-Christendom. Our main battlefront used to be with other Christians (those of Protestant liberal ilk) not the current cultural void of disbelief. Now, with the rug of the Christian cultural consensus pulled out from under our feet, evangelicalism is groping for a place to stand from which it can gather a people. Many of the younger evangelicals are tired of gathering around negative causes, whether they be fighting against the political left, those who don't believe in absolute truth, or those who sexually undermine our family values. To them, evangelicalism as an integral way of life no longer makes sense in the new post-Christendom cultures of North America. Its reason for being and its very politic is unraveling. In large parts of North America, evangelicalism is failing as a viable Christian "politic" and we must take stock of why.

For these reasons, evangelicalism needs a political theology. Political theology brings together the study of politics (how and why people come together) with the study of God. It asks how our beliefs about God (and the way we practice those beliefs) order the way we live politically (our way of life together) in the world. This is the kind of question evangelicals should ask given the current state of evangelicalism in North American society. Yet we need a particular kind of political theology—one akin to the ideological analysis proposed above. There are many kinds of political theology. In fact, for many theologians today, "all theology is political theology," meaning there can be no separation between theology and politics. Nonetheless, political theology means different things to different people. There are, for instance, political theologies that seek to address how certain beliefs about God translate into normative claims concerning the way societies should organize themselves. There are political theologies that seek to directly theorize about the relationship of religion or church to society. There have been political theologies (so-called public theologies) built to impact social policy (Reinhold Niebuhr). There have been political theologies built to interpret the gospel out of the particular experience of certain socially and politically marginalized groups (Liberation theologies, Black theologies, feminist theologies).[23] Each of these approaches has borne much fruit in the past fifty years and evangelical scholars have offered versions of these various approaches. In contrast to these approaches, however, I want to focus directly on how evangelical theology and practice form a community. How do evangelical beliefs bind people together (into a politic) and shape them for the work of Christ's mission in the world?[24] The study of evangelicalism as an ideology in crisis focuses on this question of political theology. Given that our ways of being together and the kinds of people we have become are not meeting the challenges of our existence in North America's new post-Christendom culture, this is the kind of political theology evangelicalism needs.

In what follows, I show how the core theological beliefs of evangelicalism function as ideological objects around which evangelicals rally. These core beliefs then shape us for a particular kind of political existence in society. As I will soon explain, these core doctrines of evangelicalism include a) a high view of Scripture (the Bible is inerrant); b) a conversionist understanding of salvation centered in the doctrine of the substitutionary atonement; and c) an activist engagement of church with culture for evangelism. These are all laudable doctrinal emphases that have played a significant role in renewing Christian faith in North America in the past century. Yet, as these beliefs and practices have developed within changing cultural conditions, they have reified (they

23. Michael Kirwan explores several taxonomies of political theologies in his *Political Theology*.

24. Arne Rasmusson divides his book *Church as Polis* into a discussion of "political theology," political theologies that seek to correlate beliefs about God to current political situations, and "theological politics," political theology that seeks to determine what kind of politics itself is birthed by our belief in God. It is the latter that I pursue here in this book.

have become hardened and accepted as fact). A people with a specific way of life has formed around them. Evangelicals need to understand both how these doctrines have formed us as a people and to question whether indeed the resultant character of that community is congruent with the gospel we evangelicals have been called to proclaim to the nations.[25] We need to recognize where things went wrong. We must then seek to renew the social presence of evangelicals for the witness of the gospel.[26]

What is Evangelicalism?

Of course, to put these three words together, "evangelical political theology," assumes there is a cohesive group of people we can call evangelicals in North America. Many cultural and/or sociological observers doubt this assumption. They view the label "evangelicalism" as a confused one that is hard to pin onto any sociological grouping in American culture.[27] Certainly, the label has been in constant negotiation over the last thirty years, even among its own theologians.[28] Further muddying

25. Ironically, to my knowledge, there has never been a constructive political analysis of evangelical doctrine and practice. There has been of course many political theologies based on the doctrine of the Trinity and the way it should shape us politically or socially; see most notably Moltmann's *Trinity and the Kingdom*; see also Boff, *Holy Trinity, Perfect Community* who follows a similar line of thought. There have also been political theologies that work out the political implications of Christology; see Kathryn Tanner *Jesus, Humanity.* The doctrine of creation has formed the basis for a constructive ecological theological politics in the work of Scott, *Political Theology of Nature.* Moltmann has written on the political implications of eschatology. See again his *Theology of Hope* as well as Yoder's *Politics of Jesus* and *Original Revolution* where some have argued that he makes eschatology (or apocalyptic) the basis of his Christian politics. To my knowledge, however, no one has examined systematically the specific emphases of the evangelical doctrine and practice for how they have shaped and/or should shape the very character of evangelical political existence in society.

26. In a sense, a push for an evangelical social engagement for the gospel should be seen as a renewal of something that was previously there in evangelicalism. Donald W. Dayton, for example, has written extensively about the powerful social presence of evangelicals for justice prior to the 1920s in North America. Dayton, *Discovering an Evangelical Heritage.* See also Moberg, *Great Reversal.*

27. For example, see Donald W. Dayton's comments in this regard in "'Evangelical': More Puzzling."

28. The publications on this topic are too numerous to give a fair representation. A place to start might be Dayton and Johnson, *Variety of Evangelicalism.* Also see an

the issue is that evangelicalism is not a single defined institution or church denomination. Many of its most representative organizations, such as the National Association of Evangelicals, are loosely organized and always in flux. Its churches employ diverse worship forms and organize around different doctrinal emphases. Many evangelicals worship in distinctly non-evangelical places such as Protestant mainline and even Roman Catholic churches. To make matters more complex, many of the sons and daughters of evangelicals largely repudiate the term because its cultural baggage embarrasses them. Consequently, to put it mildly, the label "evangelical" has its problems.

Nonetheless, despite its problems, I still maintain that there remains a large constituency of people who gather around the label of evangelicalism in North America. I contend that they largely coalesce around its three doctrinal emphases as described by historian David Bebbington. As previously mentioned, these doctrinal emphases are 1) a high view of the authority of the Bible; 2) a strong belief in a personal conversion experience; and 3) an activist engagement with culture (in ways peculiar to evangelicalism itself). Bebbington, as does Mark Noll who follows him in this trajectory, traces the history and identity of evangelicalism to these three doctrinal distinctives plus an additional one.[29] For the purposes of this study, I have collapsed Bebbington's two emphases on conversion and the substitutionary atonement theory into one—the conversion experience based upon faith in the substitionary work of Christ on the cross. I contend that many evangelicals still unite around these three central commitments and the practices associated with them.[30]

---

historical attempt at responding to the issue by Stone, *On the Boundaries*.

29. Mark Noll describes these characteristics as an unwavering commitment to Biblical authority, an aggressive adaptive engagement with surrounding culture, an emphasis on a conversion experience, and the atoning work of Christ on the cross as central to the evangelical faith and identity in *American Evangelical Christianity*, 13, and his *Rise of Evangelicalism*, 19–20. He follows David Bebbington who argues a similar case describing the priorities of the evangelical movement of the nineteenth century as biblicism, activism, crucicentrism, and conversionism in *Dominance of Evangelicalism*, ch. 1. I am following both of these scholars, except that I am conflating the conversion experience with the centrality of Christ's atoning death into one core attribute. See also Collins, *Evangelical Moment*, chs. 1–2, where Collins identifies evangelicalism in very similar terms to Bebbington and Noll.

30. This is not to deny the diversity of and different degrees of all these beliefs among evangelicals. Many evangelicals have "gone high church" yet remain evangeli-

Statistical data can confirm that such a people exists. The Pew Forum, for instance, delineates how as many as 50 million people gathered around these central ideas in their report of 2004.[31] The American Religious Identification Survey (ARIS) of 2008 records similar numbers for self-identifying born-again "evangelicals" who belong to specifically evangelically defined churches.[32] David Gushee summarizes interesting data that at least shows the influence of evangelicals as a sociological force in the 2004 election of George W. Bush to the presidency. Although he does not correlate evangelicalism with these three belief characteristics, the organizations he points to all possess a well-defined allegiance to all three of these criteria.[33] In addition, Mark Noll outlines statistical evidence for a large population of evangelicals who follow these beliefs in his *American Evangelical Christianity*, published in 2001.[34]

---

cal. Many evangelicals stay within Protestant mainline denominations while others reject all denominational affiliation.

31. Per the Pew Forum's Measurement of the Size of Religious Communities in the U.S. 2004 Survey available at http://pewforum.org. There is much overlap between the way this study defined evangelicalism and the way I am defining it.

32. Statistician Michael Bell calculates, using the ARIS data, that if you took all of the self-identifying evangelicals (via "born again" term) who congregate at explicitly evangelical denominational churches (subtracting the mainline Protestants and Roman Catholics) you would have 56.5 million adult evangelicals in the United States. Although the Bebbington criteria are not used per se, the "born again" self-chosen-identity together with institutional identity (members of institutions which largely adhere to the Bebbington criteria) argue for this large number falling in some way under the evangelical umbrella as I am defining it. See his report at http://eclecticchristian .com/2009/03/17/the-coming-evangelical-collapse-a-statistical-support-part-2/. Bell gives a compelling analysis of just why this data reveals evangelicals are at a crisis tipping point heading for a major decline in North America. The ARIS (American Religious Identity Survey) Survey can be found online: http://www.americanreligion survey-aris.org/.

33. Gushee and Phillips, "Moral Formation and the Evangelical Voter," 32–36.

34. If you take the main institutions and key figures of evangelicalism, including the magazine Christianity Today, Campus Crusade for Christ, James Dobson and his radio empire Focus on the Family, the National Association of Evangelicals as well as evangelical activists such as the deceased Jerry Falwell, Pat Robertson, the evangelist Billy Graham, as well as the evangelical megachurch leaders of the last thirty years, they all adhere to these basic beliefs. Together, these identifying beliefs mark a large body of people in North America labeled as evangelicals. See Noll, *American Evangelical Christianity*, ch. 2.

Statistics alone however do not legitimate this definition of evangelicalism. Though helpful, any statistical data would require a much more exhaustive defense and interpretation than I am able to offer in this study.[35] Instead, by using these three emphases as the basis of this study, I hope to show how this description of evangelicalism best explains what has happened to it. I hope to show how these three doctrinal emphases were changed into de-personalized concepts (what we will call "master-signifiers" later) that evangelicals gave their political allegiance to. The resulting ideological formation, I hope to show, best explains the evangelical cultural impasse that is so evidenced in the culture today. I hope to display as well how these evangelical doctrines produced the kinds of people evidenced in numerous embarrassing cultural episodes on the cultural plane of American media and culture (as I will be explaining, I will call these episodes "irruptions of the Real"). All together, this description of evangelicalism, if compelling, should itself demonstrate the validity of the way I am defining evangelicalism.

Following Bebbington's doctrinal emphases provides an added benefit as well for a political theology because each one of these emphases can be followed within the history of evangelicalism. This history provides a compelling explanation of the evolution of evangelicalism as a form of politics. David Moberg (together with Donald Dayton and others) once isolated a moment of "reversal" in evangelicalism's history where it turned against its own commitments towards the justice of the wider society and became more pessimistic towards culture.[36] The politics of evangelicalism changed dramatically here in reaction to what many have called "modernist-fundamentalist" controversies of the 1920s in American church history. I propose that we can locate in this history the development of each one of these doctrinal emphases and understand further why evangelicalism's politic formed the way it did.

---

35. As with any statistics, these are prone to being manipulated and interpreted in order to build a certain case. As Mark Noll took note of, much of the available data are often tainted by an agenda to define "norms of political conviction or action." Noll, *Scandal of the Evangelical Mind*, 226.

36. On this reaction see Moberg, *Great Reversal*, Dayton, *Discovering an Evangelical*, ch. 10; Marsden, *Fundamentalism*, chs. 9–11.

Each one of Bebbington's three doctrinal emphases has been shaped by the "modernist-fundamentalist" controversy. In regard to evangelicalism's high view of Scripture, many of evangelicalism's churches and institutions resulted from the split within mainline Protestantism over this issue in the 1920s. Over against the German historical-critical attacks on the reliability of Scripture that was happening in many seminaries, these "evangelical" churches asserted various doctrines of "the inerrancy" of Scripture. The famous B. B. Warfield defense of inerrancy was adopted as an evangelical litmus test for many within evangelical orthodoxy.[37] Likewise, in regard to the evangelical emphasis on personal conversion, evangelicals came from a history in America's eighteenth- and nineteenth-century revivals.[38] As a result they believed strongly in personal conversion. This was firmly welded to a commitment to the substitutionary atoning work of Christ on the cross during the modernist-fundamentalist controversies. Here, over against the threat towards this doctrine of atonement during these controversies, the emphasis upon the cross was forged. Likewise, in regard to evangelicalism's "activist" stance towards evangelism and cross-cultural missions, much of this was shaped in reaction to the same modernist-fundamentalist controversy. In particular evangelicals resisted the "social gospel" form of cultural engagement as proposed by Walter Rauschenbusch and mainline Protestantism.[39] They rejected it because they perceived a diminishment of the work of Christ on the cross for the forgiveness of our sins. Consequently, they sought all the more to engage culture with the gospel of personal forgiveness of sins. An evangelicalism that was stunningly engaged in social-justice reforms up to this point underwent a "great reversal" turning towards personal salvation as the way into culture. In many ways, this has marked the ways evangelicals view church and social activism to this day. Together, these three emphases are part of the "fundamentals" that

37. See George Marsden's work on this including *Understanding Fundamentalism*, 31–35, *Fundamentalism and American Culture*, 171–77, *Reforming*, 4–5. To see a dissenting view of the role of "inerrancy" and the Princeton defense in the identity of evangelicalism, see Dayton, "Search for the Historical."

38. See Bebbington, *Dominance of Evangelicalism*, 22–26. On the formative influence of revivalism on evangelicalism see Noll, *Scandal of the Evangelical Mind*, 60–64, Marsden, *Fundamentalism and American Culture*, 43–48.

39. See for instance Marsden, *Fundamentalism and American Culture*, 91–92

were published in the twenties, in reaction to these same modernist-fundamentalist controversies, around which many rallied who then later became evangelicals.[40]

Focusing on these three doctrinal emphases then enables us to examine what shaped the fate of evangelical politics. We not only can construct an evangelical political theology but we can also understand its past in terms of a "fall" that led evangelicalism to this point. This proposed "fall" is not about evangelicals turning and becoming more pessimistic towards society.[41] It is not even that salvation became more personal and less social for evangelicals. Rather, what I hope to show is that evangelicalism, in reaction to the modernist-fundamentalist controversies, pursued a strategy for survival via a defense based in the autonomous structures of modern reason and politics. In the process, we gave up the true core of our Christian politics—the person and work of Jesus Christ—and set ourselves up for a fall by in essence becoming a form of "religious ideology." We in essence emptied our social politic of its core in Jesus Christ for a politics buttressed by the temporary structures of modernity. Understanding this narrative, I believe, makes the Bebbington-Noll description of evangelicalism all the more compelling for constructing and understanding evangelicalism as a political ideology.

Examining Evangelicalism as Ideology

I propose then that we examine evangelicalism as an ideology. Let us understand our theological commitments and the way they work to bind us together as a people. Let us understand how these beliefs order our various desires within our community so as to form our disposition to the world. Let us survey evangelical culture and its manifestations in the broader American culture for irruptions on its surface that not only confirm our findings but also help us further understand what is going on in our politics in the world. Let us not stop there, however. Let us

40. Torrey, *The Fundamentals.*

41. Here people like Ernest Sandeen argue that, given the impetus for inerrancy, dispensational schemes of biblical interpretation were adopted that in essence ensconced a pessimistic view of eschatology where the world would get worse until Jesus returns. See Sandeen, *Roots of Fundamentalism,* Marsden, *Fundamentalism and American Culture,* 66–70.

also ask what Christian faithfulness would look like in our political life in the midst of our crisis and what might be the basis for the birthing of a new politic faithful to God's mission. Let us examine whether the new emerging movements springing forth from evangelicalism in the last ten years—including the emerging church and missional church movements—can provide the basis for a new faithfulness in these times.

Few theorists are as equipped for helping us with the first several of these tasks as the continental theorist Slavoj Žižek. He is perhaps today's premier political and cultural theorist of ideology. I contend that Žižek's analysis exposes the way evangelicalism works as a social system. Some of his most basic concepts can provide the basis for studying evangelicalism as a political ideology. It is thus to Žižek that we now turn.

CHAPTER 2

Žižek and the Evangelicals: The (Psycho)Analysis
of an Ideology in Crisis

"Tolerance makes everything boring, we need more conflict!"[1]

—Slavoj Žižek

As a teenager sitting in church on a Sunday evening, I would ask myself why the people in my church acted as they did. For starters, we had a Sunday evening service that in many ways repeated what we did on Sunday morning. Why would these people keep coming to church on Sunday evening to repeat the same things they did on Sunday morning all over again? Why would they come to hear teaching they already knew and in fact had already heard that same morning? Don't get me wrong. I loved my church. Yet in surveying the various behaviors of my church family, sometimes I had to wonder what drove these people to do these things they kept doing week after week?

It was not just the evangelical oddity of the Sunday evening church service either. There was an assortment of behaviors that were distinctive to us as evangelicals. Take, for instance, the regular altar calls at the end of the service that asked if you had made "a decision for Christ." After a "backslidden" episode, many of us would go forward to the altar to make the same decision over and over again. What drove our church to make this "decision" such a big deal and yet not really

1. From Slavoj Žižek's faculty page at The European Graduate School accessible at http://www.egs.edu/faculty/slavoj-Žižek/quotes/.

know if it "took" or not? There was also the strange attachment to the American flag and conservative politics that was present in my church. To be a good Christian somehow meant also to be a good American. Yet we would pray for the nations, even wars against these nations, and of course our missionaries overseas. There was a religious devotion to carrying around a large, leather-bound, black Bible. Everyone took amazing comfort from declaring that what he or she was doing was "biblical." Yet during heated church conflicts, from what I could gather, few people would actually discuss the issue in a way that was directly informed by the Bible itself. This was the culture of evangelicalism in which I grew up. These were the rituals of our belief that deeply shaped who we were and how we lived in relation to God and society. In a strange kind of way, it made us feel good.

Many years later, as I reflect back on those Sunday evenings sitting in church, I try to imagine some way of getting this church to a good psychoanalyst. Maybe a good trip to the therapist would have helped us figure ourselves out? Perhaps we could have all crowded into the office and got to the root of what provoked such anger when people disagreed over what was biblical, why so many in our congregation "went ballistic" when somebody wanted to move the flag from the pulpit, or why we were so insistent on making sure of everyone's decision for Christ, even when they continually did it over and over again.

Perhaps this is why I find the Slovenian philosopher/cultural theorist Slavoj Žižek compelling for understanding evangelicalism. Reading Žižek is like doing therapy upon an entire culture. Like few political theorists, he can get to the heart of a politic by asking what drives a people to believe certain things and then coalesce around these same beliefs. He understands that "ideology" takes place in the root practices we keep doing together even when they don't make sense. He is able to keenly observe the contradictions that irrupt within a culture and/or political ideology and then help us see what drives people to ignore these contradictions in order to believe their ideologies all the more firmly. His theory fits well with the kind of ideological analysis I believe we evangelicals need in regard to our politics and our way of life together.

In the past fifteen years, Žižek has risen to become a compelling figure in contemporary political/cultural theory as well as continental philosophy. He is a master of Hegelian thought, Marxist political theory, and Lacanian social psychoanalysis,[2] using all three together to develop his political theory. All the while he entertains and provokes with clever, if not crude, cultural observations from cinema and other pop culture. Žižek can be difficult to read for the uninitiated in Continental philosophy and critical theory. Nevertheless, he manages like few others to focus on how political systems play on human subjectivity (the way we see ourselves) and desire in order to drive people to come together and be a part of a political system. In short, Žižek is well suited for the ideological analysis I am proposing for evangelicalism.

In what follows, I seek to describe some of Žižek's most intuitive concepts concerning political ideology (from his early to middle stages of his work)[3] in the hope that we can make good use of them in understanding evangelicalism as a political community in North America. As if we were with a skilled therapist, I believe Žižek helps reveal how certain beliefs and practices function in our life together. He helps expose the drives behind their peculiar hold over us as a people in North America. In saying this, I do not wish to imply that our beliefs as Christians are somehow necessarily false or illusory. Rather, the ways in which we articulate and practice them can take on a peculiar shape and reify (become hardened and accepted as fact) for ideological purposes. We can abstract our beliefs out of real life and make them concepts to be used for certain social agendas. They effectively become ideology. In the process, our beliefs and practices cover over antagonisms at work in our life together. These beliefs can keep on going ignoring the

2. Jacques Lacan (1901–1981) was a French psychoanalyst who sought to re-write much of Freud and in so doing applied his resultant reinterpretation of Freud's psychoanalytic theories to many social, political, and cultural disciplines. Much of his early work is interpreted as post-structuralist. His later work as found in his *Ecrits*, is post-post-structuralism and is the focus of Žižek's appropriation.

3. As far as actual appropriation of Žižek, I will be staying mainly with Žižek's earlier period from *Sublime Object of Ideology* (1989) to *Tarrying With the Negative* (1993) although some of Žižek's later turn towards Badiou in *Ticklish Subject* will become important. I find Adam Kotsko's "periodizing" of Žižek's work helpful in this regard. *Žižek and Theology*. Though somewhat antipathic to Žižek himself, Kotsko sees Žižek's development as falling into three periods of which the last period is preoccupied with developing a reading of Christianity as part of his defense of a dialectical materialism advancing both Hegel and Lacan. Here is Žižek's famous turn towards theology and the more thorough development of his "materialist theology." This third "period" of his work, as Kotsko labels it, does not really figure into this project. Indeed, I might be working Žižek against himself and these latest theological developments in his work.

contradictions that are the source of our unraveling. Like few others, Žižek can expose these antagonisms. Like a satisfying "session" with a therapist, our goal in coming to Žižek is to come away with a deeper understanding of what drives evangelical belief and practice in order to understand our current unraveling.

As with any good therapist, however, Žižek can only get us so far. Good therapy helps a patient become aware of what he or she is doing destructively and what motivates him/her to keep doing it. Yet therapy (as a secular practice), I contend, is limited for aiding Christian formation towards the reordering of our lives towards God.[4] In similar ways, we will see that Žižek's political theory has its limits for Christian theology. For the work of Christian theology, Žižek can certainly clarify how disordered and broken (and hence ideological) political systems work. Yet because of his ontological commitments, he offers little direction for how a broken Christian political system, i.e., the church, might be more faithful.[5] For this, we will eventually need to turn elsewhere. For now, however, we turn to understanding Žižek's political theory and a few of his key concepts as the means for understanding evangelicalism as an ideology.

WHAT DRIVES OUR SOCIAL EXISTENCE?

Žižek's political theory (his earlier period[6]) portrays political systems almost as if they have personality (reflexivity). For Žižek, political systems have an inner social consciousness wherein there is a constant

4. In this vein, John Milbank argues "If, therefore, psychoanalysis can never help you to an adult fulfillment of desire (as Freud partially hoped), neither can it truly cure you of desire. For your symptomatic desire is not a sign of a psychic disease—it is rather a sinthome, what you are, and it is this alone which analysis helps better to reveal. Therefore desire, which cannot be cured, must also be tragically persisted in—regardless of social chaos thereby caused—because the alternative would be suicidal abandonment of selfhood." Milbank in Žižek et al., *Monstrosity of Christ*, 120. A similar line of thought can be found in Milbank, "Materialism," 395–96.

5. It should be noted, I do not intend a serious critical engagement of Žižek's ontological or theological proposals in this book. Instead I aim for an appropriation of Žižek's earlier work on political theory. Granted, it will be necessary to engage his construal of social reality (political ontology) for what it teaches us concerning the "lack" in ideological systems and what this might reveal about the politic of evangelicalism itself. This comes later in this chapter.

6. From *Sublime Object* (1989) to *For They Know not* (1993).

working out of conflicts, the ordering of desires, and the sustaining of meaning. In his own words, "Tolerance makes everything boring we need more conflict!"[7] The task for political analysis is to reveal the antagonisms at the core of these systems and the structures that smooth them over.

Central to Žižek's political theory is the idea of the Symbolic Order. He assumes political/social systems are linguistic structures composed of institutions, rituals, social norms, and language itself. He (following Lacan) calls the given social system (one finds oneself in) the Symbolic Order. It is this Symbolic Order that actually births the individual as a subject (via the Imaginary[8]) into the political system.[9] Here we find ourselves in relation to "the big Other" of the system, that societal "group think" that enables us to believe in something and find our way within it. The subject/person is always-already mediated by the linguistic world/Symbolic Order he/she finds herself in. It is at this intersection of the subject and the Symbolic Order that Žižek conducts his social psychoanalysis.[10] Žižek is ever analyzing the given Symbolic Order to uncover the way it works in compensating for conflict and consolidating power within the status quo, all the while holding subjects together in the social system. Here we can see how beliefs function to stave off antagonisms and play on people's deepest desires and insecurities, yet hold a people together and maintain the status quo.

7. From Slavoj Žižek's faculty page at The European Graduate School accessible at http://www.egs.edu/faculty/slavoj-Žižek/quotes.

8. The "Symbolic Order" is brought into being via the "Imaginary": this realm of appearances, ideas and conflicts that the Symbolic Order organizes for the ego. Beyond the Symbolic Order and the Imaginary is "the Real"—the untamed forces that resist all final symbolization. This is the famous triad of Lacan that underlies Žižek's political theory.

9. The individual is "interpellated" into the political system thereby granted an identity. "Interpellation" is a term Žižek borrows from Marxist philosopher Louis Althusser describing the way an ideology addresses the individual thus absorbing him/her into the ideological field. Once the individual recognizes him/herself in the address, she effectively has become a subject (an ego with an identity) of the ideological system.

10. The subject is formed by in essence giving up immediacy for the mediation of the Symbolic Order. The subject receives an identity but is always split, never complete. It is at this intersection that much can be revealed in terms of what drives the Symbolic Order. See Žižek, *Indivisible Remainder*.

Yet Žižek does not encourage us to confront the Symbolic Order directly. This is not the way to provoke change. Traditionally, Marxist theory advocated that we directly critique ideology, revealing it as a "false consciousness." Let us show, so the standard approach goes, how capitalism is a ruse for the wealthy proletariat exploiting the bourgeoisie! Žižek says this accomplishes nothing. Instead, a central piece to Žižek's early political theory is his notion of "ideological cynicism."[11] Subjects of the developed world, Žižek says, are too smart to become duped by the political ideologies of Western states. They are wise to the fact that all political speech is just more "political spin." It is accepted that ideologies are offered to appease us (its subjects) and to make us feel better about ourselves (morally) so that all of us, including those in privilege, can keep on conserving what it is we really desire. So now, as Žižek tells us, political theorists do not analyze ideology by observing "they do not know it, but they are doing it." Instead they observe "they know it, but they are doing it anyway."[12] Today's citizens listen to all the new political speeches and know nothing will really change, yet they participate in it anyway. Žižek therefore emphasized, in his early work, that ideology serves this kind of cynical function: giving the citizenry a Big Other to believe in and assuage our guilt while, beneath what we say, we are content with the status quo. Ideology provides a big lie with which we can all cooperate in order to keep our lives going. As we look at evangelicalism as an ideology, we must also ask whether some of our most basic beliefs and practices have become soothing ideologies. Far from calling us into a gospel faithfulness, have our beliefs become the means to maintain the status quo while at the same time comforting us that we still believe?

Foundational to Žižek's ideological analysis is that there is no ontological truth or ideal around which to form a political system. Drawing on Marx, Hegel, and Lacan, Žižek argues that political systems are held together by ideology and its sustenance of a way of life around certain drives/appeasement of antagonisms. There is no truth that defines its core. Ideology is indeed empty at its core. All political systems are founded upon an inaugural (primordial) trauma that

---

11. As found first and foremost in his *Sublime Object*, 28–30.

12. Here Žižek is quoting Sloterdijk, *Kritik der Zynishen Vernunft*. See *Sublime Object*, 29.

establishes what "we" are for versus what "we" are against.[13] Playing on the fears and insecurities of people, an antagonism is created that sustains the System. For Žižek (to oversimplify) this is what is real, this is "the Real" that drives the System.

American democracy, for instance, does not embody any transcendent ideal such as the inalienable rights of each individual person to pursue "life, liberty and the pursuit of happiness." Instead, this ideology is driven by the antagonism between those who wish to accumulate wealth in freedom and the disadvantaged people who are victims of this wealth accumulation. This antagonism, covered over by the idea of "freedom," founded the American system of democracy as it rebelled against the monarchy of the British commonwealth at the time of the American revolution. The American ideology of "inalienable rights" and "freedom" holds together a people around this antagonism. One could say that this is the antagonism behind the ongoing back-and-forth cycle between Democrat and Republican politics year after year, election after election.[14] It is this antagonism (at least one of them), "the Real," that lies at the core of the American ideology and keeps it going. It drives the ideology of capitalism and democracy, and it is covered over by the ideology. Uncovering this antagonism, and the inner contradictions that drive it, exposes the why, the how, and the powers behind it. It can be a maneuver towards loosening the ideology's hold on a group of people.

In similar ways, we can examine evangelicalism as a social system operating via an ideology. We can explore whether evangelicalism has become a politics founded upon such an antagonism. Many trace today's evangelicalism to the trauma of the modernist-fundamentalist controversies of the 1920s (already discussed in chapter 1). Here, Protestant mainline theologians denied the historical veracity of Scripture and minimized the atoning sacrifice of Christ on the cross as the means for

13. Žižek is a "dialectical materialist" believing that "the way things are" is not derived from a transcendent source. Instead the truth/reality of our life together is totally immanent to our structures. Furthermore, this truth is ever worked out dialectically in an ongoing reflective logic à la Hegel. Žižek, it should be noted, interprets Hegel in ways that go significantly beyond traditional account of Hegelian dialectics. For a good exposition of Žižek's use of Hegel and his dialectic, see Žižek, *For They Know Not*, 31–36. Adam Kotsko also explains this in accessible form in his *Žižek and Theology*, 9–12.

14. All of the above draws on Žižek, *The Sublime Object*, 6, 28–30.

our salvation. The forbearers of evangelicalism, the so-called "fundamentalists," founded Bible churches all across North America in protest against the Protestant liberal agenda. In the throws of defending their Christian faith against these so-called "modernist" attacks on the Bible and personal salvation, a new form of church, i.e., politics, was birthed labeled later as evangelicalism. These fundamentalists at the time (who were to become the modern-day evangelicals) responded with various forms of intellectual defense built on the same "modernist" principles. Driven by fear, amidst these conflicts, evangelicalism's beliefs and practices were constructed. Could it be that this same belief and practice developed into an ideology in the Žižekian sense, driven by fear and antagonism within American society? Could it be that, as time went by, evangelicalism acquired a status-quo position in American society wherein its belief and practice became the means to maintain its status quo, à la Žižekian ideology? And so, years later, we find this evangelical belief and practice acting like an ideology in crisis. I suggest that Žižek's political theory can throw some light upon the evolvement of evangelicalism. Our task will be to unravel its ideological malfunctions so as to return it to a faithful politic in Christ for God's mission in the world. For now, however, let us sketch a few basic concepts from Žižek's political theory that we will employ in the analysis to come.

Master Signifiers

A first basic concept for our analysis is the notion of a "master-signifier."[15] A master-signifier is a conceptual object around which people give their allegiance thereby enabling a political group to form. It represents something to believe in, a badge which identifies us as part of this political cause. Given his "cynical" assumptions, Žižek says, every ideology must provide a "fantasy" wherein the citizenry can act *as if* we believe. We may, for example, know the president is a "tool" of multi-national corporate interests; nevertheless, the U.S. government

15. The term "master-signifier" of course is not original to Žižek. It plays off of the back drop of the whole structuralism/post-structuralism movement in political theory including the early work of Levi-Straus and Saussure. The "master-signifier" as Žižek finds it, as well as the role of antagonism at the core of ideology, is indebted to political theorists Laclau and Mouffe, *Hegemony*, as well as Marx himself. See also Laclau *Emancipation(s)*, ch. 3 and also his preface written for Žižek, *Sublime Object*.

provides the fantasy of "the Will of the People" that enables us to act *as if* the president actually serves on our behalf.[16] These "fantasies" function with "master-signifiers" to hold a people (by their belief in them) together in the system. The signifiers are "quilting points" (*point de capiton*), the knots that hold together the whole quilt of ideology by which all of the subjects find their orientation in society.[17]

A key aspect of these "master-signifiers" is that they really do not refer to anything to which anyone can point. For Žižek, "the Party" in Stalinist Russia, "God" in theocracy, or "Freedom" in democracy are all "signifiers without the signified." He emphasizes that no one really knows to what these fantasmic "objects" (or political words—"Will of the People") actually refer. No one has ever actually seen it with his or her own eyes. They are "empty signifiers."[18] This quality allows for these signifiers to function on a level of vagueness where they can play into a people's desires, aligning them together towards or against certain objects. In other words, I may not understand "Freedom" or "the Will of the People" in the same way as my neighbor or the millions of other Americans who believe in them. Yet this nebulous quality allows for us all to be united together in American democracy as if we all believe in the same thing. The signifier provides enough distance between the subject and the unifying fantasy so that the signifier can bind a whole community together.[19]

Most people remember Barack Obama's campaign slogan that centered around the word "change" during the 2008 presidential campaign. Whether it was "change we can believe in" or "Yes, we can!," the dominant idea around which Obama's campaign centered was on

---

16. Žižek, *Sublime Object*; 36 see also 30–33.

17. For a fuller description of "quilting point," see Žižek, *For They Know Not*, 16–20.

18. The term "empty-signifier" is also borrowed by Žižek from LaClau. See for instance Laclau, *Emancipation(s)*, ch. 3.

19. The way a master-signifier works is best summarized in a paragraph by Žižek on Lacan in *The Fragile Absolute*: "Suffice it to recall how a community functions: the Master Signifier which guarantees the community's consistency is a signifier whose signified is an enigma for the members themselves—nobody really knows what it means, but each of them somehow presupposes that others know, that it has to mean 'the real thing', so they use it all the time . . . This logic is at work not only in politico-ideological links . . . but even in some Lacanian communities where the group recognizes itself through common use of some jargonized expressions whose meaning is not clear to anyone . . ." Žižek, *Fragile Absolute*, 114–15.

"change." But of course, in the end, no one really knew what it might actually mean. It had sufficient vagueness—sufficient distance from the subject to the signifier—that the frustrated individual could import into it whatever meaning and frustration they carried over from the previous Bush administration years, whether one was a poor African American living in the ghetto, a white educated middle-class New Yorker, or a laid-off blue-collar worker in Detroit. "Change" played well into the antagonism being aroused by the previous failed Bush administration. Master-signifiers, then, are more about the antagonisms at work in a social sphere than any specific ideal or concrete plan of action. The cynic would argue that the economic and social policies of the Obama administration leave very little room for change at all. The Obama administration could, in fact, change some things on the periphery, but it was locked into being the tool of corporatist power given the economic crisis his administration had to deal with. It was Obama's master-signifier of "change" that enabled us to believe in something righteous while at the same time allowing for more of the same, the status quo, which in the end we are all more comfortable with anyway. In so doing, these signifiers allowed us to consent to what we know is a lie, all the while bringing some release for the antagonism at the core of our life together—what Žižek calls "the Real."[20] In this way, "Change" functioned as a classic Žižekian "master-signifier."

Uncovering these master-signifiers enables us to see just what holds us under an ideology's spell. And so, in Žižek's earlier political theory, he followed a method of surveying "the fantasy" for master-signifiers. If the fantasy is an ideological field in which subjects are able to see themselves and verbalize who they are and why they continue on in this economic and political structure, one can look for its master-signifiers in order to reveal how they work to bind us as subjects into an ideology, form us as a people, and weave us into a web of social compla-

---

20. To quote Žižek in this regard, "the coordination (between the subjects in a political community) concerns not the level of the signified (of some positive shared concern) but the level of the signifier. (In political ideologies), undecidability with regard to the signified (do others really intend the same as me?) converts into an exceptional signifier, the empty signifier, the empty master signifier, the signifier without the signified; nation, democracy, socialism and other causes stand for that something about which we are not exactly sure what it is. The point rather is that identifying with the nation we signal our acceptance of what others accept, with a master signifier which serves as a rallying point for all the others." Žižek, *Indivisible Remainder*, 142.

cency. For Žižek, these signifiers allow believers to become complicit with ruthless systems like Stalinist communism or the carnivorous capitalism of late modernity. The aim of uncovering the master-signifiers of an ideology is to show how we practice these belief structures without really believing them, with the hopes we might "traverse the fantasy," i.e., break free from its hold on us as subjects thereby enabling us to renounce the Symbolic Order—the Big Other.

I propose we follow Žižek in uncovering the fantasies of evangelicalism. By isolating the master-signifiers of evangelicalism and by showing the way they work, we can reveal the ways evangelicals are passivized and become complicit in systems with which we normally would have nothing to do. We can expose the ways we really do not take our own beliefs seriously. We can see clearly the desires that shape our congregating that in themselves form our dispositions/desires in the world. By examining our beliefs in Scripture, salvation, and the church in the world in these ways we can understand how they work to facilitate our comfortable and enjoyable lives within the current society.

Yet by no means do I wish to imply that our core beliefs as evangelicals do not refer to actual realities (Scripture, salvation and the church). Rather, what I hope to show is that we have adopted certain ways of framing these foundational beliefs into "sublime objects"[21] so that our belief and practice have become, in essence, a functioning ideology. By exposing the way these objects function, we can reveal the ways we participate in evangelicalism that make us complicit with social systems we might otherwise see as contrary to the gospel.

IRRUPTIONS OF THE REAL

A second basic concept for our analysis is the notion of an "irruption of the Real." This phrase never really appears in Žižek's work directly as a means of analysis.[22] Nonetheless, I use the term to amalgamate a few ideas found within Žižek's political theory that can aid us in

---

21. A "sublime object" according to Žižek is "a positive, material object elevated to the status of the impossible Thing." *Sublime Object*, 71. It is another/yet slightly different nuanced way of talking about the master-signifier.

22. It does appear in Žižek's *Sublime Object*, 147. However, I wish to fill the term out in a way that remains faithful to Žižek's political apparatus yet diverges from Žižek's direct use of the phrase there.

understanding evangelicalism as a failing ideology. "Irruption of the Real" describes an excessive episode within a political system that reveals the drives (the antagonism and the basic lack) that lie beneath the ideology.[23]

Remembering that, for Žižek, there is a fundamental antagonism that lies at the core of every political system; there can be no escaping it. It is "the Real." When an ideology is founded, it always excludes something in order to preserve what has already been accepted. The Symbolic Order, including its master-signifiers, can never absorb entirely the conflicting forces. In the case of a common Marxist example, the ideology of capitalism is able to sustain the inequality of the poor workers over against those they work for (who were born into privilege) by promoting the ideal of "Freedom." We are all free to work for whomever we want! And yet there are challenges to this freedom. So when discriminatory practices were exposed in the 1960s that revealed grotesque economic inequality, legislation was enacted that outlawed the Jim Crow discriminatory practices (civil rights legislation). The new law forbade people from segregating public spaces into separate places for "blacks and whites," thus giving certain new freedoms to African Americans. The legitimacy of "freedom" was maintained as an ideology. The ideological cynic, however, argues that the same economic inequality continues on. Nothing has really changed. The underlying antagonism has been preserved. Indeed, by framing the problem of racial discrimination legally, the economic system actually separated economic inequality from discrimination thereby enabling economic inequality to go on in the name of freedom.[24] "You see, you are no longer discriminated against! So now your economic disadvantage has nothing to do with discrimination!" Outlawing Jim Crow actually made possible the continuance of the privileging of one group over another group for the sake of profit. And so, in the process of "ideologizing," the antagonism continues on, always in negotiation. It is this moving con-

23. The "lack" refers to the fact that there is nothing ontologically stable at the core but rather that this social system is built around what it is not, or what it has not, or the fears and hatreds generated externally thereby.

24. Waldo Martin for instance argued that the Brown vs. Board of Education decision in 1954 further ensconced an attitude in the liberal courts that economic inequality is separate from racial inequality. That indeed "legalization of the problem of racial discrimination" made possible the entrenching of economic inequalities. Martin, *Brown v.*, 34–35.

tradiction that can never be resolved. If it were resolved, there would be no reason for a political system to exist.

Political systems, therefore, are inherently unstable. We should expect irruptions of the Real that reveal the internal conflicts and drives of the ideologies. These irruptions could be awkward episodes in the lives of public figures that reflect back upon the system. They could be works of art, or cinema, or other cultural artifacts that reveal the absurdity of what we say we believe. These irruptions are almost always embarrassing, even to those who "buy into" the system, because they uncover the drive behind what we all believe and the hidden void at the core of the system. So when, for example, Senator Strom Thurmond ran for president in 1948 as the nominee for the States Rights Party on the slogan "Segregation forever!," the drive behind "freedom" was in a sense revealed. Under the ideology of freedom via "State Rights"—that each local state government have the freedom to run its own affairs— he espoused segregation! The excessive claim to preserve freedom by segregating American "blacks" was almost too embarrassing for any establishment Democrat to acknowledge. It revealed what the freedom was really about. It was an absurd irruption of the Real and it unmasked the ideology of freedom.

Irruptions of "the Real," then, reveal the contradictions at the core of our politics. Surveying a culture or political system for such irruptions can reveal much about what is being left unsaid, what is being excluded, and where the chief drive lies behind the system's very existence. Irruptions of the Real are like tears in the political fabric that reveal too much and so can prepare the way for a further unraveling. By surveying the cultural plane of evangelicalism for these kind of irruptions, I believe we can discover similar kinds of insights about what drives its politic.

Irruptions of the Real can also make an opening for what Žižek would call "a decisive revolutionary Act."[25] Here, amidst the continual revealing of its drives and contradictions, an ideology can lose its hold on its subjects. Leadership and/or movements can then emerge for a more direct engagement of the System's lack. The irruptions of the Real can set forth the space for a "revolution." By isolating these irruptions

25. I am drawing here on Slavoj Žižek's descriptions of "act" in his *Did Somebody Say?* Of course, Žižek's original understanding of "act" and "revolution" has been steadily evolving into various other less-overt tactics.

then, we can understand the new movements in terms of what they are reacting to and in what ways they emerge in fidelity to the new revealing.[26] I believe, as we look at the emerging church movement and other present-day reactions to evangelicalism (in the epilogue to this book), we can understand them better via the irruptions in evangelicalism. We can examine from whence they came and understand whether they too are repetitions of the same politic.

Two pieces of Žižek's political theory further help us recognize irruptions of the Real when we see them. They are a) overidentification, and b) *jouissance*.

Overidentification

For Žižek, an overidentification occurs whenever someone within an ideology takes the ideology too seriously, thereby exposing its absurdity. Such an overidentification cannot only be embarrassing but traumatic as it exposes what lies behind the ideology. Such an overidentification is a sure "give-away" that what we are seeing is indeed an irruption of the Real. Žižek calls for "overidentification" (a psychoanalytic term) as a tactic for unsettling a dominant political ideology.

To remind us, for Žižek, ideology is immune to overt criticism because even its progenitors do not believe its own declarations, and they know its constituents do not either. The strategy of overtly criticizing ideology, therefore, misses the point, because every ideological discourse has already internalized its own critique. Each overt criticism merely affords the ideology another opportunity to re-create itself. Žižek therefore proposes that we believe the ideology so much that its incoherence is exposed. He proposes we push the implications of what the ideology proposes to its extreme in order to reveal its absurdity and in the process, what it is hiding. This is the tactic of "overidentification."

The farcical figure Borat, in the movie of the same name, illustrates the tactic of overidentification. In a typical scene, Borat walks in to a Texas rodeo full of "red-necks" supporting the Iraq war (he is posing as a journalist from Kazakhstan coming to sing the National Anthem). Borat shouts "Can I say first that we support your war on terror!" where

---

26. Or as French political theorist Alain Badiou labels such a move internal to the history of a revolutionary politics of Truth, "in fidelity to the event."

upon loud cheering emotes from the crowd. He then shouts "May we show our support to our boys in Iraq!" and again loud cheering comes forth. He then proceeds to shout "May the USA kill every single terrorist!"—loud cheering comes forth again with shouts of YEAH!! He then shouts, "May George Bush drink the blood of every man, woman, and child in Iraq!" and there's even louder cheering. Lastly Borat shouts "May you destroy their country so that for the next thousand years, not even a single lizard will survive in their desert!" The cheering is less enthusiastic. He then sings a fake Kazak national anthem to the tune of the American national anthem that gets him booed roundly and brings him dangerously close to being killed. In a certain sense, Borat has taken the logic of the Iraq war too seriously. By doing so he has gotten too close to the truth of the logic of the war and exposed its heinous drives and contradictions. It nearly gets him killed.[27] He illustrates the process of overidentification.

When we over-identify with an ideology, the distance is removed between the subject and the master signifier and its false drives/contradictions are revealed. The subjects, in essence, get too close to the Real and an irruption occurs, and the ideology's inconsistencies (idiocies) come to the surface. An example Žižek cites is the artist group NSK in Slovenia. They would put on shows during the time when Slovenia was still part of the Soviet Union. Instead of overt critique of "the Party," the NSK would perform unabashed displays of support for the current fascist regime. They would in essence support fascism more than even the fascists themselves would support it. They would begin concerts by performing an explicitly excessive nationalist speech on protecting the purity and honor of the Serbian people. They would dress in military uniforms, enact Mussolini gestures, and read from their "manifesto." They would occasionally slip in some speaking in German, which to every Slovenian meant fascism. These performances were so bald and uncompromising that they in essence disallowed anyone in the theater any critical distance from what they were doing. It was either join in or be repulsed! As the audience viewed this display, they were horrified with the actual reality of fascism as well as their own complicity with

---

27. This scene comes from the movie *Borat: Cultural Learnings of America for Make Benefit Glorious Nation of Kazakhstan*. Thanks to Ben Sternke for giving me this reference.

it. Žižek believes this kind of overidentification created a space for the audience to now resist.[28]

Another way to describe overidentification is "subversive conformity." Žižek says that in order for an "ideological edifice to occupy the hegemonic place . . . it has to compromise its founding message."[29] He says "the ultimate heretics are amply those who reject this compromise."[30] It is not the act of non-conformity, therefore, that disrupts the system and reveals the lack at its core. It is rather the act of total conformity. This is because subversive conformity occurs fully within the ideology instead of from without. In so doing, one must give up the point of distance that actually supports the ideology. According to Žižek, this is what the ruling ideology fears the most. It is the fanatic who overidentifies without keeping an adequate distance. Such acts of subversive conformity make explicit the implications of an ideology. They cause an irruption of sorts that reveals to all what could not be spoken if the ideology was to go on reproducing itself.[31]

Overidentification can happen intentionally through "acts" of provocation by individuals such as the NSK. On the other hand, overi-

28. In an example I heard Žižek give in a lecture, he tells of being a member of a dissident group in Slovenia, publishing a newspaper the day after a rigged Soviet election, with the headline reading something like "Surprise Landslide Victory for Communist Party!" This headline is an example of over-conformity in that the elections are supposed to not be rigged, yet it is a gesture because everybody knows (but is not allowed to say) that the elections are rigged: the headline reveals the absurd behind the acting ideology of the elections.

29. Žižek, *On Belief*, 8.

30. German art curator Inke Arns explains this well stating "According to Slavoj Žižek and Peter Sloterdijk, overtly criticizing the ideology of a system misses the point, because today every ideological discourse is marked by cynicism. This means that every ideological discourse has internalized, and already anticipated, its own critique. Ideology does not "believe" in its own declarations anymore; it assumed a cynical distance towards its own moral premises. Consequently it became impossible to adequately encounter cynicism as a universal and diffuse phenomenon through the traditional means of critique of ideology (e.g. through enlightened engagement). Vis a vis cynical ideology, according to Žižek, the means of irony becomes something that lays into the hands of power. The public declarations and values of an ideology are 'cynical'; they are actually not to be taken seriously. But as soon as 'adequate distance' no longer is kept, when an 'over-identification' with ideology takes place, the so-called ruling ideology has a problem." Online: http://medinatweimar.org/2008/06/17/over-identification-with-the-hidden-reverse-of-ideology.

31. I am drawing here on Slavoj Žižek's words in his "Why are Laibach," 4.

dentification can also happen quite unintentionally through irruptions of a public figure, a piece of art, a piece of media, or a cultural symbol that takes the ideology too far and too literally. It is these unintentional, unprovoked, yet glaring irruptions of overidentification that I wish to focus upon in the analysis of evangelicalism that follows. I contend these kinds of irruptions happen all too often in evangelical culture. An evangelical person makes the news by killing an abortion doctor while calling abortion "murder" and decrying "murder as just plain wrong!" An evangelical public figure acts out his/her belief in a way that makes obvious the inner contradiction at the core of their belief and practice. Such episodes act as irruptions of the Real, revealing the full implications of evangelicalism that somehow remain unspoken. They also open the space within evangelicalism for change.

Jouissance

Žižek asserts that there is always a kind of enjoyment that holds a people together under the domination of an ideology. Žižek labels this enjoyment *jouissance*. *Jouissance* is a French word most often interpreted by "enjoyment." This kind of enjoyment, however, is much more intense than the word "enjoyment" implies. Associated in French with sexual pleasure, it is an excessive, irrational, almost perverse enjoyment that drives the very core of the ideological system.[32] We can often tell an episode is an irruption of the Real by the emoting of an irrational, excessive *jouissance* that accompanies it.

We recall again from Žižek that when an ideology is founded, it must always exclude something. There is always a tradeoff for those who subject themselves to the ideology. I might get the comfort of knowing I have a job and a paycheck as guaranteed by the government, but this means I must give up the freedom to make as much money as I want. The ideology, via fantasy, compensates for this loss with the promise of another enjoyment, a *jouissance*. For Žižek, every ideology has a founding event that requires a traumatic loss.[33] This traumatic

32. "Perverse" in the sense that the defying of the "law" through this enjoyment is what makes possible the very existence of the "law" in the first place.

33. When you think about it, every ideological system requires of its members that it must give up something—a pleasure of some sort that founds the existing order. Such a system must promise a compensating enjoyment in its place. It is out of this

founding event often leads to the displacement of the lost enjoyment towards an object outside itself. This object is what Lacan, and Žižek via Lacan, often calls the *objet petit a*.

This *jouissance* can take different shapes. One of the shapes *jouissance* can take is that of a kind of enjoyment driven by antagonism. For example, after I fail at getting a job promotion, I now become motivated to prove my employers wrong at all costs. The satisfaction of doing well at my job has been replaced by a revenge, "I'll show them" type of drive. On the group level, *jouissance* often takes this same form of displacing a resentment onto the other—my boss—who somehow has immediate access to the pleasure/enjoyment that we ourselves want so badly but have been unable to attain. This "other" is the *objet petit a*—a small other—a remainder that represents what we want that could not be subsumed by the Big Other—the Symbolic Order. This object becomes that which is unobtainable, that which I want/pursue all the more. It becomes the cause of our desire.[34]

A central way to diagnose the *jouissance* is to locate this object (*objet petit a*) upon which the *jouissance* is focused. As an example, recall the fascination that gripped everyone on 9/11 as we watched the airplanes entering the Twin Towers again and again. The nation was galvanized as never before in a display of reverence and patriotism. There was a self-glorifying sense that we are not those Islamic fundamentalists who do not believe in freedom and respect for every individual. The "Islamic fundamentalist" became the *objet petit a* against which we aimed our enjoyment. They had stolen our freedom from us, making us want it all the more. "Freedom" became an even more powerful Master-Signifier that organized that desire. We enjoyed with a vengeance that we are the greatest, bravest, most free nation on earth! Yet ironically, there was a new-found willingness to give up certain freedoms ("the

---

lack that *jouissance* materializes in the ideology and this enjoyment is promised. Yet this promise can never be consummated for to do so would dissolve the ideology. As Žižek puts it, "Desire is constituted by "symbolic castration," the original loss of the *Thing*; the void of this loss is filled out by *objet petit a*, the fantasy-object; this loss occurs on account of our being "embedded" in the symbolic universe . . ." *Tarrying With*, 3.

34. This *objet petit a* is also sometimes called "the symptom." It is itself a part of the overall fantasy (in this way it is not outside the ideology) within the ideology used to coalesce a people. It is the "object-cause of desire" and is a universal feature of desire for Žižek through Lacan.

Patriot Act") in order to join together to protect our country against these horrific Islamic terrorists. The vengeance here was more than outrage over injustice. It was indeed an excessive, lustful pride at being an American and the feeling that we have something to live for again. Chants of "we will never be the same" were heard everywhere, but no one knew what it actually meant (the sure sign of an "empty-signifier"). There was a sense of energy and purpose to America to the point where we felt more alive and almost glad this all happened. This was all the manifestation of *jouissance*, and a tell-tale sign of this was the way the Islamic terrorist was made into an object for our "enjoyment."[35]

This *objet petit a* is, therefore, that "other" that we displace our loss of our enjoyment onto within an ideology. It represents what we think we want but always seems unreachable. In a way, it holds together the ideology. As we fail to attain the promise of our ideological beliefs, we project our own enjoyment (or lack thereof) onto an object, i.e., the Radical Islamist who stole our secure American dream (freedom). In so doing, we sustain and even intensify the *jouissance* that sustains the ideology.[36] Žižek calls this the "theft of enjoyment."[37] The lack/the emptiness that lies at the core of the system and drives the focus of the *jouissance* towards this object is thus revealed.[38]

Sometimes "the Thing" (for example "American freedom") for which we strive is conceived of as "something inaccessible to the other" while at the same time "threatened by" the other.[39] The formulation of the *objet petit a* can be, therefore, irrational. We can both blame this object/other for our failure or lack in the system, while, at the same time,

---

35. For Žižek's brilliant take on 9/11 see his *Welcome to the Desert*.

36. When one fails to satisfy a desire, this desire becomes the source for more *jouissance*. A fantasy is constructed in each case that supports and sustains this *jouissance*, "if I only could do this . . . if I only experienced this . . . ." There is an ideological object that materializes that becomes the focus of the *jouissance*. This is the ideological process of *jouissance* for Žižek. See *Ticklish Subject*, 296–97. See also Žižek, *Plague of*, 32–33.

37. Žižek, *Tarrying With*, 201–5. This section is one of the best and most accessible summaries of what Žižek means by *jouissance*.

38. Žižek sees this as displacement in the psychoanalytic sense. He says therefore that the "easiest way to detect ideological surplus-enjoyment in an ideological formation is to read it as a dream, and analyze the displacement in it." Žižek, *For They Know Not*, xci .

39. Žižek, *Tarrying With*, 203.

suspecting him/her of already having it (what we lack) at our expense. Žižek often uses the example of the Jew in pre-WWII Germany who got blamed for everything that was wrong with the German system.[40] It was the Jew's fault that "our Deutschland" is bankrupt, or corrupt or so driven by greed! They're the ones always trying to make money off us! "The Jew" was the object that gave an excuse for the great German nation's failures yet it was irrational. No matter what the evidence might be, nothing could disprove the German blaming of the Jews.

As we will find out, there is much to learn about evangelicalism via its own *objet petit a.* "The liberals," for instance, or "the homosexual" can be understood as such an object for evangelicals: we blame them for threatening the veracity of the Bible or our country's sexual orthodoxy. "The liberals" signify a confidence in truth that we secretly long for but can never have. "The gay/lesbian groups" signify an unabashed freedom that threatens our morally superior status. In the process, these objects become a source of *jouissance* as we perversely enjoy the feeling of proving ourselves in either case. It is almost more enjoyable than if we actually did have the truth or felt totally comfortable in the integrity of our sexual orthodoxy before the world.

Much can be learned about what drives an ideology by paying attention to its *jouissance.*[41] The objects toward which we organize our *jouissance* towards reveal our lack but are so hard to give up. They define so much of who we aren't and yet want to be while, at the same time, enabling us to keep on going. Whenever *jouissance* irrupts, it often comes too close to revealing the "what I really fantasize about" that lies behind the beliefs and practices we follow as ideology.

Jouissance, by definition, is unrecognized. This unrecognition keeps the subject fixed within the grip of ideologies.[42] Yet if the emp-

40. In *Sublime Object* 124–25, Žižek labels "the Jew" in pre-WWII Germany the *objet petit a.* The remainder of the enjoyment that cannot be consummated is projected onto a symptom, "a small other." This signifier enables us to project our loss of enjoyment onto (organize our *jouissance* towards) the other object with a sense of vengeance yet relief, almost satisfaction. Žižek says, "What 'bothers' us in the 'other' (Jew, Japanese, African, Turk) is that he appears to entertain a privileged relationship to the object- the other either possesses the object-treasure, having snatched it away from us . . . or poses a threat to our possession of the object." *For They Know Not*, xc–xci .

41. Žižek, *Tarrying With*, 205.

42. It is a repeated theme of Žižek that the subject has no choice or rather a forced choice. Caught in the fantasy, the subject is incapable of extricating him or herself. As a

tiness (lack) of this *jouissance* were to be revealed, it would be very disruptive to the ideology, for it is in *jouissance* where the real political power resides. Žižek, in his earliest works, hopes that simply revealing the *jouissance* can loosen the hold that ideological beliefs have upon us. The task, then, is to survey the culture/ideology for these irruptions of *jouissance* and expose the hidden drives that uphold the ideology. The *jouissance* then dies, and a space for change is opened up.

Evangelicalism as a politic in North America is ripe for such a survey. It has its own versions of *jouissance*. Revealing the *jouissance* when it irrupts exposes the Real behind the Master-Signifiers at the core of our life together—the drives, the lacks, the antagonisms that lie behind the things we say we believe about Scripture, salvation, and the church's relation to society. Recognizing the *jouissance* in such irruptions can help open up space for change. As part of our ideological analysis of evangelicalism, then, we will survey evangelical culture for irruptions of *jouissance*. We will follow Žižek's method in surveying the cultural public figures/artifacts of evangelicalism that expose the Real of our political life as a people.[43] The goal is to uncover the drives/antagonisms that lie behind the way we practice our faith. In so doing, we gain a new understanding of the ways our belief and practice shape us a kind of people in the world and a space for change is opened up.

---

result, the fantasy must self implode through provoked acts from within the fantasmic structure.

43. This follows Žižek's own penchant for perusing culture for empirical illustrations. As Adrian Johnston claims, Žižek is accumulating a "formidable number of empirical illustrations" with the goal that his central analytic claims will be hammered home through a veritable deluge of data. This serves to buttress his metapsychological framework. Johnston, *Žižek's Ontology*, xv. Likewise, I also hope to buttress my own claims concerning evangelicalism as an imploding ideological framework by providing numerous empirical illustrations of its overidentification and self-revealing *jouissance*. In the same vein, Adam Kotsko argues that Žižek's cultural examples work in ways similar to Paul Tillich's correlational theological method. They elicit from culture evidences of a theological/ideological truth. For Žižek, every cultural product falls within the purview of ideology. And since "ideology is an inherently contradictory realm, . . . as the goal of Tillich's analysis is to elicit existential questions, the goal of Žižek's ideology critique is to expose those contradictions." Kotsko, *Žižek and Theology*, 142. In this same vein, I will use cultural examples both from within evangelical culture and from evangelicals in American culture to reveal the inherent contradictions that are being exposed in evangelicalism and undermining it as an ideology.

Evangelicalism as an "Empty Politic": On Using Žižek's Political Theory as a Diagnosis of a Fallen Politic

We can see the potential that Žižek's political analysis offers for understanding evangelicalism. As already alluded to, however, there are limitations to Žižek's usefulness for the constructive task of Christian political theology.

One of these limiting factors is Žižek's political ontology: the way he understands political reality itself. As already stated several times, Žižek understands all socio-cultural political systems as fundamentally structured around a core antagonism. There is "nothing" at the core. It is an "empty" politic. Ideology swirls around competing forces that produce drives that propel the system forward. There is no stable ontological core that can ground an ideological system. For Žižek, we are driven by what we lack.[44] In essence, political systems function to coalesce a people by organizing their desire for something that always lies beyond reach.[45] The question is, then, can such an understanding of politics be compatible with the Christian faith and the sociality that we (the church) have in Christ?

Another way to pose this same question is to ask whether Žižek's metaphysics are compatible with Christianity. Žižek is after all an atheist. He is a dialectical materialist.[46] He is a materialist in that he sees the material (the immanent) as all there is. He is a dialectical materialist in that for him there is always an ongoing, reflexive, dialectical movement of history within this material realm that is ever revealing what is true ("Real").[47] There is no transcendent beyond the material realm.

44. For an excellent introduction to this concept of a "political ontology of lack," see Tonder and Thomassen, "Introduction," 1–13.

45. Žižek, *Sublime Object*, 5–6.

46. To some degree the phrases "political ontology of lack" and "dialectical materialism" are interchangeable as descriptors of the ontology that undergirds Žižek's views of reality, ideology, and God. The latter, however, represents a later focus of Žižek's. "Political ontology of lack" was more often used as part of/to describe Žižek's early work. Note the subtitle of *The Ticklish Subject*—"the absent centre of political ontology." The refining and defense of a "dialectical materialism" has become more prominent in the focus of Žižek's later work. See, e.g., *Parralax View*. For the most part, however, things said more explicitly by Žižek while discussing dialectical materialism are at least implicit in his earlier ontology.

47. Žižek is intensely Hegelian, yet his interpretation of Hegel's dialectic deviates from the "standard account." Žižek sees Hegel as the philosopher of "the nega-

The material world is enclosed in its own immanence. Yet this material world is non-reductive. It is an immanence capable of spawning thought, subjectivity, and meaning. There is a dialectic at work within the material that yields consciousness and "personhood." When a subject speaks (enunciates), when the Symbolic takes shape via intersubjectivity (between many people's interactions), reflexivity happens. The subject is birthed into the System.[48] Yet there is always a remainder that cannot be captured.[49] There is always something outside language that resists symbolization. This again is the antagonism, the "self-contradiction" that is the "motor of dialectics."[50] This is the "Real" that keeps the ideology going. The question here again is, can a Christian buy into a view of the world that is devoid of the transcendent in this way?

John Milbank, one of the first significant theologians to engage Žižek, answers these questions with a manifest "No."[51] He labels Žižek "a mystical nihilist."[52] Certainly Žižek is not the first figure to be labeled a nihilist by Milbank, and it is often difficult to decipher exactly what this charge might mean for Milbank. In this case, however, Milbank's charge of nihilism gets at a problem in Žižek's metaphysics (or lack

---

tive." His dialectic is one that moves through negation, not the oft-rehearsed higher unifying movement of the *Aufhebung*. As opposed to the traditional account, where the *Aufhebung* is where the thesis and then the antithesis lead to a higher unifying synthesis, Žižek counters this emphasis by seeing the movement of history/reality as more like the thesis, being contradicted by a negation which then collapses the entire framework for a more radical thesis entirely. See Žižek, *Tarrying With*, ch. 4.

48. Or to be more exact, according to Žižek/Lacan, the subject is annihilated as he/she becomes absorbed into the "I" of the enunciation by the Symbolic Order.

49. We can never know it *in toto*, for no one subject can be removed above reality to be in such a position. Reality is, in Lacan's terms, "non-All." There is always a remainder. We are always in the process of the dialectical unfolding. The very production of subjectivity reveals the "non All" of this reality. To quote Žižek in describing Lacan over Badiou, "'This precarious reality is 'non-All', ontologically not fully constituted, so it needs the supplement of the subject's contingent gesture to obtain an embrace of ontological consistency." *Ticklish Subject*, 158.

50. Žižek, "Dialectical Clarity," 247.

51. Milbank provides a substantive critique of Žižek's political ontology of immanence in his "Materialism and Transcendence," 421–23. In addition, he offers his clearest critique in the essay entitled "Double Glory." One should also be aware that Graham Ward, another Radical Orthodoxy theologian, engages Žižek substantially in his *Cities of God*, 147–51.

52. Milbank, "Materialism and Transcendence," 423.

thereof) that I suggest is essential to understanding the limits of Žižek for Christian political analysis.

Milbank claims that Žižek's dialectical materialism provides no "ontological basis" for a progress that can lead to a stable political practice.[53] This can be seen in both Žižek's ontology (his view of the way things are) and, more derivatively, in his theory of subjectivity as well. On the ontological level, Žižek's Hegelian negative dialectic is trapped within an immanence from which it cannot escape. Since Žižek's Hegelian dialectic is a "traversing with the negative"—basically an ever unfolding of the negation of the negation—politics cannot in essence get anywhere.[54] Trapped within the material, there is nothing that can take it beyond itself. Antagonism and negation are inscribed into its very being.[55] The Real is, after all, an antagonism—a void at the core.[56] As a result, Žižek's ontology, according to Milbank, reduces the goal of politics to an "agon around an empty fetish."[57] Political reality cannot sustain the reality of a peace or justice. It is "hell-bent" on "mutually assured destruction."[58] According to Milbank, this nihilism is inherent to Žižek's system. To paraphrase the words of Connor Cunningham, a theological ally of Milbank's, the "logic of something as nothing" can get us nowhere.[59]

In the same vein, subjectivity and consciousness for Žižek are projected purely from within the material out of this same antagonism.[60]

53. Milbank claims Žižek's dialectical materialism in the end repeats the same reductive and nihilist errors of prior Marxist materialism. It fails, according to Milbank, to provide a more fulfilling and non-reductive ontology. Milbank, "Materialism and Transcendence," 393–95.

54. Milbank, "Double Glory," 136–39.

55. "[F]or Hegel this agonism is inscribed at the most ontological level." Ibid., 138.

56. Again, in Milbank's words, "there is no fundamental 'totality' for beyond the supposed 'all' lies a 'not-All' . . . which reappears on the surface of our world as 'subjective' interference... this 'not-all' is . . . like the anarchic power of the void . . . it has no content of its own, even if it may negatively reveal itself in the circumstance that physical reality appears." Milbank, "Double Glory," 120.

57. Milbank "Materialism and Transcendence," 395.

58. Milbank, "Double Glory," 166.

59. The "nihilistic logic" is among other things "a series of negations which will give rise to a fully immanentised realm, one that may accommodate the nihilistic logic of nothing as something." Cunningham, *Genealogy*, 5.

60. It is an "immanence of transcendence" in Adrian Johnston's words. *Žižek's Ontology*, ch. 11.

Desire is born out of lack and is incapable of fulfillment. Yet it must tragically be persisted in, for to not do so is the suicide of the self.[61] Our subjective identity, therefore, Milbank says, is created ever always out of conflicts and negations. Our organizing "fantasies" can only ever cover over antagonisms and repressions. Desire can never go anywhere. And purpose is at best a superficial illusion. There is therefore no basis for progressing forward.[62] For Milbank, again, Žižek's Hegelian negative dialectic cannot sustain an account of the subject.[63] All we can have with Žižek is a politics based upon what we are not that will always lead to a collapsing in upon itself. In terms of our subjectivity, Milbank's critique is again that Žižek is a nihilist and provides no basis from which to construct a positive Christian politics.

Others have voiced this same concern as well. Marcus Pound, an admitted friend to Milbank's school of thought, calls Žižek's work "*transgression without progression,* i.e., a revolutionary act that is unable to sustain itself as anything other than a moment of profound rupture."[64] Matthew Sharpe and Tony Myers criticize Žižek in similar manner as having a negative dialectic incapable of advancing a politic in the world.[65] According to these and others, Žižek's ontology relegates

61. Milbank, "Double Glory," 120.

62. "[O]ne cannot will the true human future in the name of the fulfillment of the real—except as an entertaining illusion—but can see it only, at best, as an honest collapsing back of the human illusion into prehuman sequences." Milbank, "Materialism and Transcendence," 395.

63. For Milbank, this problem is inherent to the negative logic of the Hegelian dialectic: "The more one advances from extrinsic design in inorganic nature to life and then to consciousness, the more the reserve of the ideal, over and against the objective which it shapes, is removed . . . and the more the original immediacy of the physical object and the mediated immediacy (synthesizing parts into a stable unity) of subjectivity start to coincide." Milbank, "Double Glory," 153.

64. Pounds, *Žižek*, 75. He agrees with Milbank saying, "once humanity accepts the realm of "pure nature," the very idea of teleology ceases to hold weight and creatureliness begins to be thought of, not in terms of its "normative maximal flourishing". . . but "minimal sustainability" which for Milbank leads to a Hobbesian ontology of violence. Pound, *Žižek*, 90.

65. See Myers *Slavoj Žižek*, 121–24. Matthew Sharpe points to the irony that Žižek finds himself in "odd parity with the Derridian 'deconstructionism' he elsewhere dismisses because he allows one to remain permanently dissident without being able to conceptualize the possibility of anything genuinely politically redemptive at all." Sharpe, *Slavoj Žižek*, 16. Pound, in *Žižek*, 96, as well as Milbank, in "Double Glory," 117–18, makes the same observations about the irony of Žižek's stance towards the

us to forever "swapping one set of lacks for another."[66] Using Žižekian political theory, therefore, structures politics for endless repetition, if not an eventual collapse in on itself.

It is not within the purview of this book to engage in a full treatment of the debate over Žižek's versus Milbank's versions of ontology and the political.[67] To be sure, Žižek has responded to this critique.[68] Rather than rehearsing the debate, however, I simply affirm, with Milbank, that Žižek's political theory is incompatible with a Christian politic. In other words, the Christian life together, our very politic, cannot be empty at its core, for it is formed around the fullness of Jesus Christ. As a result, the Christian politic is not driven by conflict but rather by reconciliation.[69] Ideology, therefore, as Žižek has fashioned it, is a fallen politic, a politic that is on its way to collapse, if not visibly in the process already. If the church, therefore, begins to resemble such an "empty" politic, it confirms that it has in some way left its calling as the church, the people of God in Christ in the world.

Derridians.

66. These words come from James K. A. Smith's response to a presentation I made of some of these ideas at an AAR meeting of the Christian Theological Research Fellowship, November 2, 2008, in Chicago, IL. Žižek of course sees this "swapping of lacks" as a type of nirvana to be strived for. He describes this goal as the state of "Nothing humbly aware of itself, a Nothing paradoxically made rich through the very awareness of its lack. Only a lacking, vulnerable being is capable of love: the ultimate mystery of love is therefore that incompleteness is in a way higher than completion." Žižek, *Fragile Absolute*, 146–47.

67. The analysis of these two very different ways (Milbank's versus Žižek's) of ontologizing the contradictory exceeds the purview of this book. Indeed, it is a book unto itself. Instead what I am after with Milbank's engagement with Žižek in both "Materialism and Transcendence" and "Double Glory" is the manner in which he illumines a basis for using Žižek's political theory for the furthering of a Christian political theology. This will become clearer in what follows.

68. Most prominently in Žižek, "Dialectical Clarity." One of the more direct responses to the charge of nihilism against political ontologies of immanence is delivered by his ally of sorts, Alain Badiou, *Manifesto*, ch. 4. Of course Badiou and Žižek also have significant differences. See Žižek, "Politics of Truth."

69. In the last chapter of this book, I will argue that the true politic of the church is birthed in the Incarnation of God in and through Christ and his material work in the world. Christ is at the very core of the Christian politic. The church's politic is an outworking of its reconciliation in Christ (2 Cor 5:17–19; Col 1:19–20). Any politic that is Christian therefore must be founded "in Christ"—the church being the primary manifestation of this politic—"the fullness of him" (Eph 1:23). Such a politic is founded on reconciliation as opposed to antagonism.

The way forward, however, is not to discard Žižek's political theory for the Christian political task. Rather, it is to understand his political theory of ideology (in relation to the church) as the means for diagnosing such a false politics.[70] If Žižekian ideology is what politics looks like when it is empty at its core, Žižek can help us diagnose the church as such an ideology. He can help us identify when and how the church left its calling to be the politic of Christ in the world.

We approach, then, the next three chapters as an execution of a form of Žižekian therapy upon evangelicalism. We seek to diagnose the presence of Master-Signifiers and irruptions of the Real within evangelicalism that expose the emptiness at the core of our politic. In the process we discover how our belief and practice have become reified so as to shape us into something self-contradictory to who we say we are. Of course, I realize this is to make a presumptuous move. Žižek would certainly disavow such an appropriation of his work.[71] At the very least, he would protest against there even being a place from which to step outside and make such claims. And of course, everyone must to some degree agree that we can never see this emptiness until the seeds of its own contingent conditions have been brought forth into plain view for all its subjects to see.[72] Yet it is precisely this space I seek to inhabit in the chapters to follow. As a journeying theologian deeply ensconced within evangelicalism, I believe we have arrived at a point where Žižek's social psychoanalysis can help us see the emptiness of what has become our politic in the world.

70. I am not the first to suggest that Žižek is at his best as a political theorist of ideology in critique of faulty political systems as opposed to an ontologist of religion and subjectivity.

71. Adrian Johnston reports, for example, that "Žižek complains, "Indeed part of the message doesn't get through" because his audience prefers to dwell primarily on the cultural and political dimensions of his writings—or else, if the philosophical component of the Žižekian oeuvre is addressed, it's almost always Hegel who is the center of exegetical attention." The appropriation of Žižek I am proposing puts me squarely into the group he is criticizing. Nonetheless, because of his ontological commitments, I am suggesting that Žižek is at his best when he works in "culture, politics and ideology."

72. See Žižek, *Fragile Absolute*, 90–91 on the inescapability of the present in "the future."

TOWARDS AN EVANGELICAL MISSIONAL POLITICAL THEOLOGY

We do this, however, not as an "end" in itself. As already described in chapter 1, the politic of evangelicalism may very well be imploding as an unsustainable way of life in North America. Yet I propose this need not be an ending *in toto*. It can be an ending of a different sort. I suggest that this very collapse, if examined rightly, can open up a space in evangelicalism for a new faithfulness.[73] It can be a moment in which evangelicalism reclaims Jesus Christ the Incarnate Son in the life of the Trinity as the core of its politic in the world. As defined above, this is the true politic capable of progressing towards peace, one that does not repeat past antagonisms but participates in our very source: the Incarnate Son sent by the Father, extended into the world via the Holy Spirit. This is a "politic of fullness." By exposing evangelicalism's empty politic, Žižek sets the table for such a reclaiming, which I pursue, then, in chapter 6.

The goal of the next three chapters is to make a space for this new faithfulness. Like a long journey with a good therapist, Žižek will help us examine the events of the past, our behaviors, our motivations, and the ideological objects we just can't let go of. Just like a person in therapy eventually comes face to face with the person he/she has become, so we evangelicals can come face to face with "the kinds of people" we have become and with why we have become them. We can discover how beliefs we so desperately hold onto have become ideological objects (Master-Signifiers) that, in effect, drive us away from God's Mission. We get a view of just how much we have lost the core of our faith in the process of defending a high view of Scripture, a conversionist cross-centered salvation, and an activist engagement with culture for the gospel. To be sure, in themselves (I would argue) these commitments are crucial to our life as evangelicals and must be preserved. Yet before we can reclaim these beliefs, a space must be opened up whereby we see the emptiness behind the ways we have practiced them as a way of life. Only then, out of this space, can we reclaim a politic centered in the

---

73. If we follow Žižek's interpretation of the Hegelian dialectic, the third moment occurs at "the negation of the negation" whereby the old system vanishes making way for a entirely new political form. At such a collapse, what Badiou calls the Event, a new faithfulness can appear, a new social coalescence embodying what Badiou calls the "fidelity to the event."

person and work of the second person of the Trinity, the Incarnate Son, Jesus Christ. And in reclaiming our lost core, not only is a high view of Scripture, a true conversionist faith, and an activist church upheld, but each one of these doctrinal commitments becomes the basis for a participation in the life of the triune God through Jesus Christ as the core of our politic in the world. These beliefs and practices birth a way of life together that is the very social presence of the gospel in the world, a truly missional evangelical politic.

CHAPTER 3

"The Inerrant Bible": The Politics of the Evangelical Belief
and Practice of Scripture—How It Shapes Us For Arrogance

"The Bible says . . ."
—Billy Graham

There is a story—deeply embedded in the psyche of evangelicalism—
that reveals the place of the inerrant Bible in the evangelical church. A
young Billy Graham, the archetypal figure of evangelicalism in North
America, finds himself doubting the veracity of the Scriptures.[1] His
close friend and partner in evangelism, Charles Templeton, has become convinced by the achievements of German higher criticism of
the Bible and its assessment of the historical inadequacies of Scripture.
He informs Billy that he is incredibly naïve regarding the accuracy of
Scripture, and Billy in turn becomes overwhelmed by the unanswerable
problems raised by Charles. In a moment of crisis, Billy must decide
whether to take the Bible "at face value as the Word of God," or to probe
deeper, looking for rational answers and definitive proofs. In a moment
of profound significance, Billy decides to put his faith and trust in the
total veracity of the Bible. On that day, so the story goes, Billy Graham's
famous mantra "the Bible says . . ." was born. He went on to his now
famous career as worldwide evangelist. Templeton, on the other hand,

---

1. For an account of this story, see Drummond, *The Evangelist*. For a fictionalized
account supposedly based on the true story, see McKay and Abraham, *Billy*. For a
scholarly slant on the meaning of this story, see Sparks, *God's Word*.

went on to further study at Princeton Theological Seminary. He became a thrice-divorced reclusive media personality/writer.

This story speaks to the hold that the inerrant Bible has had on
the imagination of the people called evangelicals in North America. In
the 1960s, 70s, and 80s, the prime years of evangelicalism, this story
was legend—"the stuff fathers would tell their sons and daughters." For
evangelicals of his time, Billy Graham's no-holds-barred faith in the
Scriptures was heroic. He was the exemplar for how we all should put
our faith without reservation in the inerrant Bible as the unshakable
foundation for all truth.

Evangelicals have always defined themselves by their commitment
to a high view of Scripture. Church historian David Bebbington calls
"the supreme value of the Bible" one of the four "enduring priorities of
the evangelical movement."[2] North American evangelicalism's version
of this commitment is the doctrine of inerrancy, and it first came to
prominence during the so-called fundamentalist-modernist controversies of the 1920s and 30s.[3] During this time, so-called modernist
professors and pastors within mainline Protestantism were teaching
the higher criticism of the Bible. They were asserting that the Bible
was fallible, containing many errors. Fending off this gathering herd
of scholars/teachers/pastors "trampling" on the Bible, the so-called
fundamentalists responded much like Billy Graham did to Templeton.
They avowed unequivocally "the inerrancy doctrine" that affirms "we
hold the Scriptures to be infallible and inerrant in their original autographs." During this time, a coalescence of Christians nationwide gathered around this affirmation who would later become the evangelicals.

B. B. Warfield of Princeton Theological Seminary (along with A.
A. Hodge, Charles Hodge, and then later J. Gresham Machen) provided
the theological language for this new constituency.[4] In his classic statement entitled *The Inspiration and Authority of the Bible*, Warfield defended the Bible's authority in terms of its divine verbal inspiration by

2. Bebbington, *Dominance of Evangelicalism*, 23.

3. On this period see Marsden, *Fundamentalism and American Culture*, chs. 13, 14;
Marsden, *Understanding Fundamentalism and Evangelicalism*, 36–39. For a broader
history, see Marsden, *Reforming*, 111–16, 198.

4. Also known as the Princeton Theology. On its influence during the fundamentalist-modernist controversies, see Marsden, *Fundamentalism and American Culture*,
ch. 13; and Noll, *Princeton Theology*.

the Holy Spirit (God-breathed) whereby it must be historically, and in every other way, inerrant in every word. Unique to Warfield's apologetic was that he added the words "in its original autographs" to "the Bible is verbally inspired by God, it therefore must be inerrant."[5] Warfield's work became one of the cornerstones of the foundation for what would later become the evangelical doctrine of the inerrancy of Scripture.

Amidst the birthing of (what would become) evangelicalism during this time, the belief and practice of the inerrancy doctrine took on a new prominence.[6] The fundamentalist-modernist controversies became the founding event that firmly established the inerrant Bible as a cornerstone of evangelical belief and practice. The doctrine remained the mainstay of evangelicalism as it morphed from the fundamentalism of pre-WWII into the post WWII neo-evangelicals to the polymorphic stream of evangelicalism that exists in North America today. *The Fundamentals*, published in 1909, established "the Inerrant Bible" as one of the basics for those who would later become the evangelicals.[7] This five-volume work served as the theological guidepost for this early coalescence of organizations/churches as it established its identity over against the modernist "liberals." After World War II, the National Association of Evangelicals was founded (actually in 1943) with "inerrancy" prominent in its doctrinal statement. Hundreds of independent evangelical churches were begun simply under the name ABC Bible Church, making the inerrant Bible the key issue for their coalescence.[8] The major leaders and theologians of the post-World War II evangelicals strongly espoused the inerrancy of Scriptures, including Carl F. Henry, the first editor/founder of the evangelical standard-bearer

---

5. See for instance Warfield, *Selected*, 2:583–84.

6. I am not suggesting that the inerrancy doctrine did not exist previously in some version. See for example Balthasar, *Glory of the Lord*, 1:33–36. I am suggesting that this arose in its peculiar form within evangelicalism for the first time here during the fundamentalist-modernist controversies.

7. Approximately one third of the articles in *The Fundamentals* defended the Scriptures against "higher criticism." Testifying to their enduring legacy, *The Fundamentals* have been reprinted with an introduction by Warren Wiersbe, Kregel Publications, Grand Rapids, 1990. For a history on *The Fundamentals*, see Marsden, *Fundamentalism and American Culture*, ch. 14.

8. This is often referred to in evangelical historiography as "the Bible church movement" beginning during WWII and thereafter in the United States as a reaction to Protestant liberal views of the Bible.

magazine *Christianity Today*, evangelical apologist Francis Schaeffer, and of course Billy Graham himself along with his evangelistic organization. In 1978, former editor of *Christianity Today* and evangelical leader, Harold Lindsell made a controversial plea for the holding fast to the doctrine of inerrancy in his now infamous *The Battle for the Bible*.[9] It caused a storm that roiled traditional evangelical seminaries into the modernist controversies all over again causing renewed debates in evangelical churches and seminaries nationwide. It kept biblical inerrancy at the forefront of evangelical identity. In October of that year, a group of two hundred evangelical leaders met in Chicago to write and endorse the "Chicago Statement on Biblical Inerrancy," an extremely influential statement upon the politics of evangelical institutions. Thirty years later, the two most widely used systematic theologies in evangelical seminaries, Wayne Grudem's *Systematic Theology* and Millard Erickson's *Christian Theology*,[10] maintain a strong stance on the inerrancy of Scriptures much in the same vein as Warfield did a hundred years before.

To be sure, "inerrancy" has receded as a strategy among intellectuals in many evangelical denominational and academic settings in recent years. Many organizations and churches have traded words such as "infallible" or "accurate" for "inerrant." Others have dropped "the original autographs" phrase. Nonetheless, the idea of "the inerrant Bible" as well as the coinciding idea of "verbal inspiration" linger on in the majority of doctrinal statements of organizations, academic institutions, denominations, and churches that wish to identify as evangelical. Even more to the point, the inerrant Bible is evidenced in some central core practices of many evangelical churches. For instance, many evangelical congregations regularly practice this understanding of Scripture through the practice of "expository preaching" in Sunday services.[11] This style of preaching reflects the evangelical doctrine of Scripture by emphasizing word-for-word exegesis, staying as close to the text as possible, putting a lot of trust in seeking the original au-

---

9. Lindsell, *Battle for the Bible*.

10. Grudem, *Systematic Theology* and Erickson *Christian Theology*. These two texts remain best sellers and in multiple printings. Over 200,000 of Grudem's books are in circulation and Erickson's was going into its twelfth printing in 2009.

11. A classic representative statement on expository preaching is John MacArthur's *ReDiscovering Expository Preaching*.

thor's single intent through the aid of historical-critical exegesis.[12] This reflects the belief that "every word is inspired" (i.e., that every word is inerrant and communicates truth propositionally). In addition, many evangelical churches practice a form of Bible study, both group and personal, described as inductive Bible study. Word studies are prominent in these Bible studies. Both of these evangelical practices make sense when one considers the manner in which this founding evangelical doctrine emphasizes the verbal nature of inspiration. Indeed, regarding the inductive study of Scripture, B. B. Warfield and the Princeton theologians introduced this very method of Bible study in the 1920s, seeking a hermeneutical objectivity in biblical interpretation. With an almost scientific zeal for objectivity, they sought a method that allowed "the data of Scripture" to speak for itself.[13] Behind these practices of Scripture, therefore, lies the founding doctrines of inerrancy and verbal inspiration of Scripture, which remains the operative doctrine of Scripture for many evangelicals.

The belief in the inerrant Bible, then, has been central to the coalescence of evangelicalism in the twentieth century. While this belief has diminished in recent years as a stated article of confession in many evangelical settings, its vestiges remain. It remains a central tenet around which evangelicals gather as a people and practice their faith. It has formed the ethos of the evangelical Christian community's presence in society.

"The Inerrant Bible" as Master-Signifier

How then has this allegiance to the inerrant Bible functioned to bind us together and form us as a people in the world? How has it shaped our character as a people?

In many ways, "the inerrant Bible" functions as a Master-Signifier for evangelicals in the classic Žižekian sense. We can see this, for instance, in the ways evangelicals confess their belief in the inerrant Bible (or at least practice it in their rituals) yet few really know what it might mean. This is a clue that in effect it has taken on the "elusive" quality of

---

12. For a fuller treatment of this, see my own *Great Giveaway*, ch.5.

13. See Clark, *To Know*, 48 for a summary of the roots of inductive Bible study.

a master signifier—that it serves as an "object" to rally us together as opposed to actually meaning anything in our daily lives.[14]

This elusivity, for example, is represented in the phrase "inerrant according to the original autographs." The phrase was part of the original articulation of the doctrine by B. B. Warfield.[15] It lingers on in many evangelical doctrinal statements to this day. Yet its meaning is hard to pin down. For no one has yet to see these original artifacts, and no one expects to. It makes the inerrant Bible into "a sublime object" that forever lies beyond our reach. We simply don't have nor ever expect to see these original documents. In this way, "the inerrant Bible" exposes itself as an "empty-signifier": a signifier with no referent. Instead, the notion of a perfect replication of the original autographs lies in the future as continued textual research provides more and more clues and the hope for the perfect text. "The original autographs" therefore offer an object that we are in constant pursuit of yet is simply unattainable.

Of course there are other ways "the inerrant Bible" proves elusive. The idea that we can locate the one true interpretation of these inspired words is elusive. Yet this also is implied in the idea of "the inerrant Bible." And so we continue to pursue the "authorial intent" of each text, yet that one meaning that was in the head of the original author, which guides interpretation of the single meaning of the words, ever eludes our grasp. It is mocked each time another set of evangelical commentaries multiplies the possible interpretations for each text in the Bible. What good then is having an inerrant text? In all these ways, at its earli-

14. This question should not be confused with another question: How does the evangelical approach to a high view of Scripture set the Bible up as an object of allegiance above the Lord of the church? Many have accused evangelicals of a Biblicism, a Biblical positivism and/or Bibliolatry. In this case, the Bible achieves almost divine status among evangelicals so as to become the center of the Christian life replacing the living Christ Himself. Although this criticism may have had merits at several moments within evangelicalism's history, and dovetails with some of the engagement that follows in this chapter, this well-worn style of engagement with evangelical doctrine is not what I am interested in this chapter. Most evangelicals are more careful along these lines. There is already a certain cynicism towards inerrancy among evangelicals. Instead, what I am interested in is the peculiar way the notion of "the perfect book" lingers on in doctrine and practice within evangelicalism and holds ideological currency in the ways Žižek describes. I am interested in how inerrancy (along with several ideas germane to it) persists as a Master-Signifier in the Symbolic Order that is evangelicalism in America.

15. Warfield, "Inerrancy." The fascinating machinations behind "the original autographs" phrase is debated in John Woodbridge's "Biblical Authority," 59–60.

est founding (at the traumatic event of the fundamentalist-modernist controversies), the evangelical doctrine of Scripture was dematerialized in Žižekian terms: i.e., made into something of no actual use in our concrete lives together. It serves us well, however, as a Master-Signifier that "rallies the troops" against the liberal deniers of biblical truth.

Žižek asserts that when we make the Master-Signifier invisible, it strengthens its hold on the believers. The Master-Signifier becomes an object that can never be nailed down specifically enough to topple it from its commanding position. It can mean many things to many people. Its invisibility therefore makes for a more powerful spectral domination. It creates sufficient distance between the individual and the object to allow a space for a much more expansive imaginary. In the process, the object becomes all the more immovable within our ideological fantasy.[16] This is what makes "the inerrant Bible according to the original autographs" such a powerful ideological "sublime object."[17] No one can really nail down what it might mean to find an error in the original autographs—which makes it all the more invincible. In fact the worst thing that could happen would be the actual discovery of the original autographs. In Žižek's terminology, we would be getting too close to the Real and the reason for our coming together to search the Scriptures would be evacuated. This Master-Signifier quality of "the inerrant Bible" is therefore revealed whenever someone comes too close to actually finding something approximating the original autographs. Many remember, for instance, the feeling of horror we evangelicals felt at the appearance of the Dead Sea scrolls. What would happen to us if indeed our Bible proved inauthentic? The elusiveness of "the Inerrant Bible" makes it a durable Master-Signifier.

Another way "the Inerrant Bible" functions as a Master-Signifier is the fact that it does little work in actually directing the biblical interpretation that affects evangelical doctrinal/ecclesial practice. "The inerrant

16. Across his voluminous work, he can allude to the Master-Signifier's various nuances with terms like "the object of ideology" or "the fetish." On "the dissipation of the materiality of the fetish" in the fantasy, see Žižek, *Plague of Fantasies*, 102–3.

17. A "sublime object" according to Žižek is "a positive, material object elevated to the status of the impossible Thing." *Sublime Object*, 71. This Thing is "the material leftover, the materialization of the terrifying, impossible *jouissance*." If we were to catch a glimpse of this forbidden domain, it would be terrifying for it has a potential to unravel out entire "self" as formed within the Signifier, within the Symbolic Order. According to Žižek, this is "a space that should be left unseen."

Bible" in essence allows us to interpret the Bible to mean anything we want it to because after all we believe it to be "inerrant." To exaggerate, we can say just about anything based on the Bible and then declare our allegiance to the Bible's inerrancy. No one then can dare question our orthodoxy! In this way, "the inerrant Bible" functions once again as an empty-signifier. As a result, "the inerrant Bible" (and its variants) holds together a wide variety of institutions and churches that have very little in common in terms of their practice except of course the desire to self-identify as evangelical. Groups as diverse as National Association of Evangelicals, many Pentecostal groups, *Christianity Today*, numerous televangelists, Joel Osteen's Lakewood Community Church, Willow Creek Community Church, Saddleback Community Church, the Billy Graham Evangelistic Association, Moody Bible Institute, World Vision, and Wheaton College all claim one of the evangelical inerrancy variations to articulate what they believe about the Bible.[18] Yet the differences in versions of the gospel preached and their actual practice of it in each setting are multitudinous. They have many more differences among them in matters of actual practice than they have in common. Yet somehow they all adhere to a perfect book that is verbally inspired and propositionally true. Since rarely are any doctrinal or pragmatic issues influenced by an appeal to inerrancy, these organizations essentially use "inerrancy" as a badge to self-identify as evangelicals. "Inerrancy" (along with its variants) acts powerfully as a classic Žižekian Master-Signifier within the ideological quilt of evangelicalism to hold this people together into a given politic.

The belief in "inerrancy" is rarely talked about in evangelical churches or organizations except in moments when an organization has to prove its orthodoxy.[19] Yet the term is continually found in doctrinal statements that seek to prove the church credible for those seeking a church to which they can be loyal. "Inerrancy" is often buried in these statements until there is a need to appeal to donors for money or prove one's conservative orthodoxy. The assertion of "inerrancy," therefore, acts an identifier used to assert the organization's, church's, or one's own

18. Most of these doctrinal statements can be investigated for the inerrancy clause, and/or its variants, via their respective Web sites.

19. For instance, Rick Warren, in his famous *Purpose Driven Church*, says, "Personally, I consider the inerrancy of Scripture as a non negotiable belief, but the unchurched don't even understand the term."

personal evangelical orthodoxy. It serves to generate a certain ideological identification that we are conservative Bible-believing Christians who can be trusted. It serves to identify a group as "not-liberal." The actual belief, however, in "the Inerrant Bible" means little in terms of what each evangelical organization or church actually believes about biblical interpretation, the manuscripts, and/or internal contradictions as exposed by higher biblical critics. It instead functions purely as a symbol, an "empty-signifier," that binds evangelicals together for certain political purposes.

We could summarize then the evangelical ideological stance towards inerrancy following Žižek's famous quote of Peter Sloterdijk— "They know inerrancy doesn't mean anything, yet they use it (in their doctrinal statements) anyway." Among most evangelicals, no one appears to be interested anymore in the inerrancy defenses of old, except in the most entrenched of apologetics-oriented evangelical seminaries. Nonetheless, in all these various places, it functions in a way that self-identifies one as an evangelical and it holds evangelical constituents firmly fixed within the evangelical ideological edifice. It makes us feel comfortable with one another and sets us over against those who don't "believe in the Bible," even though we really have no idea what that might mean according to our own definition.

Some may say that the ideological hold of "the perfect book" is diminishing in recent days. We should be careful, however, not to imply that its hold has loosened merely because the words "the Bible inerrant in the original autographs" are spoken less in evangelical churches/academies. Žižek says there is a dimension to ideological cynicism that implies that the illusion of ideology "is not on the side of knowing." It is in "what the people are doing."[20] In other words, the hold of ideology upon the subject is perpetuated in the illusion as structured in the practice. Contrary to belief being something interior for Žižek, belief is exterior, "embodied in the practical effective procedure of the people."[21] As a result, one should best look for the ideological hold of "the Inerrant Bible" upon evangelicals in the core practices of their churches and institutions. In this regard, as I have already mentioned, expository preaching and personal and group "inductive Bible" study

20. Žižek, *Sublime Object*, 32.
21. Ibid., 34.

are examples of such practices. The continued proliferation of these practices among evangelicals through their emphasis on "word studies" and the scientific precision of studying propositions reinforces the conviction that this Bible is inerrant in every word and is to be learned rightly and cognitively as a fundamental practice of the Christian life. It is a belief that gives the expository preacher an inherent ideological authority in the pulpit.

Žižek helps us see the danger inherent in "the Inerrant Bible" as a Master-Signifier for evangelicalism. The Master-Signifier, we remember, weaves the subject into the ideological system by providing sufficient distance from the object for the subject to in essence be shielded from what his or her beliefs might actually demand of them.[22] It becomes an object that can mean many things to different people, thereby uniting people around the illusion that they all believe in the same thing when they don't. The "signifier without the signified," in other words, allows us to believe without believing. Perhaps worse, it allows us to be complicit in systems we know are not righteous while acting as if they are. Could the "inerrant Bible" function in this way within the communal life of evangelicalism?

I suggest this is so. For in a strange way, "the inerrant Bible" allows us to believe we have the truth while at the same time remaining distant from actually engaging in it as a way of life. We assent unabashedly to the perfect book without it truly meaning anything. It acts as an "ideological fantasy" wherein we live in a projected world where we can believe we have the truth, but in real life have to make little or no changes to the way we live.[23] To crassly over-simplify, we can be prosperity gospel preachers indulging in avaricious capitalism, or megachurches

22. The term common to Žižek for this process is "interpellate." Borrowed from Marxist political theorist Louis Althusser, "interpellate" describes the way an individual is absorbed into the Symbolic Order thereby receiving an identity. This subjectivization happens when we as subjects accept the call (most of the time unvolitionally) of an ideological product to recognize ourselves in it. See *Sublime Object* 2–3, *Ticklish Subject*. 257–60.

23. I am using the word "fantasy" in the technical Lacanian sense, used by Žižek and already mentioned in the previous chapter. According to Žižek, every ideology must provide a "fantasy," an imaginary in which the subject can finds his or her place and thereby organizes his/her desire. By calling "the Inerrant Bible" a fantasy then is to say this is the way we imagine the Bible so that it makes us feel/gain some satisfaction/comfort which enables us to go on living within the comfortable status quo with no guilt.

selling a self-help gospel, we can be complicit with societal values of consumerism, materialism, and wealth accumulation at the expense of the poor, all the while affirming "we believe the Bible is true and the inerrant word of God." Surely this is not the majority of evangelicalism, yet there is no denying that in the process of the Bible becoming this Master-Signifier for evangelicalism, evangelicals lose the means to determine and converse what biblical faithfulness might entail.

It is this distancing aspect of the empty signifier within Žižek's political theory that should give us evangelicals pause as we contemplate the role this belief and practice play in forming us into a people in the world. We must ask whether "the inerrant Bible" as Master-Signifier keeps us from embodying the truth, living into the Story, indeed the mission that God is working in the world. The perfect book, in almost too subtle of ways, becomes a distraction leaving us unable to see the living reality of the mission of God recounted and extended to us through the Scriptures as handed down to us in the church. Instead, through the way we speak and the way we practice Scripture as evangelicals, we are held fixated by the sublime object of "the inerrant Bible." We parse it, exegete it, defend it, uphold it, inductively study it, take notes on it, all the while distracted from ever fully participating in the story it tells of the mission of God. If this is evident among us evangelicals, we are seeing the signs that evangelicalism has become an empty politic, an ideology that has lost its core.[24]

"The Inerrant Bible": Signs of an Empty Ideology

There are signs among evangelicals that reveal the "emptiness" behind our politic of "the inerrant Bible." They appear in the form of "irruptions of the Real": episodes of overidentification or excessive *jouissance* in the culture of evangelicalism that reveal the inner conflict and/or drives that lie behind our belief and practice. These irruptions reveal how our belief in "the inerrant Bible" is no longer about the place of the

---

24. To talk about an ideology "that has lost its core" is to deviate significantly from Žižek's political ontology. Žižek says every politic is and always will be built around a lack at its core. Hopefully the reader begins to see here the way I have started to use Žižek to diagnose when a social body has taken on the characteristics of Žižek's empty ideology all the while assuming something else about the nature of a "true politic in the world."

Bible in our lives but about inner antagonisms that have taken over our reason for being together.

According to ideological theory, if evangelicalism is an unraveling ideology losing its hold on its people, we would expect to see more of these episodes. The instability of the core of the ideology cannot be contained. "Irruptions," then, are inevitable. They expose the antagonism (the Real) that lies at the core. As more of these exposures eat away at the political fantasy's credibility that has sustained the ideology for so long, more people "act" on the obvious. The "irruptions" increase in intensity as an ideology loses its grip. At this point the ideology enters a crisis.

In relation to "the inerrant Bible," evangelicalism for years has been populated with "irruptions" of over-identification. For instance, in 1970, when Hal Lindsey's book *The Late Great Planet Earth* became a best seller, proclaiming that the inerrant supernatural Bible could predict the future, he was carrying the logic of inerrancy further than most evangelicals ever intended. The fact that the book sold an unheard of 35 million copies suggests it was tapping into a certain *jouissance* (vengeful enjoyment) among the evangelicals. After all, evangelicals were saying when Israel was rebirthed "See! We told you so! The Bible is supernaturally inerrant and predicted this whole thing!" When, however, Lindsey had to revise and re-revise his predictions based on the events of Israel's Six-Day War in sequel after sequel, he embarrassingly revealed the hazards of "believing inerrancy too much." Inerrancy was revealed to be more about "being right!" than a belief that we inhabit with our daily lives.

Similar episodes have plagued evangelicalism for decades. Recall when famed "creation scientist" Henry Morris chastised the Chicago Conference on Inerrancy. He was appalled when the conferees refused to incorporate the "literal seven day creation" into their statement on the Bible.[25] An over-identification had taken place. He had assumed inerrancy meant we would all agree on interpretation—his interpretation! He had taken the logic of "the inerrant Bible" too seriously and in the process revealed the true antagonism at work—that inerrancy is a Master-Signifier used to enforce that my interpretation is right![26]

25. As well as the worldwide flood hypothesis. Henry Morris talks about this in his book, *King of Creation*.

26. Ironically, his "creationist hypothesis" would have been rejected by the archi-

In similar fashion, evangelicals often look askance at the KJV-only Baptists: those who believe the King James Version is the only true inspired translation of the Bible. Yet, amidst the publication of hundreds of translations of the Bible in the 1970s and 80s, were not the "KJV-only" people only saying what made sense? They were saying "Hey, if we really do believe in the inerrancy of every word then how can we have multiple translations that contradict themselves? Of course there must also be a God-breathed, infallible translation!" And so when fundamentalist evangelist Jack Hyles stated that no one can be saved without the King James Version, he had dared to take the evangelical belief in the inerrant Bible too seriously.[27] An irruption of the Real had taken place revealing the absurdity behind the object that "the Inerrant Bible" had become.[28] To exaggerate, it became the means to assert "we are the ones who have the truth and anyone else is going to hell!" All of these episodes illustrate the way the inerrant Bible became "over-identified." Each time the contradiction that lies at the core is uncovered. Yet "the inerrant Bible" continues on as an evangelical Master-Signifier because it feeds on a certain emptiness—the need to be right, to control the truth—that drives our political existence.

In more recent times, the not-so-subtle "good-evangelical-Bible-student-turned-agnostic" Bart Ehrman became a public figure and a New York Times bestselling author. Ehrman made no secret that he was a pristine evangelical student of the paragon evangelical schools Moody Bible Institute and Wheaton College, Illinois. So when he closed his bestselling book *Misquoting Jesus* with a slam against inerrancy by saying, "Given the circumstance that [God] didn't preserve the words, the conclusion seemed inescapable to me that he hadn't gone to the trouble of inspiring them," something of a revealing had taken place for evangelicalism's belief in "the inerrant Bible."[29] Certainly Ehrman was not the first evangelical to disavow *en toto* the historical

tects of "the inerrancy doctrine" themselves. B. B. Warfield and Charles Hodge were both known to be professing evolutionists. See Mark Noll, "Charles Hodge and"; Livingstone, *Adam's Ancestors*, 159–62

27. Jack Hyles famously said "I have a conviction as deep as my soul that every English-speaking person who has ever been born again was born of the incorruptible seed; that is, the King James Bible." Hyles, *Enemies of Soul*, 47.

28. I owe this example to a suggestion made by my fiend Gordon Hackman.

29. Ehrman, *Misquoting Jesus*, 208, 211.

divinely inspired inerrancy of the Bible.[30] Rather it was Ehrman—the publishing event—that was so telling. This popularly written book, along with others like them,[31] had become a best seller. Why would a rather eccentric but boring New Testament academic author become a best seller? It is because of the excessive performance of inerrancy before his originating family. He was a true evangelical who tried and failed at proving "the inerrant Bible," and now he tells "his personal testimony" and makes a spectacle of it. In the words of the ideology itself, "didn't he know he wasn't supposed to try to do that? Inerrancy was never about that? Yes we assert that the Bible is accurate according to any scientific historiographical test out there, but that's not the real point!" And so Ehrman reveals to the world what happens when you believe inerrancy "too much": become you a bestseller! In the process, he gets dangerously close to the drives that lie behind evangelicalism's "inerrant Bible." In Žižek's terms, the publishing of Ehrman's books stirred up some "perverse enjoyment." Evangelicals and ex-evangelicals (Protestant mainline people largely paid no attention) alike clamored around this piece of dirty laundry, in essence revealing that "the inerrant Bible" is really about the drama as to whether the evangelicals get to tell the liberals "I'm right."

Certainly, this list of irruptions is anecdotal. They prove nothing. Yet just as Freud depended mostly on illustrations and examples to substantiate his psychoanalytic diagnosis, so we also point out episodes in the cultural world of evangelicalism that, as they accumulate, help us see the pathology of our life together. We begin to see the lack that drives our beliefs as evangelicals.

The "Enjoyment" that Drives Our Allegiance to "the Inerrant Bible"

Ehrman illustrates another aspect of the ideology at work in evangelicalism's politic of "the inerrant Bible." Most of the hoopla surrounding the publishing event of Erhman was among the evangelicals. The irony at play is that we evangelicals have always been able to blame "the lib-

---

30. It wasn't the content of Ehrman's books that was new, rather it was the tone. Reams of similar books have been published by "Protestant-liberal" scholars that never made it passed a small first printing.

31. Most notably *Jesus, Interrupted*.

eral" for undermining the Bible, except that now "Ehrman is (or at least was) one of us!" In a way, then, Ehrman materializes for us the fear that says "We have to believe in 'the Inerrant Bible' lest we become the victims of 'the liberals' (who don't believe the Bible) or worse we become one of them."[32] Ehrman in essence reveals how "the inerrant Bible" is the Master-Signifier for evangelicals (or else why would we care about such nit-picking?) And the "dreaded liberals" are the *objet petit a*: the object that makes us want this certainty all the more. Ehrman helps us see how the ideology of "the inerrant Bible" plays on a *jouissance* that is aimed at "the liberals," that perverse enjoyment we experience when we blame "them" for stealing our certainty. The liberals thereby embody that elusive goal that we all seek: perfect certainty and control of the Truth. They emulate the certainty we can only aspire to![33]

As we recall from the last chapter, for Žižek any political system plays on a perverse enjoyment built on the lack within it. The system keeps going based on its ability to compensate its people for some loss by projecting that loss of enjoyment onto an object. To repeat a previous example, recall the 9/11 attacks on New York and the resultant figure of the Islamic terrorist. The Islamic terrorist now symbolizes our loss of freedom as Americans (they attacked us on our land!). Through the terrorist, however, we are able to give up freedom (the Patriot Act) in order to keep pursuing the freedom we don't have—all of which is symbolized in the Islamic terrorist. The Islamic terrorist becomes the object symbolizing the unobtainable desire that keeps us pursuing it. We become defined more by what we are against (and what we do not have) than by the particular freedom we possess. They are the ones who have stolen our freedom. And yet there is a perverse enjoyment in having something to live and die for once again (and go to war for). There is something pathological about the way the object (the Islamic

---

32. The making of "the liberals" into an object to fight against at all cost was symbolized most famously in Harold Lindsell's book *Battle for the Battle*, where he tried to show how various small moves towards acknowledging errors in the Bible led down the slippery slope to becoming "the dreaded liberal."

33. But of course, as we will see, there is something perverse in wanting this certainty in the first place in the way we seek to establish it. In the end it is a kind of certainty we should renounce because it separates us from God.

terrorist) supports the Master-Signifier (Freedom).[34] Žižek calls this enjoyment—*jouissance*—and this object is the *objet petit a.*

For evangelicals, I contend, the *objet petit a* of our belief in "the inerrant Bible" is "the liberals." There is a perverse enjoyment we feel in being the ones who still believe the Bible over against "them": the ones who do not. We foist on them our resentment and we "enjoy" it. They are the ones who would steal the certainty of the truth from us. The doctrine of the inerrant Bible, therefore, originally created to fight against the modernist deterioration of the Bible's authority perpetrated by Protestant liberalism, has now become a badge by which we are defined as "not them." A lustful pride bursts forth among us whenever a fulfillment of biblical prophecy is announced, whenever an esteemed university professor agrees with the Bible, or whenever a discovery in creation science vindicates the supernatural accuracy of Scripture (as we have interpreted them). Instead of being content and quietly confident in what we already knew (the Bible can be trusted), we shout with glee, "See! We were right!" Somehow, via the object of "the liberal" we seem to want this certainty all the more. This is a kind of *jouissance.* Every time such *jouissance* is emitted among evangelicals, it is a signal that "the inerrant Bible" has moved from being a substantive doctrinal commitment around which we embody a way of life to being a Master-Signifier that gathers us around an empty shell.

For Žižek, *jouissance* covers over the conflict at work in the ideology. The ideology has promised too much so as to please everybody. As a result, different forces will eventually conflict as they compete for their specific, yet incompatible, goals. This can all be overlooked as long as people get caught up in the perverse enjoyment of it all. The belief in "the inerrant Bible" dares to promise certainty regarding truth about God independently of God. In other words, it dares to say we can know this truth objectively, through modern science and historiography, and we can prove it by these means! In its excess, it puts the true believer in the false position of making God an object of our own control—a truth we can know without knowing Him.[35] This over-exuberant claim

---

34. "[T]he pathology of the *objet petit a* has to support S_1, the Master-Signifier." Žižek, *Fragile Absolute,* 48.

35. And this in essence incites us to put the Bible into a perverse universalizing logic among those who have never read it, submitted themselves to it, or lived within in. Emergent theologian Pete Rollins in *How (Not) to Speak of God* and Karl Barth

to "objective absolute truth" in effect fetishizes the Bible. Yet the knowledge of God can only be approached in humility out of dependence upon God as a gift from Him. This danger of false hubris is as old as the garden (Gen 3:4). The excessive claim inherent in "the inerrant Bible," therefore, contains the contradiction of this false hubris. This very contradiction is ultimately unsustainable yet goes unchallenged by making "the inerrant Bible" into an ideological object. The hubris is covered over by the sanctimonious energy of believing in "the inerrant Bible."

Living with these various contradictions, then, is facilitated by the fantasy as projected by "the inerrant Bible." The fantasy puts forth the sublime object of "the inerrant Bible" whereby we can believe in absolute truth while never truly being able to test it or even having to live it. It enables us to believe cynically in absolute certainty while never actually having it.[36] It does this by creating an object—"the liberals"—so that whenever the arbitrariness of inerrancy is discovered, we can blame the object (*objet petit a*). We sustain the fantasy by diverting the blame for not having the truth onto this object. The "liberals" are the reason we don't have it yet. They keep stealing it from us! By either saying the Bible has errors or by being better scientists or philosophers than we are, the "liberals" become the *objet petit a*, the leftover (of the ideology) that reminds us we don't have "certainty" yet. We therefore keep pursuing being better at academia and historiography to prove the inerrant Bible. We are proud whenever an evangelical makes it to the halls of Harvard (unless he/she turns into a Bart Ehrman). Ironically we pursue being better "liberals" than they are by adapting their methodologies. This hides the false hubris behind "the inerrant Bible" that, if ever revealed, would undercut the very nature of the God we proclaim.

each get at this each in their own yet very divergent ways. Both argue that we cannot know God (and truth) as our own Cartesian possession separate from our involved faith-participant relationship with God.

36. Again, I do not use the word fantasy to confer doubt upon the status of Scripture in the life of church. Neither do I doubt its historicity or divine inspiration. My point is that the Bible can act as a Žižekian fantasy wherein the citizenry can act *as if* they believe. We may know the Bible has errors (in Enlightenment terms) yet in order to really know and understand the Bible we must sink ourselves into its story, be shaped by it, to understand it and make sense of it. "The inerrant Bible" gives us the wherewithal to bypass all that and in essence act as if we believe it, all the while having to change nothing about our lives. On the way fantasy works in these ways, see Žižek, *Sublime Object of Ideology*, 36, 30–33.

Every once in a while, however, this hubris irrupts. One version of this is the boisterous outcries by various evangelical spokespersons against the purveyors of postmodernity in the Emergent church. They decry "the loss of absolute truth" as devastating to the cause of Christ in the world.[37] Yet it is these objects of disdain, "the dreaded liberals" or the Emergent church, that keep us doggedly in pursuit of certainty in truth. If it weren't for them, we would have no reason to gather. But with them, we can debate and excoriate them over their apostasy towards "the inerrant Bible" (or "Absolute Truth") thereby avoiding ever having to live into it.[38] It all reveals the contradiction at the core of evangelicalism. As Žižek might say, "which is worse, believing in absolute truth or actually having to act like it?"

In summary, then, when this hubris appears as *jouissance*, it reveals what "the inerrant Bible" is really all about (in its recent development). It is about being right! It is not about the Truth, it is about "being in control of the Truth!" It is about possessing the Truth as an object instead of it possessing us. When therefore a burst of arrogant enjoyment springs forth from evangelicals, it often reveals this drive over against the object of disdain that has been nurtured at the core of our politic by "the inerrant Bible." The "dreaded liberal" has become the symbol we resent because they have what we don't have (and maybe we shouldn't have). As a result, evangelicalism comes off as an empty disingenuous politic whose very reason for existence is to fight against someone for something it really doesn't have itself.

The recent history of evangelicalism is strewn with excessive irruptions of this perverse drive to be right. Whether it be exorbitant outcries against the Emergent church, Jack Hyles telling the world they

37. Some of the more notable evangelical spokesman who decry the loss of absolute truth and speak out against the Emergent church in this regard include Albert Mohler, president of Southern Baptist Theological Seminary, in *The Disappearance*, evangelical pastor John MacArthur, in *Truth War*, evangelical theologian Donald Carson, in *Becoming Conversant*, as well as other notables such as apologetics evangelist Ravi Zacharias and evangelical spokesman Charles Colson.

38. Remembering that according to Žižek, "The easiest way to detect ideological surplus-enjoyment in an ideological formation is to read it as a dream, and analyze the displacement in it." *For They Know Not*, xci. In this case, then, the fantasy is to have complete direct unmediated knowledge of God plagued with no uncertainty of the modernist variety. The displacement takes place in resenting the "liberals" as the ones most confident in what they know and thereby stealing this certainty from us, the evangelicals.

can't be saved apart from the King James Version of the Bible, or aw-
ful violence enacted against abortion doctors in the name of protecting life, our tendency as evangelicals is to chalk these instances up as
outliers that exist in every group and therefore should not be counted
against us. When, however, these incidents are magnified by public attention and media frenzy, we should pay attention. Here, in magnified
form, via media-driven frenzy, we can see how American onlookers see
us. These incidents can act as "an ideal projector screen,"[39] a mirror, in
which we can then examine who we have become. We can test our way
of life as to whether it can stand the scrutiny or be revealed as empty at
its core. President George W. Bush's performance of evangelicalism over
the past decade in many ways played this kind of role for evangelicals.

In this regard, one would be hard pressed to find a more public
display of the evangelical *jouissance* that we have been describing. It is
true that George Bush himself never publicly declares his allegiance to
"the inerrant Bible," yet his media persona as an evangelical is firmly
ensconced in this belief. His evangelical identity is beyond question.
He was so aligned with evangelicalism in his campaigns that he became the primary symbol of evangelicalism for his day. As a result, no
president has ever been so visibly supported and elected by evangelicals.[40] His outbursts of hubris, therefore, whether we liked it or not, are
a reflection of evangelicalism to the world. Indeed, the event of George
W Bush's presidency may have been the definitive tipping point for
evangelicalism as an ideology in the world, laying bare the worst of
the drives that lie behind our beliefs and practices. I suspect that many
American Christians under the age of thirty-five refuse to be called
evangelical because of the presidency of George W. Bush.

---

39. The phrase "an ideal projector screen" is from Žižek, *Fragile Absolute*, 60.

40. Bush captured the allegiance of evangelicals in the 2000 presidential election.
He did it again in 2004. In 2004 he carried the white evangelical vote over John Kerry
by a margin of 78 percent to 21 percent. It was roughly the same in terms of percent-
ages of evangelicals voting for Bush in the 2000 election. This led to at least the perception in the media that George W. Bush had been put into the presidency by the nation's
evangelicals. The late Jerry Falwell therefore pronounced that "the church won the
2004 election" at the Southern Baptist Convention pastor's conference in June 2005.
For Rev. Falwell, the church he was speaking about was most certainly the church of
the evangelicals. Falwell's words are reported by AP reporter Rose French, as reported
by Gushee and Phillips, "Moral Formation," 23–24.

It's no exaggeration to suggest that Bush performed evangelicalism before the watching American public. His "walk with Billy Graham," his personal conversion, and his regular church attendance were all recorded regularly in news media. His personal devotion to reading Scripture, inductive Bible study, and prayer was widely and regularly reported as part of his overall campaign strategy.[41] Most peculiar to Bush's life as a Christian were the two years he spent studying the Bible in a national evangelical program of "inductive" Bible study called Community Bible Study: a defining mark of those who believe in inerrancy. Carefully orchestrated then, Bush was seen by evangelicals as one embodying their habits and beliefs, one of those beliefs being "the inerrant Bible." George Bush then became a symbol of evangelicalism for both evangelicals and non-evangelicals alike. He acted as the ideal "projector screen" for evangelicals to see the fulfillment of their fantasy of "the inerrant Bible"—someone who reads the inerrant Bible, prays, and via the Holy Spirit can know truth (because of the perspicuity of Scripture) who is now in charge of the world! Likewise, for other on-lookers and skeptics, George Bush became their target, their own *objet petit a*. Surely every negative drive and antagonistic thought anyone had ever had towards the conservative evangelical Christians in their neighborhoods was foisted upon George W. Bush.

Therefore, when George Bush told a senior Palestinian leader on a BBC News documentary that "God told him to invade Afghanistan and Iraq," his words amplified the evangelical belief that one can know individually a truth as it comes directly from God.[42] The words became an international sensation. The White House made every effort to get the BBC to retract the statement but failed. What ensued, however, reflected back to the whole world the worst fears of the world concerning evangelicals—that we believe that we alone have the truth directly

41. All of these things were recounted in depth in Newsweek by Howard Fineman. "Bush and God." Much of this was fully documented in the 2004 PBS Frontline program "The Jesus Factor." In 2003 Stephen Mansfield's *Faith of George W. Bush* was published as a deliberate part of the campaign strategy to attract more evangelicals to his re-election. A virtual media explosion over George Bush's evangelicalism enveloped him associating him as a card carrying evangelical.

42. See the BBC press release concerning the documentary entitled "Elusive Peace: Israel and the Arabs." Online: www.bbc.co.uk/pressoffice/pressreleases/stories/2005/10_october/06/bush/shtml. The title of the BBC press release was "God told me to invade Iraq, Bush tells Palestinian ministers."

from God and now we have bombs to prove it! In ideological terms, the words reflected the over-identification that happens when evangelicals take "the inerrant Bible" too "seriously." Who among us, after all, have not heard these very same words in our own evangelical church meetings, or in daily conversations with other evangelicals: "God told me . . ."? The real ideological impact of president Bush's statement is that his words are so familiar to us all as evangelicals. They reveal to us the excessive implications of what might drive the evangelical belief in "the inerrant Bible": the belief that if we have an inerrant Bible together with the perspicuity given to us by the Holy Spirit; we can be right, we can be in control.

The same kind of episode had already occurred a few months earlier in the Bush administration. Journalist Bob Woodward famously asked the president whether he had talked with his father about invading Iraq (and Afghanistan), referring to his father the former president of the United States. George W. Bush replied, "He's the wrong father to go to . . . there's a higher father that I appeal to."[43] Reported on the TV show "60 Minutes," as well as numerous media outlets across the country,[44] evangelicals had to wince as the world saw us in this light. We could not avoid the implicating question: does he really believe he can know the "words of God" directly with enough certainty to lead an entire nation into war?[45] Again, the excessive implications of the evangelical epistemology (the way we know and understand truth) are revealed on a national scale. There is an excess hubris that dares to declare that I have a direct line to God. I can know truth for certain and therefore I am in control.

This drive to be certain and to be right came to define Bush as president. He was universally lauded and/or despised (depending on

43. Woodward, *Plan of Attack*.

44. 60 Minutes, April 18, 2004. Online: www.cbsnews.com/stories/2004/04/15/60minutes/main612067.shtml

45. Mansfield's *Faith of George W. Bush* was written a year before the 2004 election as part of Bush's campaign. It was a NY Times Best Seller for many weeks. The book reiterated his personal conversion as well as his intense devotion to inductive Bible study as the basis for his relationship with God. It told the now-famous story of how Bush and Tony Blair read Scripture and prayed together before long walks at Camp David. The book dared to imply that Bush was "God's man for the presidency," that president Bush (together with Blair) had prayed and read the Bible thereby leading to the decision to invade Iraq.

which side you were on) for his stubborn certainty and/or his decisiveness. In unusual fashion, the pro-Bush evangelical Robert Draper wrote a book entitled *Dead Certain* in 2007 in which he called Bush "The Decider."[46] Evangelicals seemed to be enamored with this quality about him. Yet many reputable journalists wrote about this trait in Bush in unflattering ways, attributing it to his religious commitments within evangelicalism and referring to him as "Bush the Infallible."[47] In his first post-9/11 address to Congress on September 20, 2001, he proclaimed, "Either you are with us, or you are with the terrorists" using biblical-like language. To many it was a burst of excess enjoyment at having a cause, something to be against. It revealed an antagonism at work. For many it identified Bush as an evangelical.

In 2003 president Bush took the extraordinary measure of donning a U.S. Navy flight suit and flew as a passenger in a jet that landed on the U.S.S. Lincoln Aircraft Carrier off the shores of California. In full view of network news cameras, he emerged from the Navy jet in a show of bravado hard to exaggerate. He proceeded to the deck to the cheers of hundreds of marines. He then ascended to a platform where a large banner hung behind him with the words "Mission Accomplished." This stunned the American media and many political pundits, for one could hardly assess the future of Iraq at this point in the operation. Nonetheless, from the deck and with full press coverage, he declared victory in Iraq and a ceasing of major combat operations in Iraq. Over the next few weeks, the White House denied having anything to do with raising that banner. They claimed it was the work of the U.S. Navy sailors on board at the time. Other White House personnel were supposedly caught photo-shopping the sign out of the press photos.[48]

---

46. Draper, *Dead Certain*.

47. In 2003, Jeffrey Tucker, an editorialist with the conservative libertarian think tank the Mises Institute, wrote an article entitled "Bush the Infallible." Online: http://www.lewrockwell.com/tucker/tucker29.html. He attributed Bush's arrogance to his religious commitments within evangelicalism. In October 2004, journalist Ron Suskind wrote a famous article entitled "Without a Doubt" that was published in the *The New York Times Magazine* where Suskind alluded to similar things.

48. The reports on these activities are multiple. For a summary, read the CNN account: http://www.cnn.com/2003/ALLPOLITICS/10/28/mission.accomplished. On November 2006, the video "White House Caught Doctoring 'Mission Accomplished'" was posted on YouTube that took the viewer step-by-step through the process of discovering that the White House had indeed cropped the photos and videos of that

This entire flurry of activity smacks of *jouissance*. The excess of the flyer jacket and the claim to have flown the plane, the hurry to proclaim victory, and then the White House embarrassment over the brashness of it all, can really only be explained as a sign of an excessive drive working at the level of ideology. One can hardly imagine Dwight Eisenhower doing the same after the victory at D-Day—the prevailing atmosphere was one of immense sorrow and relief. Yet here, the hoopla and the ensuring press reaction hints at an excessive "perverse" enjoyment revealed. For one can see in this "act" an almost excessive "in your face," "I was right," almost as if to say this was more about me being right that winning any war.

It is not possible to draw a direct link between the doctrine of inerrancy and the performance of president George Bush as an evangelical on the world stage. Yet to the extent that a) we evangelicals recognized ourselves in the mirror that is George Bush; b) George Bush is a performance of evangelicalism for the American public for which we must now answer; and c) George Bush himself is a product of evangelical culture and its formation around "the inerrant Bible," there are some things we should acknowledge as evangelicals. George Bush held the allegiance of evangelicals for so long because we recognized and associated ourselves with his evangelical behavior. We should, in a sense, ask whether it is his *jouissance* or our *jouissance*? The fact that so many evangelicals continued to fight for his presidency because "he is one of us" suggests that we were not only enduring but in fact vicariously associating with his behaviors. In a way, then, the excesses of his beliefs (in "the inerrant Bible" for one) are ours. His drive for certainty, to be right over against those who would steal the truth from us, is revealing of what lies behind our life together as well.

Perhaps then the forty-third president has pushed evangelicalism into an ideological crisis. In the same manner as Borat ratcheted up the intensity of the over-identification in the rodeo scene in the movie, making the absurdity of the war obvious even to the pro-Iraq War fanatics, so the performance of evangelicalism by President Bush has done the same for evangelicals and our ideology of Scripture. Perhaps he has

---

speech to remove the Mission Accomplished sign. The video was later removed for unknown reasons. There still is however sufficient media available on the Web to compare original media coverage of the speech with the coverage released by the White House several weeks later.

so unabashedly over-identified with the drives behind evangelicalism and "the Inerrant Bible" (among other doctrines) that he has made visible the excesses behind our belief for all. Perhaps more damaging to our own life together as evangelicals, these same excesses have become apparent to us as well. As a result, many evangelicals are beginning to turn away from this vision of what we have become.

Arrogance and Exclusion:
The Spiritual Formation of an "Empty Politic"

Žižek's political theory shows us how an "empty" ideology operates. Via Žižek, we see how a belief in the Bible's authority expressed through the doctrine of inerrancy can misshape a people's life together. "The inerrant Bible" can act as a fantasy that holds evangelicals in its grasp by playing on a *jouissance*, an enjoyment of sure knowledge of God over against those who would steal it from us. It can be used to help define us as "against" the liberals. As Master-Signifiers will do, "the inerrant Bible" works to turn the Scriptures into an ideological object, thereby distancing us from participation in it. We do not need to live it but merely swear our allegiance to it! "The inerrant Bible," therefore, shapes us away from actually participating in God's kingdom and towards complicity with the existing social status quo as a false future. Through observing (what we have called) the irruptions of the Real within our politics, we have caught a glimpse of what is driving our life together.

Surely this is not all of evangelicalism. Yet via "the inerrant Bible," we can see how the Bible can become a Master-Signifier for evangelicals that in turn shapes us into an antagonism with the world instead of gathering us into the life of the triune God and his work in the world. As a result, we often tend toward a false posture of arrogance and a perverse enjoyment of exclusion. And we do this all with a passivity bred by the confidence we have in "the inerrant Bible."

Arrogance can be defined as seeing with undue certainty. The disposition to exclude sees the world in terms of "either you are for me or against me." It results in an unwillingness to listen and discern with others. It sets us up (as a politic) over against any one who might disagree. Strangely, these two dispositions into which "the inerrant Bible" shapes us are the opposite of what we need if we want to engage the world with love, the embodiment of truth, and the hospitality that invites the world into the redemptive ongoing work of God in Christ to reconcile the world to himself. The ideologization of "the inerrant Bible" works against us being shaped into the hospitable politic God inhabits for his mission in the world.

If the defining questions for this political theology are "What kind of people is our belief and practice shaping us into?" and "is this consistent with the very gospel we seek to embody in the world?" then the evangelical belief and practice of "the inerrant Bible" must be critically examined. The task, in going forward, must be to reform our belief and practice of Scripture so as to shape a life together in the gospel. We must recognize the emptiness at the core of our belief and seek to recover the core of our life together: the incarnate Son of God, the Sent One from the Father whom by the Spirit reigns over all things until "all things are made subject" (1 Cor 15:25–28).

In the language of Žižek, we must traverse the fantasy of "the inerrant Bible"[49] and recognize the lack that is behind it, detach ourselves from it and work towards a reconfiguration of our belief and practice of Scripture. We surely want to uphold "a high view" of Scripture as truth bearing, reliable, trustworthy, and dare I say infallible. But we need a way of both articulating this belief and practicing it in a manner that restores Jesus Christ to the core of our politic. Žižek, no doubt, would have us find a better way to live with the void.[50] Contrary to Žižek, however, I propose the way forward is to fill the void via a restoration of the incarnate Christ to the core of our political life together—via our belief and practice of Scripture. Scripture, in other words, must be practiced as a living political extension of the living incarnate Christ who lives and reigns within the triune relation and what God is doing in the whole world. Reclaiming the core of our politics in Jesus Christ in this way provides the basis for a politics of mission. This will be the

---

49. According to Žižek "the ultimate goal of psychoanalysis is to enable the subject analysand to accomplish the passage from S(1) (Master Signifier) to *objet petit a* so as to identify the remainder that sustains the dignity . . . ." Žižek, *Fragile Absolute* 48–49. In other words, once we see the object that we are projecting our perverse enjoyment on is really a fantasy, the ideology's hold is released, we break from it, detach from it, making for a new truer form of political existence.

50. His modus operandi is to learn to live with the void, come to peace with it, as opposed to somehow escaping it and recovering a core, since either is metaphysically impossible for Žižek.

task of the last chapter of this book. Before we get there, however, we must turn to the next evangelical doctrinal distinctive: how evangelicals speak about and practice the salvation we have in Christ.

CHAPTER 4

"The Decision for Christ": The Politics of the Evangelical Belief
and Practice of Salvation—How It Shapes Us for Duplicity

*"I'd rather die today and go to heaven than live
to be a hundred and go to hell . . ."*
—Sonny Dewey, *The Apostle* (1997)

In a notable scene in the 1997 movie *The Apostle*, pastor Sonny Dewey
(played by Robert Duvall) is driving with his mother, fleeing the police
after he has committed a terrible act of violence. Along the way he happens upon a severe car accident. He stops his car, grabs his Bible, and
approaches one of the cars, where he finds a dead young woman and a
dying young man. He tells the boy that it looks too late for his companion, but he might still have a chance for salvation before he slips away.
Sonny tells the boy that Jesus is waiting so that the boy, whether he lives
or dies, can have eternal life in heaven. He asks the boy if he wants that,
and the boy nods in assent. Sonny asks the boy if he is ready to follow
Jesus for the rest of his life, whether his life were to last for years or just
for a few minutes. The boy again nods. Sonny leads him in prayer while
kicking away a police officer who is telling him that he isn't supposed
to be there. Sonny gets back into his car and tells his mother that they
won one for Jesus.

The scene plays on a stereotype of evangelicals and their understanding of salvation. Evangelicals, the stereotype suggests, are
primarily focused upon one's escape from hell—God's punishment of

sin—rather than the present life. The character of Sonny illustrates the duplicity of our lives that forms the unfortunate backdrop for this practice of salvation and how indeed we seem oblivious to it.

"The altar call" is the symbolic practice for this version of evangelical salvation. Most evangelicals of the boomer generation know its cadence. The preacher preaches a sermon, some music begins (most often the hymn "Just as I Am"), and then the "invitation" is made. The preacher invites those who have "not received Christ" to come forward and make a "decision." Though perhaps an over-characterization, this used to be standard fare in evangelical Sunday services as recently as the 1960s and 70s. For many of us who "went forward" early in our lives and "made a decision" to put our faith and trust in Christ, we went home afterward and wrote the date and time of it in our personal Bibles (at the prodding of our parents). These practices, so pervasive in the evangelicalism of even a generation ago, speak to the central importance of "the decision for Christ" for understanding the belief and practice of salvation for evangelicalism in America.

Evangelicalism was birthed out of the revivalism of the eighteenth and nineteenth centuries. The signature ritual of this revivalism was (some form of) "the altar call," where one made a decision to put one's faith in Christ. Amidst the burgeoning individualism of a new democracy and the new religious freedom unimpeded by the traditionalism of the European Reformation, the Great Awakenings called countless thousands across the American frontier into a decision to commit their lives to Christ. These populations of the newly "saved" funded the generations who would later walk through the modernist-fundamentalist controversies and become the evangelicals. From the Methodist camp meeting preachers, to Charles Finney and his "new measures" revivalism, to evangelists Billy Sunday and Charles Fuller all the way up to the more recent "crusades" of Billy Graham, all of these preachers were evangelists calling people forward to an "altar" of some kind to make "the decision."[1]

The basic message of salvation which emerged during this time was as follows. 1) God created us and loves us; He created us for "relationship" with Him. 2) All humanity, however, has sinned and lies

---

1. Of course for Finney it was the "anxious bench." For a history of the "altar call," see Sweeney and Rogers, "Walk the Aisle."

fallen under the judgment of sin. Every individual therefore is separated from God and condemned to hell (Rom 3:23). 3) God, however, has made a provision for our sin through Christ's sacrificial death on the cross; Christ took upon himself our sin as a substitute, thereby paying the penalty for our sin, propitiating the wrath and judgment of God (1 Pet 3:18). 4) By putting our faith and trust in Christ alone through his atoning work, we are saved from eternal damnation and are gifted with eternal life (John 5:24, Eph 2:8–9). Every one, therefore, needs to make "a decision for Christ" to recognize their own sin and to put their faith in Christ and His work on the cross in order to then receive eternal life.[2] There was then usually a decision that followed afterward. Upon making the first decision, the individual was called into the "Spirit-filled life," an additional decision to live daily in dependence upon the Holy Spirit.[3]

This basic "salvation message" melds together two of evangelicalism's defining characteristics, as defined by historian David Bebbington: conversion and the cross. Evangelicals, Bebbington says, have always placed a central importance on one's personal conversion. Someone might do all the right things, lead a good life, go to church, and help the poor, but all of this is for naught if he/she has not personally made a decision to "receive Christ."[4] In this way, everyone must be born again! One must acknowledge that he/she is a sinner and then put his/her faith in the atoning work of Christ on the cross. Essential to this personal conversion was the second of Bebbington's characteristics: the cross. Evangelicals, as described by Bebbington, have been committed from the beginning to the substitutionary view of the atonement over and above other theological explanations of Christ's atonement.

The call to holiness and life in the Spirit was also central to the revivalist evangelicalism of the nineteenth century leading up all the way to World War I.[5] Regeneration by the Spirit was always presented

---

2. For a summary of this message, see Graham, *How to Be*, 167–68.

3. "The Spirit-Filled Life" is the title of a tract by Bill Bright, the author of "the Four Spiritual Laws."

4. Bebbington, *Dominance of Evangelicalism*, 32.

5. It is theological historian Donald Dayton who sees the holiness movements rooted primarily in American Methodism as the source of the true classic evangelicalism. But according to Dayton, and in distinction from prominent evangelical historian George Marsden, something happened in the 1920s with the fundamentalist-modern-

as a next step that came after the decision. The call to holy living in and through the Holy Spirit was emphasized and took the shape of a second and separate decision. Something happened however with the modernist-fundamentalist controversies of the 1920s that exaggerated the split between the decision to receive pardon for sin in Christ (justification) and the second aspect (sanctification), the decision to receive and live in the Spirit. As a result, there was an increase in emphasis on the decision to receive pardon for one's sin in and through Christ. The active decision to engage in the life of the Spirit fell more to the wayside or was left for the Pentecostal movements who were emerging in that day.[6]

No doubt, the fundamentalist-modernist controversies of the 1920s and 30s played a key role in this development. During this time, mainline Protestantism began to question and down play the "bloody" sacrificial aspects of the atonement. Likewise, Protestant mainline pastors put less emphasis on personal conversion versus recruiting participants for the social transformation of society.[7] Fundamentalists complained that "the social gospel" was diminishing the importance of personal salvation. They stood staunchly in the camp that affirmed that Christ—on the cross—had taken our place as a substitute and borne our sins. Through faith, Christ's righteousness is thereby transferred to our account. We thereby have been pardoned from hell and declared righteous before God.[8]

As a result, both conversion and the substitutionary atonement of Christ took renewed prominence as a defining marker of the emerging

---

ist controversies that shifted the whole evangelical movement towards the categories of a new Reformed emphasis on inerrant Scriptures, substitionary atonement and away from the experiential aspects of salvation in the Holy Spirit. For the debate between Dayton and Marsden see the entire issue of *Christian Scholar's Review* 13:1 (1993).

6. So someone like Donald Dayton can complain that George Marsden has lost the true identity of classic evangelism in the Methodist holiness roots by seeing evangelicalism almost entirely through the lens of the modernist-fundamentalist controversy which took evangelicalism towards a decidedly conservative Princeton emphasis on inerrancy, subtitutionary atonement, and individualist conversionist evangelism. See Dayton, "Search for Christian America."

7. On the fundamentalist reaction to liberal versions of the Christian life by strongly defending the substitutionary atonement and conversion, see Carpenter, *Revive Us Again*, 76–80; Kyle, *Evangelicalism*, 137–38, Marsden, *Reforming*, 4–6.

8. Bebbington, *Dominance of Evangelicalism*, 27–29.

evangelicalism.[9] The "life in the Spirit," though still present (even to this day), receded in prominence. The stage was set for this group of people (who would later become the evangelicals) to firmly coalesce around "the decision" as defined by these two characteristics: conversion and subtitutionary atonement.

"The decision for Christ" reached its zenith as a hallmark of evangelicalism during the "crusade" ministry of Billy Graham. Graham called his radio program "The Hour of Decision." He labeled his magazine *Decision* magazine. He made famous the altar call, inviting hundreds to "make a decision" to the singing of "Just as I Am." Yet Graham was not alone in demarcating "the decision" as the evangelical hallmark of how one entered into salvation in Christ. Several developments contemporary to Billy Graham and his evangelistic crusades developed their own tools that furthered the centrality of "the decision" as defining the belief and practice of salvation among evangelicals. For example, Bill Bright, the founder of the evangelical para-church ministry Campus Crusade for Christ, created the *Four Spiritual Laws* booklets in 1952. This evangelistic "tool" led a person through the basic salvation message recited above and then invited him/her to pray a prayer to "receive Christ." This booklet became emblematic of how to lead one into salvation in Christ through arriving at "the decision" to say the prayer at the end of the booklet.[10]

Other, similar versions of this technique were developed such as the Romans Road and the Bridge Illustration, the latter being the form of gospel evangelism adopted at the lead evangelical megachurch in America, Willow Creek in the Chicago area, for use in both evangelism and children's ministry programs. In each case, the presentation followed the outline of the message above and then invited the individual to make a commitment and pray a version of "the sinners' prayer." The famous *Evangelism Explosion* outreach method reached national prominence among evangelical churches as a door-to-door evangelism program. Thousands of door-to-door teams were trained to take

9. The first place to see this emphasis is in volume three of *The Fundamentals* where several articles are devoted to both the substistionary nature of the atonement and the necessity of the decision for faith in Christ.

10. *The Four Spiritual Laws* is the most widely distributed of the tools with over 100 million in print with an influence much wider. On the scope and influence of *The Four Spiritual Laws*, see Hunter, *American Evangelicalism*, 75.

surveys in the neighborhoods that led to the same message and again asked for a similar decision. To this day, these programs, although continually revised, continue to dominate the evangelistic programs of the evangelical church.[11] The term "decision for Christ" may have changed over time, yet the concept of a life-changing moment from death to eternal life sealed by a decision to trust in Christ's atoning sacrifice "for my sins" still dominates the evangelical landscape.

In recent years, Billy Graham crusades, "the altar calls," and evangelistic sermons asking "do you know where you are going when you die?" have been on the wane in large parts of evangelicalism. The popular *Evangelism Explosion* methods of evangelism have come under critique because they focus too much on one's personal decision regarding eternal destiny.[12] Yet we still lie under the spell of "the decision." The practices of the evangelical megachurch movement, for instance, testify to the reality that these most visible of evangelicals still operate under the assumptions of "the decision." "The decision" assumes salvation is individual, begun through a voluntary act, and then nurtured through individually acquired learning and worship. The large megachurches are built around this version of Christianity. Baptism for these churches, therefore, functions only to make a public declaration of one's "decision" to follow Christ. There is little understanding of the corporate aspects of baptism. Large groups of people come to these settings anonymously as individuals and receive the "materials" they need to grow. They receive the goods and services necessary to lead individual Christian lives. It all makes sense because of the backdrop of "the decision."

Wayne Grudem's *Systematic Theology*, still the most popular present-day textbook among evangelicals studying theology, illustrates the importance of "the decision" and "the altar call" to the evangelical understanding of salvation. In the book's section on salvation, Grudem focuses upon conversion as a repentance-faith response to the Word strongly centered around justification by faith and the substitutionary

11. *Evangelism Explosion*, for instance, has enhanced its evangelistic tools with a new booklet using more relational/meaning of life questions as opposed to questions that concentrate on getting a person to realize their sin. The booklet in the end still leads to "the decision." See the "life starts here" booklets available online: http//www .xeelife.com.

12. See Lawton, "Evangelism Explosion."

view of the atonement. His chapter on conversion (chapter 35) ends with the hymn "Just as I Am," the closing hymn of "the altar call," the symbol of "the decision" in evangelicalism.[13]

As a result of this history, evangelicals focus on the cognitive when it comes to the practice of salvation. In other words, despite an emphasis on "the heart," "the Spirit," and "the experience," we put the most emphasis on "the mind" when it comes to salvation.[14] Given the right information (e.g., "The Four Spiritual Laws"), we believe the Spirit can convict the soul and move the person towards a decision. Evangelicals are thus Cartesian in their assumptions about how salvation works. In the same way, evangelicals have largely practiced discipleship as an "informational" practice. It is true that we regularly instruct new converts to depend upon the Holy Spirit for everyday Christian life. Yet, by and large we focus on cognitive practices versus the mere holistic spiritual disciplines offered in church history as the means to growth in Christ. After "the decision," we emphasize regular Bible study (inductive) alongside personal prayer. Regular fellowship and witnessing follow as essentials to personal Christian growth.[15] We emphasize going to church, which is largely an informational gathering centered around the sermon. Underlying it all is the belief that if we give the right information to individuals, they will grow. Just as we are urged to make a decision that responds to cognitive as well as spiritual conviction, so it is hoped the mind can learn what it needs to learn and then tell the body (with the help of the Spirit) what to do. In all these ways, evangelical discipleship reflects the Cartesian assumptions of "the decision."

13. Grudem, *Systematic Theology*, 721.

14. Descartes famously located "knowing" and the moral agency in the individual human mind. He set off modernity's emphasis on "the cogito" as the center of the subject that thereby inhabits the body. The dualism inherent therein led to the proliferation of Enlightenment individualism as well as numerous social and political developments. Evangelicalism, in my view, inherits this Cartesianism.

15. The famous Navigator wheel of discipleship is a wheel based on four practices that an individual does. The wheel places each of these four practices as spokes (under the rubric of obedience) around the center of Jesus Christ. They are taught as disciplines individuals do. See online: https://www.navigators.org/us/resources/illustrations/items/The%20Wheel%20-%20Illustration. *The Four Spiritual Laws* also follow the same approach with the added element to depend upon the Holy Spirit for daily living. These things are listed in the final button one clicks after making a decision on the Four Spiritual Laws website. Online: http://4laws.com/laws/english/flash.

Despite then the numerous evangelicals who have left behind the practices of "the altar call," the lingering reality is that "the decision" remains a hallmark of evangelicalism. It endures as a major factor in the forming of the people called evangelical in North America. It organizes our coming together in a peculiar way. It has shaped what kind of people we have become.

"THE DECISION FOR CHRIST" AS MASTER-SIGNIFIER

The question here again is, what kind of political formation has resulted from this evangelical belief and practice of "the decision for Christ"? How has "the decision" shaped us as a people for inhabiting the gospel in the world?

Once again, I contend that "the decision for Christ" functions in many ways as a Žižekian Master-Signifier for evangelicalism, with all the political ramifications implied by that. It possesses, for instance, the same elusive quality that all Master-Signifiers must have to function politically. It is hard to define in terms of what it actually might mean for our practical lives. In terms of its practical effects, it means different things to different people among evangelicals. This was illustrated for me in 2008, while I was speaking at a conference of mostly evangelical pastors in Toronto, Canada. I was with a group discussing the place of "the decision for Christ" in church life among evangelicals in Canada. Much like telling a joke that everyone knew, several of the pastors told me about a statistic that was recently generated by one of the main statisticians of religious life in Canada. Evidently, this researcher surveyed several thousand people in Canada and found that 20 percent of the sample checked the "box" that they had made a decision for Christ. This same 20 percent, however, *also* checked the "box" that said they did not believe in God. Although I have not been able to verify the reliability of this research, this "story" had attained a mythic status among evangelical Canadian pastors. It gets at the Master-Signifier quality that "the decision for Christ" has taken on within evangelicalism in North America. "The decision" has coalesced a large group of evangelical people around it, but fewer and fewer of them really know what it might mean for their concrete lives.

There is enough imprecision as to what "the decision for Christ" might mean that it makes for a good banner for people of all types to gather around. Evangelicals certainly have detailed explanations/ booklets concerning the doctrine of justification by faith that undergirds the practice of making a decision. We who make such a decision are instructed as to what "happens" forensically before God when the person says "the sinners' prayer." But on a concrete level it is hard to locate what this decision might actually mean for the way we live. In one sense, the largest "political" impact of "the decision for Christ" is that evangelicals are able to gather large numbers of people around a belief (they've made a decision) that asks little of them in terms of concrete ways of life.

The recidivism rate of those who make "the decision for Christ" is famously high. *Eternity Magazine* reported as far back as 1977 that evangelistic crusades among evangelical churches could locate only 3 percent of those claiming to have made "a decision" as being found in any kind of Christian church.[16] Billy Graham said publicly on David Frost's PBS show in the 1990s that he believed only 25 percent of the decisions recorded in his crusades resulted in people actually being born again.[17] At the time, this shocked evangelicals. One of the largest evangelical denominations reportedly disclosed that there had been 384,057 decisions for Christ within their churches in 1995, but only 6 percent could be accounted for in any way the following year.[18] Figures like these reveal the nebulous quality of "the decision."

Yet it does not matter. We keep on counting! Despite its elusiveness, evangelicals stubbornly persist in holding onto "the decision" as a unifying practice. Recidivism figures, even considering the few cited above, are notoriously difficult to acquire from local church organizations. This works to enhance "the decision" as a good Master-Signifier. It is difficult to measure what the decision might actually mean for people's everyday lives.[19] Nonetheless, the ideological power of "the

16. As reported by Comfort, *Hell's Best Kept*, 9.

17. Frost and Bauer, *Billy Graham*, 72.

18. McIntyre, *Graham Formula*, 12.

19. Several years ago now, over a cup of coffee, a major leader in evangelical missions told me of two large campaigns that went into Indonesia and Thailand with the Jesus film. After these campaigns, and the presentation of "the gospel" as outlined above, they recorded 35,000 conversions in Thailand and 85,000 conversions in

decision" continues to manifest itself as organizations and independent churches continue to record decisions for Christ on an annual basis.[20] The "decision for Christ," despite its slipperiness, continues to capture the imagination of evangelicals and drive our understandings of salvation.

The elusive quality of "the Decision" is represented by the iconic street preacher who asks the passersby, "Do you know where you are going when you die?" His/her message is that if they make "the decision," then they will know they are going to heaven! Yet this well worn tactic of revivalist evangelicalism proves less capable of delivering the personal "assurance" it sells. Do we really know? Were we sincere enough when we made the decision? Did we mean it? How did that work anyway? Furthermore, on another level, it is impossible to know because you'll only really know after you die. And how can something this momentous hinge on something that seems so frivolous? And so the certainty surrounding "the decision" is something evangelicals are ever pursuing but never quite arriving at. We recognize this elusiveness of "the decision" in that one particular church member we have all seen go forward to the altar time and again ever pursuing the assurance that she/he "is in." The repeated trip to the altar symbolizes the constant pursuit of something that "the decision" promises but always seems to elude our grasp.

The ideological drift of "the decision" into an elusive signifier became exposed in the 1980s with a theological infight among evangelicals provoked by theologian-pastor John MacArthur. In a book, on his radio program, and in several national addresses, MacArthur argued vehemently that "the decision" had to actually mean something for the Christian's life. In what was later to be called "Lordship salva-

---

Indonesia. They had "decision cards" for each one and two years later were shocked to find that literally no one could be located in a local church. When faced reporting this back to the board of this organization, this leader told me, the board was shocked but nonetheless still convinced that at least these "conversions" were no longer condemned to an eternity in hell. I tried to get this prominent leader to put this in writing to me but was never able to acquire an account of this episode in writing.

20. The Campus Crusade for Christ's Global Media Outreach (GMO) division, for instance, recorded with much fanfare one million decisions for Christ in one month over their GMO-hosted "Gospel Web sites" in June 2009. See Young, "CCC Media records." Most evangelical denominations still require their churches to report this statistic as part of their annual report.

tion," he asserted that one "cannot accept Jesus Christ as Savior without also accepting him as Lord." The Christian, therefore, should exhibit some behavioral changes upon becoming a Christian. Zane Hodges, a professor at evangelical stronghold Dallas Theological Seminary, took the opposite side. He had already argued that one must first accept Christ as Savior and only thereafter (separately) as Lord. To place the added demand that the unsaved dedicate themselves to do God's will at the same time as they make "the decision" would confuse salvation from being anything other than by faith alone.[21] This debate set off a controversy with a flurry of evangelical publishing, conferences, and various other media surrounding this issue. In setting forth his position, MacArthur, in his book *The Gospel According to Jesus*, famously quoted theologians who wrote that you could become an atheist, but as long as you believed for one moment that Jesus was Savior, you were in fact saved. For the onlooker, the so-called "Lordship salvation controversy" might seem obscure, yet it illustrates the ideological hold that "the Decision for Christ" still had on evangelicalism as recently as twenty years ago. The attempt to put too much definition upon what it might mean for real life threatened its status as a Master-Signifier. "It must be by faith alone!" "We must protect it against any added on works requirement!" It is this logic which maintains "the decision's" elusive quality as a Master-Signifier for evangelicalism.

As Žižek often details, it is the ability of the signifier "to stand for that something about which we are never sure what" that enables it to rally people together without requiring them to agree on anything. The adherents can pretty much remain comfortable with whatever status quo they are already in while believing they have more.[22] The empty signifier allows us to believe without really believing. In this case, "the decision" enables the formation of various kinds of churches that can appeal to various status-quo lifestyles, making little to no demands on changing one's life, all the while claiming allegiance to the gospel. It

---

21. See MacArthur, *Gospel According to Jesus*. See Zane Hodges's original statement, which MacArthur criticized, in his *Gospel Under Siege*. See also Hodges's response to MacArthur in his *Absolutely Free!*

22. See Žižek, *Indivisible Remainder*, 141, where he notes that by accepting the signifier, "we signal our acceptance of what others accept" without really knowing what that might truly mean. We get pacified into thinking this is what it is, the waiting for what is to come.

allows for Christianities to emerge that remain complicit with social systems of self-fulfillment, consumerism, or for that matter excessive sexual desire. It becomes the means for Christians to bypass the malformation of their own desires and instead keep their existing desires under the banner of being a Christian. "The decision for Christ," in other words, becomes the perfect empty signifier, unifying a body of people around competing desires while requiring nothing of them.

Of course, this kind of accusation towards evangelical soteriology—its belief and practice of salvation—is nothing new. Indeed, John MacArthur is beating on drums that go as far back as Luther. Luther himself may be exempt from these charges against the evangelical "decision." Luther's theology, however, has been criticized for sowing the seeds that later led to the folding in of justification into a moment unto itself in separation from sanctification in the Protestant doctrine of salvation. Separated from sanctification, the criticism goes, salvation then gets absorbed into the occasion of forensic pardon where one's culpability for sin is forgiven on the merits of Christ's substitutionary sacrifice. In fact, it must be separated lest one be tempted to think "works" can gain you entry to God's grace. In the process, the self acquires a static status that is distanced (passivized) from God's salvation active in the Christian's everyday life. Luther's emphases on a) the individual and his/her justification in Christ by faith alone, not by works; b) *simul justus et peccator*: that each one is simultaneously righteous and a sinner at the same time; and c) the self caught between two kingdoms (the world of personal faith versus civic duty, gospel versus law), forged the way towards this divided self.[23] Luther himself should be held exempt from this criticism; his later followers, however, isolated these particular Lutheran themes and detached them from Luther's deeper understanding of union with Christ.[24] Calvin, also blamed regularly

23. In the words of theologian Stanley Hauerwas, in order to assuage the Protestant concern "to deny any significance to the actual shape of a man's [sic] life for the attainment of his righteousness . . . Protestants have emphasized the dual nature of the self. . . . it has frequently implied that what a man does and how he acts have relatively little to do with his real 'internal,' justified self." Hauerwas, *Character and the Christian Life*, 4–5.

24. David Aune suggests that Luther and Calvin were not proponents of what has become the standard Protestant account of justification. They were proponents more of union with Christ. Aune suggests one should look to Melanchthon as the one primarily responsible for developing the forensic notion of justification we are discuss-

for this development, likewise should be pardoned from endorsing this bifurcation within the later Protestant developments of the doctrine of salvation.[25] Revivalist evangelicalism, however, following in the wake of the Reformation, front-loaded salvation into the moment of justification.[26] This later became "the decision." It opened the door towards a belief and practice of salvation that is detached from our real lives and our bodies.

Many years later, "the decision," as Master-Signifier covers over this inconsistency at the heart of popular evangelical salvation. The saved person proclaims, "Yes, I am saved! For I am forgiven for all my sin against God's law. But not because of any attempts to keep the law, for that would be earning my salvation!" The conflict emerges at the point where the saved person then asks, "What should I do now? For surely I shouldn't try to keep the law now as a means to my further salvation." A dissonance follows when I realize I'm saved, and yet I continue to desire the things that the law tells me is wrong. But if I say that's just alright, the law doesn't matter anyways, then why did I need this salvation in the first place? Yet, on the other hand, if I dare try to keep the law, I have slipped into depending on it for my salvation and I am now condemned all over again. This contradiction at the core of the evangelical development of salvation is covered over in "the Decision." By separating "the decision" from everyday life, it is able to make it possible to both keep the law in place as the condemner of the unrighteous yet defy it at the same time as having any relevance for my day-to-day life.[27]

---

ing here. See David Aune "Recent Readings" as referred to by Gorman *Inhabiting the*, footnote 12, 44. For others who agree with this general theory of the development of Protestant soteriology, see McGrath, *Iustitia Dei*; Mannermaa, *Christ Present*.

25. The debate on Calvin's role in this bifurcation is much debated. See, for instance, McCormack, "Justitia Aliena," 169–72, who asserts that Calvin affirmed a forensic view of salvation separate from one's union with Christ. J. Todd Billings argues the opposite in his "John Milbank's Theology."

26. Karl Barth provides some helpful insights into the division between justification and sanctification that occurred post Calvin and Luther in *CD* IV/2, 499–511.

27. Žižek's approach to Pauline anthropology, although still guided by what he sees as Paul's perverse logic of the law and desire, nonetheless sees the essence of Christianity, specifically Pauline Christianity, as the law vanishing as a mediator for desire. That is when in Christ we die to the law, instead of playing into the perverse organizing of desire by the law, in Christ the law vanishes making way for the order of Pauline agape. See *Fragile Absolute*, 100.

In this way, "the decision," as it has become ideologized, enables us to bypass the issue of desire in our lives. We are "saved" through a "decision," but we are unsure of what if any connection this has to our bodies. The believer can now navigate his/her desires as best he/she can—to live "your best life now"—without really having to worry about the status of "the decision."[28] It in essence accomplishes a political necessity, that we can all gather to be saved without really having to change our lives—that's up to each person individually. All are accepted here. We do not judge! "The decision" is part of a fantasy (a way of construing our identity and the way things work) which organizes us politically in order to feel good about our belief without having to change anything. It shapes us for duplicity.

There is some irony in "the decision" developing in this way. In its earliest beginnings, amidst eighteenth- and nineteenth-century revivalism, the altar call to a decision/commitment was meant to pull people "back" into the actual living of the gospel more intentionally. The anxious bench and the altar call were meant to revive Christians who had fallen into a stale orthodoxy.[29] In the same way, the English Puritans, concerned that the Reformation had only been a half-Reformation, introduced a stress on conversion. Their goal was a more serious, intentional living of Christ's salvation.[30] The preachers of the various Holiness movements preached repentance for the sake of renewing backslidden Christians to holy living. They preached "the second work of grace"/"the second blessing"/"entire sanctification" that separated sanctification from justification for the purpose of calling people into an intensified experience of it.[31] In virtually all of its revivalist origins, "the decision" was meant to call people into a more intentional Christian living—not separate them from it. But as historian of evan-

28. *Your Best Life Now* is the title of televangelist and prosperity preacher Joel Osteen's best seller of 2007.

29. "Revivalism is generally understood in terms of the dramatic conversion of profligate sinners, but such is not true to the literal meaning of 'revival.' Finney's message was directed primarily to church people or 'professors of religion' not living up to the fullness of Christian existence. The revival was the means of 'breaking with the power of the world and of sin over Christians.' This involved the accusation that many (perhaps most) church people were less than vital Christians, a suggestion vigorously resisted by the traditional clergy." Dayton, *Discovering an Evangelical Heritage*, 17.

30. Lovelace, *Dynamics*, 233–34.

31. Dayton, *Theological Roots of Pentecostalism*, ch. 2.

gelicalism Richard Lovelace describes, a "sanctification gap" emerged. The later revivalists "disconnected sanctification from conversion and made it easy for men to enter the kingdom based on simple faith and repentance."[32] "The decision"—meant to call Christians into the actual living of Christ—became a Master-Signifier for the movement, the means to actually separate the believer from the embodying of his/her belief.

In summary, then, we see how "the decision" functions as a Master-Signifier in evangelicalism. It symbolizes for the individual that he/she has confessed sin, "has put his/her faith and trust in Christ," and has now decided in some way to enter a "personal relationship with Christ." Yet this belief and practice have become reified into an ideological object. It has become set off and separated from one's embodied life. Surely each new "decider" is given a set of directives following the decision: read the Bible daily, pray daily, obey God daily, witness, trust God, and allow the Holy Spirit to guide you.[33] Yet, as described above, he/she remains perplexed as to what this "decision" might actually mean for his/her body. It surely calls us into a political existence with others who have made the very same decision, but means little for the actual shaping of Christian living. As such, "the decision" shapes us for duplicity as a people always aware that this thing we confess means nothing for our concrete physical lives. It is a sign of the emptiness at the core of our politic.

Signs of the "Emptiness" Behind "the Decision"

As we have already learned, an ideology begins to unravel once its inner contradictions and perverse (excess) enjoyments become so apparent that its subjects can no longer ignore them. Through repeated incidents ("acts") of "over-identification" or excessive displays of *jouissance* in the culture, the Real irrupts. A crisis of confidence follows. The ideology

---

32. Lovelace, *Dynamics of Spiritual Life*, 234.

33. As already mentioned, this is a summary of the directions given to people upon having made "the decision." Having gone through the four laws, made the decision, prayed the prayer, they are now invited to enjoy their new life to its fullest by clicking the next arrow on the website http://4laws.com/laws/english/flash/. This I contend is paradigmatic of how discipleship is viewed within evangelicalism—cognitive driven, individualist and with small groups when at all possible.

loses force. There are signs of this happening with evangelicalism and its belief and practice of salvation. A few examples.

Jessica Simpson, the MTV celebrity early in the first decade of the 2000s, represents what it looks like when someone over-identifies with the evangelical signifier, "the decision." She was a music performer of significant celebrity. She attained enormous television exposure on her own MTV reality show—the Newlyweds. Part of her novelty was that she presented herself as a Christian on her show ("Jesus is my homeboy")[34] and declared her commitment to remaining a virgin until married (a signpost of an evangelical youth in the nineties). When she exploited (or was exploited for) her sexuality on both TV and in film, evangelicals proved their cynicism and largely ignored her. For many evangelicals, she was just another "backslider," someone who didn't "get" what it means to be a Christian. When she was criticized, however, by evangelicals for appearing provocatively in the music video for the song "These boots are made for walking," she defended herself by saying, "I was always criticized for my looks in the Christian world. They said I was too sexy to sing Christian music . . . I think if they were really good Christians judgment wouldn't be there."[35] She in essence told all evangelicals, with the bravado of her larger-than-life public persona, "You have missed the point! If you were really saved, you would accept me for who I am. For we who have been forgiven (made the decision!) are free now to do anything we desire, and you should quit resenting it!" In a classic way, Simpson the television persona carried the logic of "the decision" to its extreme, exposing its emptiness. "It is not about works." In terms of real life, therefore, it means nothing.

Jessica famously complained that "they would never let me sing solos in church, because they said I made the men in the congregation lust!"[36] Here Jessica exemplified for evangelicals the quality that makes "the decision" an empty signifier: "the Decision" enables salvation to completely bypass the body as relevant to salvation. As a result,

---

34. She wore "Jesus is my homeboy" T-shirts on the Newlyweds MTV reality show and some said sparked a nationwide run on the T-shirts. Of course many other celebrities wore these t-shirts as part of the same fad.

35. Thompson, "Jessica Simpson."

36. She said these words in an interview with Michael Thompson in *Allure Magazine* (September, 2006). This was quickly distributed worldwide through numerous internet and media sites.

in heinous fashion, we see Jessica as a church-going teenager singing on Sunday morning, testifying to God's grace while being leered at by men in the pews who have been saved but have nowhere to go with their desire. [37] In so testifying, Jessica reveals for the evangelical church itself the horror of "the decision." We're saved—but it's still not safe for a shapely teenage girl to sing in church on Sunday! She reveals the lack that lies behind the evangelical belief and practice of salvation.

The holiness codes of evangelical denominations and colleges present another site for this excessive over-identification. These codes, instituted by evangelical denominations and colleges, prohibit ordained pastors and college students from using alcohol and tobacco and sometimes even participating in public dancing. These codes themselves represent an over-compensation for the lack at the core of the evangelical belief and practice of "the decision." They say "we are saved, but this does not effect how we live, therefore we must *make sure* it effects the way we live!" What is perhaps even more revealing, however, is the stereotypical appearance of obesity among these same constituencies, as exemplified in the iconic obese Southern Baptist preacher. The mythic status of this figure is evidenced by the caricature of the obese Baptist preacher showing up in movies, novels, and other areas of American culture. I have no intent to disparage the character of any preacher or anyone else struggling with his/her weight. I am merely examining these figures as products of a symbolic structure (evangelicalism). The question is, then, on a purely symbolic level, is not the overweight (and since deceased) Jerry Falwell, Chancellor of Liberty Baptist University (where all of the above holiness codes are so vigorously in force) a symbol of what we are trying to hide from? [38] Does not the southern Baptist obese preacher—the prevalence of a "Krispy

---

37. Indeed, her father, Joe Simpson, former evangelical youth pastor, symbolized this in an even more heinous fashion with his now infamous and repeated comments about his daughter's breasts. For instance, on the Paula Zahn show on August 11, 2005, on CNN, he said, "Somehow double D's don't really fit on the overall picture of what works in white Christian music." Online: http://transcripts.cnn.com/TRANSCRIPTS/0508/11/pzn.01.html. Joe Simpson was notorious for making this type of comment, most notably in an interview he did in the December 2004 issue of *GQ Magazine*.

38. As Žižek states, "we overlook the way our act is already part of the state of things we are looking at, the way our error is part of the Truth itself." Žižek, *Sublime Object*, 59.

Kreme Christianity"—symbolize for all evangelicals that the more we try to say "being saved" means something for the way we live, it really in the end does not?[39] "The decision" really doesn't affect our bodies (and its desires) the way we wish it did (tobacco, alcohol, and sex). As a result, the holiness codes just shift inordinate desire from one bad thing to another, from sex and booze to obesity.

In essence, then, we evangelicals are caught up within the fantasy of "the decision"—forced to believe it makes a difference and enacting a compensating structure to make sure it does. Meanwhile, we ignore the appearance of its very violation right before our very eyes. For here at Liberty University, in a place that prohibits alcohol, tobacco, and even dancing, the lack in "the decision" irrupts in the body of Jerry Falwell, revealing the inconsistency that cannot be ignored: that "the Decision" really does not affect our lives in the way we say it does. Instead it orders the drives that lie beneath in more hideous ways.[40]

The "Enjoyment" that Drives Our Allegiance to "The Decision"

One such hideous way is revealed in the role "the gay/lesbian" has come to play in the formation of the evangelical politic in North America. By all appearances, "the gay/lesbian" functions as a kind of object against which evangelicals define themselves. Regularly in evangelical culture, "the gay/lesbian" gets singled out as the representative of the sin we simply cannot tolerate. If, according to Žižek, every ideology has an unobtainable object of desire that supports the Master-Signifier ("the

39. Ken Ferraro wrote provocatively on this theme in the *Journal for the Scientific Study of Religion.* In his article "Does Religion Increase," he labels some Baptist and fundamentalist groups "Krispy Kreme Christianity" claiming they preach abstinence in drugs, tobacco, and alcohol but make up for it with food, doughnuts, etc., making obesity an epidemic among the fundamentalist and Baptist Protestant churches. This research received much attention in columns, blogs, and other media in 2006.

40. Žižek, following Lacan, distinguishes between drives and desires. Within the Symbolic Order, the desires of the subjects (who are subjectivized by the Symbolic Order) are ordered via the fantasy screens, the symbolic way of structuring identity and subject orientation. At the core of the Symbolic Order however is the Real, the lack, the antagonism that churns that which can never be totally encapsulated by the Symbolic structure. Here lie the drives that perpetuate what can never be totally acquiesced. On this, see Žižek, *Indivisible Remainder,* 95–99.

pathology of the *objet petit a*"[41]) "the gay/lesbian" acts as such an object for evangelicalism. "The gay/lesbian" represents both what we resent not having as well as what we fear the most: unimpeded desire with no limitations! They, in essence, present to us the lack behind our politic of "the decision."

Evangelicals simply have no way to deal with desire in our practice of salvation, so we indulge in it with guilt. As a result, there is often a perverse enjoyment aimed at "the gay/lesbian" who indulges with *no* guilt. We can at least say proudly, "at least we're not them." We feel better and morally superior. Yet they represent what we want—unimpeded sexual desire with no guilt. In the process, the duplicity of our lives—the lack of integration of the decision with our embodied lives—is exposed for all to see. No matter how orthodox evangelicals might be in rejecting the norm of same-sex relations, a position I personally agree with, our witness is hopelessly caught within a swirl of duplicity.

This is all illustrated by the episode surrounding Miss California USA in 2009. Carrie Prejean, the California representative in that year's Miss USA competition in Las Vegas, was asked a question by gay activist and blogger Perez Hilton in the question portion of the pageant. She was asked what she thinks about same-sex unions in light of the recent legalization of gay marriage in the state of Vermont. In a now-famous statement, Prejean replied, "I do believe that marriage should be between a man and a woman; no offense to anybody out there. But that's how I was raised and I believe that it should be between a man and a woman." Miss Prejean proceeded to lose the pageant (she came in second). This was viewed on evangelical media as an outrage, a retribution against Miss Prejean's position on same-sex unions. In the days that followed, she became a spokesperson for the evangelical position for heterosexual orthodoxy. Yet the picture presented by the wider American media was of a woman who had pranced before the whole world in a provocative bikini (ironically designed by Jessica Simpson), who had ("sexually enhancing") cosmetic surgery (we found out), and who had been caught in a revealing photoshoot and pornographic sex-tape of some sort.

---

41. We remember that the *objet petit a* is an object of desire that is left unfulfilled by the Symbolic Order. It becomes an object (the *objet petit a*) around which the Master-Signifier can be supported in a pathological relationship. *Fragile Absolute*, 48.

The day following the pageant Miss Prejean appeared on the NBC Today show and said, "I don't take back what I said. I had spoken from my heart, from my beliefs and for my God." "It's not about being politically correct," she said. "For me, it's about being biblically correct." The moment she said the word "biblical" she self-identified as an evangelical to the media regardless of her own church allegiances (she was a student at San Diego Christian College, an evangelical institution). From this TV appearance she went on to appear on the iconic evangelical national radio show *Focus on the Family* as a heroine for Christian morality. She was introduced at Jerry Falwell's evangelical school Liberty University to the student body during a convocation service in which she told students that the unexpected event had opened more doors than she ever dreamed possible to speak about her faith in Jesus Christ. In a few short weeks she became the darling of evangelicalism and its politic.

What do we make of this? I have no desire to disparage Miss Prejean's moral character. Rather, what we are able to see through her performance is just how much we as evangelicals don't know what we are for when it comes to sexual desire, yet we certainly know what we are against. Evangelicals can ignore how Miss California sexualizes her body in numerous ways because she is absolutely clear in her rejection of gay/lesbian sexual relations. She illustrates, therefore, how evangelicals use "the gay/lesbian" object.[42] We self-identify by what we are against as opposed to what we are for. Once more, the perverse "enjoyment" at work is exposed when we lay judgment upon "the gay/lesbian" because the object of "the gay/lesbian" enables us to ignore the disordered desire in our own lives while feeling good about ourselves for not being "them."[43] In the process, judgment against "the gay/lesbian" becomes a badge of honor that identifies us as evangelicals—we

---

42. I use "the gay/lesbian" as the object because the LGBTQ identity is still largely not in the vernacular of evangelicalism and its social engagements.

43. On the disordered state of sexual relations in evangelicalism, see the Barna Report from September 14, 2005, "Born Again Christians Just as Likely to Divorce as Non-Christians." Online: http://www.barna.org/barna-update/article/5-barna-update/194-born-again-christians-just-as-likely-to-divorce-as-are-non-christians. See also the Christianet report entitled "Evangelicals are addicted to Porn." Online: http://christiannews.christianet.com/1154951956.htm. And Winner, "Sex in the Body."

have made "the decision" and it means something! And we appear duplicitous in the worst of ways before the watching world.

To say all this in Žižek's terms, "the gay/lesbian" has become an *objet petit a* for evangelicalism. By vehemently protesting gay/lesbian relations, evangelicals maintain the "fantasy" that being a Christian (making "the decision") still makes a difference. Via "the gay/lesbian," evangelicals are able to ignore the duplicity in our own sexual lives and still say we believe in something! We maintain a level of moral superiority, and "perversely enjoy" saying, like the Pharisee looking at the publican (Luke 18:9–14), "Thank you that I am not them." Miss California illustrates all these things for us and, in so doing, reveals the emptiness at the core of our politic of "the decision."

Meanwhile, this persistent, perverse enjoyment (*jouissance*) towards "the gay/lesbian" covers over the contradiction at the core of our soteriological existence: the law (being moral) should matter (it tells me I'm a sinner) and so I need to be saved, but now that I am saved, the law shouldn't matter anymore (it's not by works). In essence, we should be able to enjoy desire, but we can't without the guilt necessary to be saved. Therefore, when the gay or lesbian, bi- or trans-sexual person comes along and says, "We have desire too! And we can indulge it to our heart's content and not feel guilty about it!" evangelicals are threatened. Part of our enjoyment is stolen. The gay/lesbian symbolizes for evangelicals what we are shooting for but can never have: unimpeded, fulfilled desire with no guilt![44] Indeed, our greatest fear is that we become them—hedonists who enjoy desire with no constraints from the law—even though it is obvious we already are them. We have no way to deal with desire and our bodies. So "the gay/lesbian" becomes the object that we must blame to hold ourselves together. They become the *objet petit a* that holds together the ideology of "the decision." It all once again reveals the emptiness at the core of our life together as evangelicals.

It should not surprise us, then, that every time the gay or lesbian person seeks to enter the church or, worse yet, to be married as Christians in the church, they threaten to unravel the whole ideology of salvation by which we live. They enjoy—but with no guilt. But if there's

---

44. As Žižek states ". . . one has to maintain desire in its dissatisfaction." *Indivisible Remainder*, 96.

no guilt, then there's no reason to make "the decision." The gay/lesbian, by disregarding the law and still "enjoying themselves," makes "the decision" dispensable. And we evangelicals must fight against it, for it is about much more than who is right, it is about our very survival.

In all these ways, Miss California reveals the duplicity at the core of our morality and that we indeed need "the gay/lesbian" as an object to hold our fantasy together concerning our lives as saved via "the decision." As a national beauty contestant, she flaunts her sexuality and says, "Sex is good, enjoy it!" while at the same time saying "but not for you gays/lesbians." In her flaunting of her body, she reveals that we evangelicals are no different than the gay/lesbian when it comes to sexual desire. We enjoy our desire! Yet in our case, we must enjoy with guilt. When "they" dare to enjoy it without guilt, it threatens our ideology. As such, the gay/lesbian, bi/transsexual represents the remainder/ the left over, the thing that always escapes us. They help us see our lack: that we have no place for desire. Again, I certainly mean nothing personal against Miss California.[45] Yet the episode of Miss California discloses the vacuity of our belief and practice of salvation in ways few cultural episodes could.

When evangelical megachurch pastor Ted Haggard's gay affairs were revealed in 2008, many of Miss California's cultural dynamics were repeated. Haggard was the president of the National Association of Evangelicals, the pastor of a successful megachurch, and listed as one of the twenty most influential evangelicals in America by *Time Magazine* in February 2005. Then he was famously exposed as being involved in an adulterous gay affair. At first glance, his moral failing is not unusual on the plane of evangelical life. Moral failure has become prevalent among evangelical pastors. The media extravaganza that ensued, however, revealed much about what drives the evangelical ideology of salvation. I seek no condemnation aimed at the person Ted Haggard, his own fall into sin, and subsequent repentance. As a symbol and product of evangelical political formation, however, Haggard is an irruption of the Real evangelicals should not ignore.

45. My own formal position on these matters agrees with Miss California's. I affirm that same-sex unions are without warrant in Scripture and that same-sex attractions are in need of Christian, embodied spiritual formation. Sadly, the current politic of evangelicalism, as revealed by the episode of Miss California, works against evangelical churches as being such a place for sexual spiritual formation.

On January 29, 2009, for instance, Haggard appeared on national television via Larry King's CNN talk show.[46] Haggard had gone on the television show to promote a documentary about his moral failing as well as to rehabilitate his image. He had been renowned for preaching conservative family values and "the evils of homosexuality" side by side with no reserve. All the while, he lied directly about his own gay proclivities. When Larry King asked him, in light of his exposed gay affair, was this hypocritical? Haggard replied, "Absolutely, it was." Then without stopping he explained the reason for his hypocrisy: "because I have a belief system . . . I believe the Bible is the word of God . . . Jesus is the son of God and I believe in being born again . . . . those things are fundamental to Christianity." Haggard called evangelicalism a "belief system" as he explained how he could both preach against it and "enjoy" it perversely at the same time. He put a distance between his beliefs (of evangelicalism) and his actual life. He then goes on to say how he believed if he would just be more spiritual he'd be okay. "I would pray and fast. I'd read my Bible. I'd memorize more Scripture. . . . And it actually made things worse . . ." Here Haggard baldly reveals how evangelicalism's "belief system" has no place to go with desire. A few minutes later, Haggard is quoted on tape, by one of his gay lover victims, as saying, "You know what, Grant, you can become a man of God and you can have a little bit of fun on the side." Here Haggard is pictured as integrating gay sexual sin into the evangelical practice of salvation, the practice of becoming a man of God. In what appears to be a working of a grand resolution to this entire series of statements, Haggard finally says, "You know Larry . . . Jesus says 'I came for the unrighteous, not for the righteous . . .' So as soon as I became worldwide unrighteous I knew Jesus had come for me." Here, in stunning fashion, Haggard presents the language of forensic justification as that which makes a final resolution possible. It is "the decision" to be forgiven and pardoned that enables him to bypass the raging duplicitous desires, make sense of the inconsistencies of his life, and come to peace.

Is this not a replay of the Miss California diagnosis all over again? Does not Haggard reveal that as long as we preach against "the gay/ lesbian," everything else is okay in the end? Does this not reveal the

---

46. The entire transcript for this show can be found online: http://transcripts.cnn .com/TRANSCRIPTS/0901/29/lkl.01.html.

contradiction at its core, which says, "Go ahead and enjoy, but be guilty about it and then forgiven. For that's where the true enjoyment lies"? Is this not the revealing of the lack behind the evangelical belief and practice of salvation: "the decision"?

Shortly after King and Haggard have finished talking about his preaching against gay/lesbian sexual relations, King shows a clip of Haggard preaching that "evangelicals have the best sex life of any other group," proclaiming about his church, "there's a lot of love in this place. You don't think all these babies just come out of nowhere, do you?" Whatever King's intentions were, one cannot miss the strange revealing that occurs in juxtaposing "Christians have the best sex!" with Haggard's prior preaching that "Gay sex is sin!" The juxtaposition reveals that we are driven not so much by the fact that gay sex is wrong (like many other kinds of sex) but that we fear you might enjoy it more! The perverse enjoyment behind the exclamation "we have better sex than you!" (or least we're striving for it) might be compromised. Once again the duplicity of the evangelical politic of salvation is repeated: "Sexual desire is good, enjoy it! Just not for you homosexuals!"

In the caller interaction portion of the King Show, someone called and informed Haggard that he had come out as a gay man. He asked Haggard, "Do you feel I can be a Christian?" Haggard, almost like a robot, repeats his earlier words, that everyone needs "to read our Bibles and pray . . . use the Scriptures as your guide and ask God to reveal things to you by the Holy Spirit in fellowship with believers. You will grow." Shockingly, Haggard recommends to the caller to do the same individualist discipleship, word for word, that he described as failing him so miserably earlier. He does not deal with the inherent contradiction—the Bible says one thing and my body tells me another. Instead, in a re-enactment of "the decision," he affirms that we need to believe in the Bible, make a decision, and keep doing it, even if it is completely separated/distanced from my body. In so doing, Haggard reveals that he remains caught within the swirl of an empty ideology. He knows of no other way to think of desire. He must keep the ideology intact. In so doing, Haggard symbolizes the state of evangelicalism's belief and practice of salvation. It is revealed as empty, yet we keep repeating it in different form, desperate to continue its ideological existence. And our duplicity comes off as even more disingenuous.

Duplicity: The Spiritual Formation
of an "Empty Politic"

Miss California and Ted Haggard reveal the emptiness that lies behind what has become of the evangelical belief and practice of salvation. "The decision" has become a Master-Signifier for our life together as evangelicals. As a result, our witness in the world is tainted by duplicity. We do not offer the world a direct witness of our own sexual broken-ness and redemption; we instead use the gay/lesbian as an object by which we hide it and see ourselves as "saved." The gay/lesbian becomes the means for us evangelicals to believe we still have some morality while in concrete terms we have a hard time defining how this makes a difference in our lives. The gay/lesbian reveals the perverse enjoyment that drives our allegiance to "the decision."

In all of this, we see the way the ideology of "the decision" has shaped us for duplicity as evangelicals in the world. It is a belief and practice that distances us from our bodies and everyday lives. Salvation becomes our own personal "assurance of heaven," not a way of life. The belief and practice of "the decision" then sets us up over against others who threaten our structures for morality. This tragically leads to a hypocrisy before the world, not just because we will inevitably be say-ing one thing and doing another—this is common to all people—but because we make demands upon others so that we can "enjoy" feeling better about ourselves. In so doing, "the decision" sets us over against those who would challenge our morality. We resent them and then preach against them while they do the very same things we end up doing ourselves. We, however, are already forgiven for doing it, yet our lives show no difference. This is the brand of duplicity we live that so enrages the world.

These are the contradictions and perverse enjoyments of an empty politic. Their revealing is what is undermining the current viability of evangelicalism as a politic in North America. As a result, we have be-come a kind of people incompatible with the gospel of redemption we seek to inhabit before the world. The task is to traverse this fantasy of "the decision." We must recognize the lack behind it, detach ourselves from it and work towards a reconfiguration of our belief and practice of salvation in Jesus Christ. We need a different politic of salvation, a politic of fullness, one that participates in the triune life of God through the Incarnate Christ.

Constructing such an evangelical politic will be the task of this book's last chapter. Before we get there, however, we must turn to the third and final evangelical doctrinal distinctive: how evangelicals believe in and practice the church in society.

CHAPTER 5

"The Christian Nation": The Politics of the Evangelical
Belief and Practice of the Church in Society—How It Shapes
Us for Dispassion

*"We must never allow our children to forget that this is a Christian na-
tion. We must take back what is rightfully ours . . . "*
—Jerry Falwell, 1993 sermon[1]

In April of 2004, as the presidential campaign was heating up in the
U.S., evangelical megachurch pastor Greg Boyd preached a series of
sermons entitled "The Cross and the Sword" at his Woodland Hills
Community Church. He preached that Christians should not claim
that the United States is a "Christian nation." He asked that Christians,
among other things, resist glorifying American military campaigns.
Shock waves rolled through the church. One thousand members (out
of 5,000) left the St. Paul, Minnesota, church. The national media reported on the church upheaval and a bestselling book was produced
from Boyd's sermons entitled *The Myth of a Christian Nation*.[2] The incident gave evidence to the strength of "the Christian nation's" hold on
the imagination of evangelicals in North America.

Evangelicals, growing up after WWII, are familiar with the sym-
bols of the Christian nation in their sanctuaries. The American flag,

1. The source for this widely reported quote is Barber, *Jihad vs. McWorld*, 212.
2. For instance, see Goodstein, "Disowning Conservative Politics."

draped on a pole, usually sits on one side of the pulpit, while the Christian flag of the cross sits on the other. Many an evangelical pastor knows the uproar from his/her congregation if he/she dares suggest that the American flag be removed. To this day, evangelical pastors are often asked to support a particular candidate for president (usually the Republican candidate) and know the conflict that erupts if the pastor refuses. This all testifies to the powerful place the Christian nation has held as an ideal in the evangelical church.

Historically, evangelicals have taken an activist evangelistic stance in society. David Bebbington, in describing this characteristic of evangelicalism (the fourth of his four main characteristics), quotes a publication from the 1800s stating matter-of-factly that, for evangelicals in those days, a profession of faith in Christ meant not only "a constant activity in cooperating with the brethren in building of the cause of Christ" but also "war against sin wherever found . . ."[3] In other words, a Christian's engagement in society meant more than working for the salvation of individual souls, it also meant working for social reform "wherever sin was found."[4] As a result, evangelicals were leaders in practically every social reform movement of the time prior to and leading up to the Civil War. They worked for the improvement of the working conditions for laborers, the abolition of slavery, voting rights for women, prison reform, humane treatment of the mentally-ill, and the temperance movement, to name just a few.[5] Behind these movements was the vision that God was working in the United States as a chosen nation. America had a manifest destiny to usher in the Kingdom of God upon which Christ himself would return.[6] In American church historian Donald Dayton's words, the revivalist and reform movements that birthed evangelicalism all "supported the broader expectation of a 'Christian America.'"[7]

This evangelical "activism" however changed into a different kind of activism after the Civil War. The evangelical emphasis shifted away

3. Bebbington, *Dominance of Evangelicalism*, 38.

4. In support of this, Bebbington cites Smith, *Revivalism and Social Reform*.

5. See Moberg, *Great Reversal*, 28–30. Dayton, *Discovering an Evangelical Heritage* is one of the classics on this subject. See also Marsden, *Fundamentalism*, 85–93; 124–32.

6. The classic on this is Tuveson, *Redeemer Nation*.

7. Dayton, *Discovering an Evangelical Heritage*, 124.

from the social aspects of Christianity to the personal. This shift materialized again with the fundamentalist-modernist controversies in the 1920s and 30s. The "Great Reversal," as David Moberg labeled it, took place.[8] Evangelicals began intentionally to separate personal salvation from social salvation. They reversed their stance on being active for the social reform of society and instead adopted a pessimistic view of society. For these evangelicals, the world was on a track to Armageddon. They now focused almost entirely on engaging society in order to extract as many lost souls out of the hellfire path of destruction upon which society was surely headed.[9]

One of the ways to make sense of what happened in this "reversal" is by understanding the conflicts surrounding the fundamentalist-modernist controversies of the 1920s. The evangelical Protestants of the time, then called "fundamentalists," were battling Protestant mainline denominational leaders/intellectuals over both the authority of Scripture and the importance of the substitutionary work of Christ on the cross. They interpreted these Protestant leaders as emphasizing the social work of the gospel to the detriment of personal salvation and Christ's atoning work. As a result, they reacted in the other direction, emphasizing personal salvation and the view that society was in a terminal state of moral decline. The Protestant mainline leaders pushed for the church's role in a post-millennial eschatology, emphasizing the coming Kingdom of God and God's present work for social justice in the world. The evangelicals rallied around a pre-millennial eschatology, which forestalled the Kingdom and encouraged overseas missions, personal conversions, and a heightened belief in the imminent return of Christ. The so-called Protestant "liberals" devalued Scripture's historicity. The evangelicals attached themselves to dispensationalist systems of interpreting Scripture that emphasized its literal interpretation. This system emphasized "biblical prophecy" that foretold the demise of this present world and shaped evangelicals with a new pessimism towards

---

8. According to David Moberg, Timothy Smith was the first to coin the phrase "The Great Reversal." Moberg, *Great Reversal*, 30.

9. Although present prior to the fundamentalist-modernist controversies, this attitude is famously represented in the following statement by the turn-of-the-last-century evangelist Dwight L. Moody: "I look upon this world as a wrecked vessel. God has given me a lifeboat and said to me, Moody, save all you can." Marsden, *Fundamentalism and Evangelicalism*, 38.

social change. The driving force, then, behind "the great reversal" was the evangelical reaction against a social gospel of the Kingdom that marginalized, even rejected, a Jesus-centered personal salvation in the cross.[10] All of this led evangelicals to separate personal salvation available in Christ's atonement from social redemption and to minimize the social aspects of salvation in favor of personal conversion.

The notion of a Christian America—of working for the improvement of just social political structures in American society—took a back seat within evangelicalism for a long period of time, approximately the 1930s to the 1960s. Evangelicals continued to maintain an activism in working for the evangelization of society through personal conversions.[11] They invented the Sunday School, the Sunday Night service, the Billy Graham crusades, and numerous radio broadcasts for these purposes. They sought to influence society by providing an intellectually viable faith. In the post-WWII period, famed evangelical radio evangelist Charles Fuller founded Fuller Seminary to provide an intellectual basis for evangelicalism to engage society and its intelligentsia.[12] By and large, however, evangelicals viewed political and/or social activism with suspicion. Billy Graham was criticized whenever he sat with American presidents. Evangelicals saw their role in terms of a passive support for the state's affairs because Christ was returning soon to begin a new age yet to come.

This all reversed once again with the emergence of Jerry Falwell as a socio-political force in the late 1970s. Here, going against his own sectarian roots, Falwell joined with a number of evangelicals across

10. Carl F. Henry states exactly this in his *Uneasy Conscience*, 26–34. See also Henry, "Evangelicals in the Social Struggles." Referred to by Moberg, *Great Reversal*, 35. Moberg summarizes the issues when he says, "the fundamentalist-modernist controversies developed . . . (*within protestant mainline churches*) carrying out Christian social responsibility through attempts to influence legislation and basic social structures that became identified with the Social Gospel movement . . . . It gave growing attention to social evils, while fundamentalists concentrated upon personal sin and individualistic approaches to social problems . . . . The sharp polarization that developed during the conflict made it politically impossible to remain both an evangelical and social gospeler . . . . Christians became either evangelistic or socially involved, not both." Moberg, *Great Reversal*, 34 (italics mine).

11. James Davison Hunter describes this evangelical commitment to change society through the conversion of individual souls in his *To Change the World*, 9–11.

12. Marsden's *Reforming Fundamentalism* describes the birth of Fuller as an attempt to reform fundamentalism in terms of an evangelical reengagement with society.

many church denominational lines and organized the Moral Majority to force moral change in society through church involvement with national politics.[13] In 1980 he wrote the manifesto for the new movement, entitled *Listen America*, which proclaimed an agenda to reclaim America as a Christian nation. In it, he said,

> I believe America has reached the pinnacle of greatness unlike any nation in human history because our founding fathers established America's laws and precepts on the principles recorded in the laws of God, including the Ten Commandments. God has blessed this nation because in its early days she sought to honor God and the Bible, the inerrant Word of the living God . . . It is God Almighty who has made and preserved us as a nation, and the day that we forget that is the day that the United States will become a byword among the nations of the world.[14]

In a total disavowal of his own heritage that separated church from state, he declared the church must work through the ballot box to "turn America around or prepare for her destruction . . ."[15]

On these grounds, an ever-expanding group of evangelical leaders promulgated the belief in the Christian nation. Among the many to join Falwell's cause were evangelical leaders such as Francis Schaeffer,[16] Tim LaHaye, D. James Kennedy, Charles Stanley, and the icon of the movement, James Dobson of Focus on the Family. The rise to social dominance of this form of activism among evangelicals was carried out through organizations such as the Christian Coalition, Family Research Council, Traditional Values Coalition, American Family Association, and, of course, the aforementioned Focus on the Family. The "Christian Right" became a dominant force in American politics by coalescing evangelicals around the notion of reclaiming America as a Christian nation. Its crowning achievement was the election of George W. Bush in 2000 and 2004.

With the Bush presidency, many evangelicals thought the moment had come for the Christian nation. Bush supported the notion in

13. For an inside account, see Jerry Falwell's former ghostwriter Mel White, *Religion Gone Bad*, 45–46.

14. Falwell, *Listen America*, 243–44.

15. Ibid., 17–23.

16. Schaeffer delivered his message famously in his book published in 1981 *A Christian Manifesto*.

many subtle ways. His support could not be missed, for example, when he addressed the nation on the first anniversary of the 9/11 terrorist attacks. He spoke with an illuminated picture of the Statue of Liberty in the background, concluding with the words "and the light shines in the darkness. And the darkness has not overcome it." Changing only slightly the tense of the verb, he used John 1:5—a text about the messianic coming of Christ—to refer to the United States as God's messianic light amidst the darkness of terrorism. In the months that followed that speech, the evangelical right wielded power in and through the White House to bring about a Christian legislative agenda. A backlash of hate literature exploded against the Religious Right and onto *NY Times* bestseller lists. This backlash culminated with atheist Sam Harris's wildly bestselling book *Letter to a Christian Nation* in 2006.[17] The Christian nation had taken on iconic status in American culture and had become a dominant theme among evangelicals as the means for understanding how Christians are to engage society.

With the ending of the Bush presidency and its widely perceived failure, many conclude today that the idea of the Christian nation has been discredited. Indeed, in its aftermath, many of the evangelical Right's leaders seem discouraged, feeling like they had "been taken" by the Bush administration with little to show for their efforts.[18] In the spring of 2009, journalist Jon Meacham of Newsweek inscribed the epitaph of the Christian nation in his cover story entitled "The End of Christian America."[19] He boldly proclaimed, "the thirty-five

17. Harris, *Letters to a Christian Nation.*

18. Dan Gilgoff charts the rise to power of James Dobson and his Focus on the Family organization as well as the frustrations of Dobson and others with the Bush administration's inability to accomplish any of their established "Christian Nation" objectives. Gilgoff, *Jesus Machine. The Washington Monthly* (April 12, 2009) and Telegraph.co.uk (April 10, 2009) recorded a widely disseminated story that James Dobson stepped down from his role as chairman of Focus on the Family conceding defeat with a farewell speech that admitted "humanly speaking" we the religious right had lost most of the battles. The religious right leader Chuck Colson also stated in a *Time Magazine* article, "We [the religious right] made a big mistake in the 1980s by politicizing the Gospel. We ought to be engaged in politics, we ought to be good citizens, we ought to care about justice. But we have to be careful not to get into partisan alignment. We [thought] that we could solve the deteriorating moral state of our culture by electing good guys. That's nonsense." This was reported in the article "Q&A: Religious Leader Chuck Colson."

19. Meacham, "End of Christian America,"

year campaign to bring the U.S. society an anti-abortion amendment, a school-prayer amendment and a ban on same-sex marriage has failed miserably."[20] Alongside Meacham, evangelical social activist Jim Wallis proclaimed that we are now living in a "post-evangelical right America."[21] Yet, despite all this, I contend that we should not write off the enduring hold of the Christian nation upon the belief and practice of evangelicalism. Polls indicate 62 percent of Americans still think of America as a Christian nation.[22] Many of these Americans are evangelicals. When President Obama suggested in 2009 that America was not a Christian nation, the backlash from evangelicals was significant.[23] James Dobson made several media appearances to refute the new president. In 2009, Thomas Nelson published a version of the Bible named the *American Patriot's Bible*. It consists of hundreds of comments on various patriotic themes, interweaving a patriotic version of American history with the biblical narrative. It rather crassly supports the idea of America as the inheritor of the mantle of God's people. Numerous evangelical Web sites and Christian nation apologists continue the exercise of defending the role of the founding fathers and the constitution in founding the nation on Christian principles. Despite its many naysayers, the Christian nation continues its hold on the evangelical imagination.

The enduring hold of the Christian nation upon us evangelicals tells us much about our ecclesiology. It speaks to the fact that we do not see the church as having a social reality on its own. Evangelicals have long understood the church as a collection of individuals saved for eternal relationship with God. We gather to encourage and edify, but we know of no earthly sociality under the rule of Jesus as Lord. The belief in the Christian nation continues this evangelical belief and

20. This statement was recorded during a television interview on the USA cable network MSNBC. The interview with Meacham can be accessed online: http://www. msnbc.msn.com/id/3036789/vp/30151678#30151678.

21. Wallis, *Great Awakening*.

22. Cited by Meacham in "End of Christian America."

23. In early April 2009, president Obama spoke at a news-conference in Turkey saying, "One of the great strengths of the United States is . . . we have a very large Christian population . . . (yet) we do not consider ourselves a Christian nation or a Jewish nation or a Muslim nation. We consider ourselves a nation of citizens who are bound by ideals and a set of values." As reported by CNN. No pages. Online: http://www.cnn.com/2009/POLITICS/04/06/obama.turkey/index.html.

practice of a church that has no imagination for seeing itself as a politic in the world. It plays on our proclivity to rally individuals as volunteers to work for a Christian version of morality outside the church. It brings together our already existing commitment to a morality based in personal conversion with our desire to engage society actively. As a result, the practice of Christian justice always takes the shape of another program at the local church. It never becomes a way of life we embody and thereby live into the world.

The Christian nation then acts as a symbol of the evangelical nonbelief in the church. It organizes Christians to do Christ's work always away from the church. It absorbs our commitments to "justice and righteousness" and orients them to the nation-at-large via political work. It is a signifier that keeps justice at a safe distance so that we rarely have to "get dirty" ourselves. We can work for the Christian nation through voting or trying to get other Christians to vote, but we do not have to work as one among the poor ourselves. We can promote voting against abortion or gay marriage issues with voter guides,[24] yet the faithful work of adopting babies in our churches or ways of fellowshipping with (getting too close to) gay and lesbian people can be ignored. We can give enormous resources to charity as individuals, more than any other single religious group in North America,[25] yet we can avoid working with the poor directly because we usually ship these resources (as white suburban evangelicals) "far away" to the poor in the urban centers. We are mostly homogenous in terms of our socio-economic class and ethnicity, and we largely keep our finances to ourselves. Rarely do we share material aid and relationship with the poor we sit next to in the Sunday morning pew or live next to in the neighborhood. The Christian nation is a way we can practice justice as a program external to the church that leaves the church itself untouched.

24. Christian voter guides are brochures printed by organizations such as the Christian Coalition that grade candidates' voting records on the key issues of the evangelical vision for a Christian America, e.g., abortion, gay rights, prayer in the schools, etc. Victoria Clark analyzes them in her *Allies for Armageddon*, 195–97.

25. This statistic is often quoted. Some of the statistical data can be found in the following: Willmer, "Evangelicals"; Barna, "New Study Shows"; Hiemstra, "Evangelical Giving." For further insight into this phenomena, see Kristof, "Learning from the Sin of Sodom."

"The Christian Nation" as a Master-Signifier

Once again, the question is what kind of political formation has resulted from this evangelical belief and practice of the Christian nation? Has the belief and practice of the Christian nation shaped evangelicals for the inhabiting of God's mission in the world? One more time, I contend that Žižek's ideological analysis can help us answer these questions. In ways similar to the previous two beliefs, his analysis helps us see how the Christian nation functions as a Master-Signifier (with all that implies). We can see what lies behind its hold on the evangelical community and why that hold appears to be unraveling in recent days.

Immediately, we should take note of the way that "the Christian nation" functions with the same elusiveness of the previous two master-signifiers: "the inerrant Bible" and "the decision." No one really knows what exactly "the Christian nation" might look like if we as evangelicals actually attained it in the public square. We know that "the Christian nation" means some very well defined legislation for people like Dobson, Robertson, and the Christian Coalition. This list includes an anti-abortion amendment, pro-family, anti-gay marriage legislation, and the restoration of prayer in the public schools. But, even if we assume all this legislation was passed, how would this nation then be Christian? Would more people be acting like Christians? Would more Americans be doing less of the "off-limit things" Christian should not do? Even if they did less of them, would this in any way suggest that the nation had somehow become more Christian? Would they not be doing Christian things for non-Christian reasons? Yet who can argue with achieving less abortion? Yes, of course we are all for that, and we can rally around that by subscribing to "the Christian nation!" Who can argue against the strengthening of American families? Yes, of course we can rally around that in the name of "the Christian nation!" But in what sense would this nation be more Christian as we evangelicals think about what it means to be one? With this lack of clarity as to what it actually entails, "the Christian nation" functions as an empty-signifier enabling evangelicalism to appeal to a wide variety of people, stirring them up about many things, all under the object of "the Christian nation," while little is actually being accomplished. As discussed previously, it is this "enigmatic" quality that makes for a well-functioning Master-Signifier. The Master-Signifier, incapable of being pinned down by anyone, can bind a disparate people together into one politic despite their multiple disagreements. Meanwhile, we are shaped for a casual disregard of the injustices that surround us. The status quo continues on.

When we are frustrated that "the Christian nation" seems to be making little headway, we simply add more things onto the list. This keeps the ideology going. Evangelical leaders will argue for restoring the ten commandments to the front of a municipal court building, putting "under God" back into the pledge of allegiance, putting "Christ back into X-mas," or even putting the words "the United States of America is a Christian nation" into the platform of the Republican Party of Texas.[26] With each new item added onto the list, we pursue a more Christian nation but accomplish little to clarify what we might actually mean by it. Each time "the Christian nation" is challenged, activist evangelicals get into long debates as to whether the founders of the United States intended to found a Christian nation when they wrote the constitution. We even argue as to whether they were themselves Christians. Yet if anyone ever finally resolved these questions, would it matter? Instead, these endless efforts illustrate how "the Christian nation" acts as a Master-Signifier, something that occupies our time but in reality can never be attained. It functions as a fantasy for evangelicalism that enables us to see ourselves as accomplishing something in terms of changing our society for Christ, while in effect nothing really happens. It is a sign of an empty politics.

In 2005, evangelical preacher and social activist Jim Wallis wrote *God's Politics: Why the Right Gets It Wrong and the Left Doesn't Get It*.[27] The book immediately became a best seller on the *New York Times* best-seller list.[28] In the book, Wallis makes a case, similar to Falwell, that religion and national politics should not be separated. Although he never invoked the language of "the Christian nation," he argued for the Christian basis of several political goals that were not on Jerry Falwell's or James Dobson's list of items for a Christian nation. Wallis advocated for just healthcare and a proactive agenda to alleviate poverty and the

26. The latter actually was accomplished by the Texas Republicans at their convention in July of 2004.

27. Wallis *God's Politics*.

28. Much to the credit of Jim Wallis' own organization's—Sojourners'—aptitude for marketing it to their constituency.

gross discrepancy between the poor and the rich in the United States. I do not wish to criticize his positions per se; I agree with most of them. What should be noted, however, is that Wallis defended these political goals (within *God's Politics*) on arguably more theocratic and biblical grounds than anyone on the Christian right defended theirs.[29] It was in every sense another manifesto for "the Christian nation." His second book was even more overtly appealing to "the Christian nation" impulse. As evidenced in the title—*The Great Awakening: Reviving Faith and Politics in a Post-Religious Right America*—Wallis used "church-language" to describe national political goals, in effect advocating another version of "the Christian nation."

The fact that Wallis could pursue the same Christian-nation tactic as Falwell with completely different goals illustrates the nebulous space that is opened up by the signifier "the Christian nation." While I may be focusing on the evangelical right in this chapter (the predominant majority of evangelicals and the ones who most vociferously promote "the Christian nation" language), the fact is that both the Christian right and the progressive evangelicals are caught in the same ideology of the empty signifier: "the Christian nation." And the stark contrast between Wallis' and Jerry Falwell's/James Dobson's visions for "the Christian nation" displays its illusiveness. Churches of any political party can support "the Christian nation" because it in essence means nothing we can put our finger on. Meanwhile both sides gather enormous energy, providing their subjects significant enjoyment (thinking I'm accomplishing something!), while in effect we see little changed. We are shaped for passivity in matters of justice. These are all signs that "the Christian nation" has become a masterful empty-signifier in evangelicalism.

We should not be surprised, then, in looking back that despite having arrived at the zenith of "the Christian ation" movement (for the evangelical right) and having elected an evangelical president complete with a strategy for implementing legislative change, little has been accomplished (perhaps some Supreme Court Judges were installed!). Its own leaders admit to its total failure.[30] Nonetheless, in its aftermath,

29. For instance Jim Wallis called for the United States Budget to be based on what he called "the Isaiah Platform," "God's vision of a good society" as found in the book of Isaiah "nearly three thousand years ago." *God's Politics*, ch.15

30. Again, details can be found of the demoralization of the Christian right in

James Dobson vows to keep up the fight despite the failures. Evangelicals Jim Wallis and Brian McLaren continue to argue on for a progressive version of "the Christian nation." They still pursue "the Christian nation," proving its enduring quality as the ever-elusive Master-Signifier. When times are changing, it feeds on some of our most inflammatory fears—"the country is heading for moral collapse and taking us with it"! And in so doing, it organizes our desires against those who would steal our morality from us, all in the name of "the Christian nation." It occupies our attention and shapes us for an antipathy towards our political opponents. Meanwhile, evangelicals seem to be treading water, accomplishing little on the ground for the gospel in the world.

As we have often seen in the prior chapters, Žižek extols the virtue of the Master-Signifier to cover over internal contradictions, thereby enabling an ideology to hold a people together. The Master-Signifier holds competing drives at bay for the sake of unifying the whole by directing those drives somewhere else. In this same manner, "the Christian nation" covers over the great contradiction at the core of evangelical belief and practice of church in society—that "transformation comes only through personal conversion" while at the same time "society needs to be transformed too!" We remember, dating back to the "Great Reversal" of the 1920s, that evangelicals rejected any social transformation that does not come via personal conversion. Yet evangelicals remain committed to an activism that affects society. Via "the Christian nation," evangelicals can have both! We can enforce socially a personal morality that is possible (so we say) only by personal conversion.

Yet the inconsistency in this is glaring. As evangelicals, we seek to enforce personal moral behavior through legislation (anti-abortion, anti-same sex, prayer in the schools, ten commandments at the court house, etc.) while denying our own premises. For we legislate a morality we think is possible only through conversion (their own decision!). "The Christian nation" covers it all over by playing on the fear that we will lose our children to the moral decadence of our nation. It is at this point that the perverse nature of "the Christian nation" raises its ugly head. For we must fabricate enemies that we can then fashion into an

---

the aftermath (and even latter stages) of the Bush Administration in Gilgoff, *Jesus Machine*. See also n. 18 in this chapter.

object to keep our "fantasy" going. In a perverse way, we feel better about ourselves because we are fighting for securing our country from "those people" who would steal our moral society from us. It promotes the fantasy that we are doing something even when we are accomplishing nothing. Within this antagonism lies the power of "the Christian nation" to hold evangelicals firmly in its grasp.

The result of all of this is an empty politic, one that relies on being against something as opposed to who we are in ourselves. Much like the other two Master-Signifiers of evangelicalism, "the Christian nation" defines evangelicals by whom we are against rather than who we are as the social body of Christ in the world. Our desires for justice are directed against the *objet petit a* of "the Christian nation," "the ones who seek to destroy the Christian foundations upon which this country was built!" As with the other two Master-Signifiers, our allegiance to "the Christian nation" forms us as a people to always work for something illusory as opposed to something real. It distracts us and organizes our energies away from (and in fact distances us from working for) the reconciliation and renewal of all things in the midst of our lives in the world. As a result, our justice proves dispassionate and our politic proves empty at the core.

"THE CHRISTIAN NATION" AND OUR "ENJOYMENT" OF MARKET CAPITALISM

The great attribute of the Master-Signifier is that it organizes our desire (through fear) towards an object (the *objet petit a*), thereby enabling us to ignore the contradictions right in front of our faces. This misdirection of energies enables our complicity with the status quo. The ideology can go on keeping things in place. For evangelicals, in terms of "the Christian nation," we fear so much "the ones who wish to steal our morality from us!" that we can ignore the fact that "the gospel should change the way we live together!" We can always say, "But hey! We are working for the Christian nation! We are staving off the demise of our moral society! We haven't achieved anything yet, but we're trying!" The elusiveness of "the Christian Nation" therefore enables us to go on acting as if we believe "the gospel makes a difference" all the while having to change nothing about our lives.[31] It allows us to work vigorously for

31. See Žižek *Sublime Object*, 36, 30–33 on this quality of the master-signifier.

justice while being complicit with existing systems of injustice under the fantasy that we are actually accomplishing something in the name of "the Christian nation."

One of the more blatant examples of this complicity is the evangelicals' alliance with market capitalism, what one author calls "Evangelical Capitalism."[32] No one should expect evangelicals to be socialists. I am not a socialist. Democratic socialism is not a better system than market capitalism. Each system has its problems and its benefits that the church must accept, live within, and work for the improvement of. When it comes to capitalism, however, evangelicals go much further. They fight vehemently for market capitalism by often making it the one true Christian system of economics.[33] Evangelicals argue that property ownership and diligence in hard work are virtues to be honored as biblical and as best embodied in market capitalism.[34] They laud the individualist economic freedoms capitalism affords and extol it as the basis for freedom of religion. They lash out against any government encroachment upon these individual economic freedoms.[35] Of course, there is some truth in all of these arguments, but there appears to be something more at work here than merely the admiration for an economic system. Evangelicals see capitalism as inherently Christian.

Albert Mohler, an evangelical leader and president of Southern Baptist Seminary, summed up "the Christian nation" version of capitalism at the height of the U.S. financial crisis of 2008.[36] He said, "The free market is not perfect, but capitalism has brought more wealth to more people than any other system. It rewards investment, labor, and

---

32. Kurtz, "Free Market."

33. For a detailed analysis of this alliance see Connolly, "Evangelical-Capitalist"; Corbin, "Impact of the American Dream." I have no desire to defend socialism as a better economic system than capitalism. Instead, I am pointing out how evangelicals have uncritically accepted capitalism as the Christian form of economic organization. It has become the primary ethos of the way we organize church life.

34. So Jerry Falwell famously stated that "God is in favor of freedom, property, ownership, competition, diligence, work and acquisition. All of this is taught in the Word of God, in both the Old and New Testaments." as quoted by Hunter, *Culture Wars*, 111. Quoted by Corbin, "Impact of the American Dream" No pages. Online: http://www.crosscurrents.org/Fall2005.htm accessed April 28, 2010.

35. William Connolly suggests this is due to the influence of dispensationalist conspiracy eschatologies. "Evangelical-Capitalist Resonance Machine," 874–75.

36. Mohler, "A Christian View."

thrift and rises on innovation. Better ideas and better products push out inferior ideas and inferior products. Given the reality of human sin, we should not centralize economic control in the hands of the few, but distribute economic power to the many. A free market economy distributes power to multitudes of workers, inventors, investors, and consumers." Mohler hereby joins the Christian doctrine of sin with democracy and market capitalism under one Christian theological vision.[37] He applies divine sanction to the "invisible hand" of the market as the distributor of power. Capitalism for Mohler has become part of the vision for "the Christian nation."

Mohler reveals that the same contradiction that underlies the evangelical belief in "the Christian nation" also lies beneath this version of capitalism. In both cases, we maintain the priority of the individual in morality while being activists in society. In our advocacy of market capitalism, we want to both promote our version of "biblical" personal morality—the virtues of hard work and individual responsibility—and to actively engage society for change. In the same way that "the Christian Nation" plays on the fear of those who would steal our morality, this form of "evangelical capitalism" plays on the fear of those who would steal our security and the efforts of our hard work—those sinners who somehow need to learn the virtues of personal responsibility and hard work. The same *jouissance* at work in "the Christian nation" is thus present here as well. In these ways, "the Christian nation" and "Evangelical capitalism" are symbiotic twins needing one another to continue existing.

"Evangelical capitalism" extends our fight against those who would steal our morality from us to the fight against "those socialists" who would steal our economic freedoms. The worst insult we can hurl at President Obama is to call him a "socialist," despite his friendly policies towards corporate America. By folding capitalism into "the

---

37. This strategy is known to those familiar with the work of Reinhold Niebuhr as expounded most famously in *Moral Man, Nature and Destiny of Man*, and *Children of Light*. His Christian Realism sequestered the Christian ethic of Jesus' absolute love to the realm of the individual while in the realm of society we had to take into account the real contingencies of original sin. He therefore affirmed democracy and capitalism as the best ways to organize a society to contain the sins of groups while making space for the individual, in voluntarist groups, to pursue the Christian ideal. It is ironic that evangelicals have now imbibed the classic Niebuhrian liberal cultural strategy from the 1950s.

Christian nation," evangelicals therefore gain a whole new set of enemies including the progressive left conspiracies, the socialists, and the environmental activists who plot a pro-abortion agenda to keep population growth at bay. It all distracts us from looking at ourselves and our relationships and whether the justice of God is indeed taking shape right here in our midst and around us in our neighborhoods. Via "the Christian nation" we are shaped for complicity with the global economics of capitalism with little wherewithal to live differently and resist economic injustice. This lethal combination of a social activism that engages legislation for a personal morality that in turn baptizes the current economic system as Christian keeps evangelicals locked in the gaze of "the Christian nation." This, in turn, keeps us from attending to righteous and just relationships among ourselves.

Evangelicals can therefore "enjoy" giving huge amounts of money to the poor. We are the most generous of all the religious groups in North America in supporting charitable causes and sending aid around the world. Upon closer inspection, however, this outpouring of generosity is often done at a distance. We are suburban congregations sending aid to the urban centers while we sit as individuals next to each other in the strange comforts of the church pew. We avoid knowing the poor among and around us. Via the pious protections of "evangelical capitalism," we can give enormous sums of money from behind the protection of our secure bank accounts and gated communities.[38] We are inoculated from the poor. We do not need to get our hands dirty in each other's lives, never mind the poor around us (if we can even find them). In an all too subtle and perverse enjoyment, we can help the poor and feel good about it. After all, we have received the "blessings" of our Christian virtue.

In these most subtle of ways, then, market capitalism has become an ideological part of the evangelical narrative of what it means to be a Christian in the world. Evangelicals run their churches as businesses, elevate successful businessmen as leaders/elders of the church, and use business principles of leadership in terms of hiring and evaluating ministers.[39] Just as with "the Christian nation," "evangelical capitalism"

38. I say private because most evangelicals would rather talk publicly about sex or anything else other than their own bank accounts.

39. For the full exposition of capitalism's influence in evangelical church see my *Great Giveaway*, ch. 2, 6.

lifts Christian justice out of our immediate local context and makes it something we can pursue at a distance. We are shaped for dispassion—helping the poor from a distance—because fighting for market capitalism is the Christian thing to do, the equivalent of Christian social justice. We can ignore our immediate social relationships where the actual reconciliation of Christ can take place among us. Ironically, the very thing we evangelicals accused "the social gospelers" of in the 1920s—pursuing justice apart from Christ—has become our own predicament through the adoption of capitalism via our allegiance to "the Christian nation."

"The Christian Nation": Signs of an Empty Ideology

As in the previous chapters, there are episodes among us that reveal the contradictions and/or false enjoyments of evangelicalism that lie at the core of our belief in "the Christian nation." They help us see the "emptiness" that lies at the core of this politic.

One such example is when prominent evangelical preachers make exaggerated pronouncements of God's judgment on the occasion of a horrific national disaster. When Jerry Falwell declared that the 9/11 attack was a visitation of God's judgment on America, many evangelicals winced, demanding an apology. Falwell specifically blamed "the pagans, and the abortionists, and the feminists, and the gays and the lesbians who are actively trying to make that an alternative lifestyle, the ACLU, People For the American Way, all of them who have tried to secularize America."[40] The day following the 9/11 terrorist attacks, Pat Robertson said in a press release that God had removed "his protective covering" over America, allowing her to be attacked. Both Falwell and Robertson were extending the logic of "the Christian nation," treating America as a singular theocratic entity out of the Old Testament. A few years later, Pat Robertson and other evangelical groups affirmed that God's judgment was unleashed upon New Orleans with Hurricane Katrina because of its gay/lesbian populations. The diatribes against gays and lesbians, so common among evangelicals, bring together the evangelical angst towards gays/lesbians with "the Christian nation."

40. This quote can be found on CNN's website reporting Falwell's apology for the statement 2 days later. No pages. Online:http://archives.cnn.com/2001/US/09/14/Falwell.apology.

Robertson was in essence interpreting the United States via the Old Testament metaphor of Sodom and Gomorrah. He had identified the USA as a religious people of the Old Testament who have corporately denied God's rule by allowing homosexuality to go undisciplined. Yet the United States has never been a theocracy. He had indulged in excessive over-identification of the U.S. with "the Christian nation." The eccentricity of some of these pronouncements reveals a perverse sense of gratification that the world is being judged for the sins we so love to fight against. Sadly, these kind of excessive pronouncements have become common among evangelicals of all types. With each occasion the politic of "the Christian nation" is revealed as "empty"—that we are more driven by what we are against—and more of the younger evangelicals turn away.

In subtle ways, the corporation Wal-Mart has become a cultural symbol of the drives at work within evangelicalism's allegiance to market capitalism and its alignment with "the Christian nation." Wal-Mart began by blending evangelical religion with free-market economics in ways that had never been done before. Starting in the Bible Belt of Arkansas, Wal-Mart played to the core values of evangelical churches.[41] It refused to sell the abortion-inducing "morning-after pill." It instituted a policy of censorship (called the Timothy Plan) that censored DVDs and kept *Cosmopolitan* magazine covers out of view of its customers. It welcomed Salvation Army bell-ringers at Christmas in protest over their treatment at rival Target. Neither its founder, Sam Walton, nor its corporate policies ever explicitly identified with evangelicalism. Nonetheless, it made sense when evangelical Don Soderquist, its chief operating officer/vice chairman, said at a Washington DC prayer breakfast, that Wal-Mart was not a Christian company, but "the basis of our decisions was the values of Scripture."[42] He was verbalizing the contradiction at the core of "the Christian nation": there is no such thing as a redeemed social entity (or corporation), only redeemed individuals (who can obey Scripture), but we still want to affect society in Christian ways!

Meanwhile the same Wal-Mart that takes such strong corporate action against "the morning-after pill" and pornographic magazines has

41. This is all detailed in Moreton, *To Serve God.*

42. This was reported numerous places. See, for example, Sellers, "Deliver Us"

been accused of failing to provide their employees affordable healthcare and selling goods made from third-world countries with exploitive labor practices. It appears they can affect personal morality but dare not cross the sacred rules of profit maximization. The documentary *WAL-MART: The High Cost of Low Prices* exposed Wal-Mart's abusive labor practices and disregard for its employees. It was a media event. Whether one agreed with it or not, Wal-Mart symbolized evangelical-ism's justice in the world as summed up in the words "the Christian nation." It symbolized how we care about personal morality while we remain dispassionate toward the claims of the gospel on economic jus-tice—because capitalism is the best way to be a Christian economically! Yet, strangely, Wal-Mart is one of the most generous corporations in America supporting anti-poverty causes while it participates in exploi-tive labor practices.[43] In so doing, Wal-Mart mimics the evangelicals of "the Christian nation." Together we say, "I will help the poor, I will be generous, but only on the terms of Christian capitalism which provide me protection, security, and distance from the poor when I need it." We see once more the contradiction that lies at the core of our politic united around "the Christian nation" and its allegiance with capitalism.

An episode in 2002 in the life of Bernie Ebbers—CEO of WorldCom—illustrates all of these same contradictions and enjoy-ments. Ebbers, a well known evangelical Christian and Sunday School teacher, led WorldCom into the largest bankruptcy filing ever in American history at that time. When all was said and done, the mal-feasance totaled in excess of seven billion dollars affecting thousands of people's pension plans and livelihoods. Ebbers was convicted and put in prison. While running WorldCom to ruin, however, this same man was an outstanding evangelical churchman, extremely generous to the poor, not only giving millions of dollars to charities but himself helping to serve meals to the homeless regularly in downtown Jackson, Mississippi.[44] He is a paradigmatic symbol of the contradictions and enjoyments that lie at the core of the evangelical belief in "evangelical capitalism" and "the christian nation."

---

43. In 2006 as reported on MSNBC, it was once again the top corporate donor in all of the U.S. to charitable causes. Online: http://www.msnbc.msn.com/id/17803920/.

44. These well known attributes of Bernie Ebbers were reported in *Time Magzine*. Padgett, "Rise and Fall"

On June 30, 2002, Ebbers made a famous appearance at his Mississippi church, Easthaven Baptist Church, Brookhaven, Mississippi, to teach Sunday school and to attend the morning worship service. At the end of the service, Ebbers walked to the front of the church and talked about his indictment for the first time on record. He addressed the congregation saying, "I just want you to know you aren't going to church with a crook."[45] The whole church erupted with a standing ovation, applauding him for several minutes. The widely reported standing ovation implied something more was at work than a mere affirmation of Ebbers' innocence. The excess in this public display could be interpreted as the congregation's exploding with a great sense of relief. They could well have been saying, "All he was doing was being a good capitalist! He was following the rules, being responsible and taking care of his wealth. And this is the Christian thing to do! Thank God Ebbers is not a crook, because now we can go on doing the same!" Ebbers' performance thus allowed the congregation to exhale in relief and enjoyment that we are all indeed still good Christians. Despite the revealed absurdity, we get to keep the security of our finances within our capitalist arrangements as well as feel good about helping the poor.

I am not arguing here that capitalism is an immoral economic system. Instead, what is troublesome is the way evangelicals are shaped by the Christianizing of it. I have no intent to disparage the person of Bernie Ebbers. Rather it is the episode of Ebbers in his local evangelical church that reveals the perverse enjoyment at the core of the evangelical belief and practice of "evangelical capitalism" within "the Christian Nation." We can "enjoy" being secure within our capitalist protections, enabling us to help the poor on our terms. It allows us to feel righteous in our wealth and to enjoy helping the poor more because we earned it via the Christian virtues of hard work. We can enjoy wealth as the accumulation of good Christian character while at the same time enjoy the position of being able to give out of our wealth while being protected from those who would steal it away from us. Perhaps this explains how an iconic evangelical businessman can make billions via malfeasance yet feel vindicated (via the rules of capitalism), all the while enjoying immensely the helping of the poor. The performance of

45. As reported by Waller, "Ebbers tells church." Picked up later in numerous publications such *The Wall Street Journal* and *New York Times*.

Ebbers prompts us to examine how we evangelicals give so generously to the poor as suburban congregations yet remain strangely detached from a relationship with the poor in our own congregations.

Surely there are several evangelical suburban churches who engage the poor in concrete, relational ways. And perhaps the Bernie Ebbers' episode is just one episode that we should treat as an outlier from the true practice of evangelical justice.[46] But the enduring prominence of "the Christian nation" among evangelicals indicates that our justice is prone towards this kind of dispassion. We therefore must continually ask ourselves after we give millions to the poor if we fellowship relationally with them as part of our everyday lives? Do we fellowship with the poor, the mentally unhealthy, and the broken in our neighborhoods (in which God can work his reconciliation and renewal incarnationally)? If the answer to these questions is "No," we must then look to the ways we have been shaped by the "Christian nation"/"evangelical capitalism." Irruptions like Bernie Ebbers reveal a lingering empty core at the center of evangelicalism's belief and practice of the church in society via "the Christian nation."

Dispassion: The Spiritual Formation of an "Empty Politic"

We have seen exposed yet again the contradictions and perverse enjoyments that drive our evangelical way of life together, this time in the way we gather around "the Christian nation." We have seen how this ideological banner organizes our belief (or lack thereof) and practice of the church in society. It plays on our fears so as to set us against those who would steal our morality or financial security from us. It enables us to enjoy affirming our belief in personal morality while staying ac-

---

46. It did not go without notice that WorldCom was just one in a series of corporate scandals at that time that took place led by American CEOs who were also prominent evangelicals The Enron scandal, for instance, that cost pension plans billions and impoverished thousands of its own retirees while its own executives made millions, was also led by a devout evangelical—Methodist Sunday School teacher Ken Lay. The fall of Enron and all the hubris of figures that surrounded it, including the extravagance of CEO Ken Lay, was reported in a media sensation documentary *The Smartest Guys in The Room* from the book of the same name by McLean and Elkind. The fact that Lay was an evangelical Christian was also widely reported. See, for example, *USA Today*'s report by Ehrich, "Not Heard From the Pulpit."

tive in the world promoting justice. We must ask, however, whether this is the justice of God inaugurated in Christ for the world. For "the Christian nation" rallies us as a people to work for a justice removed from our own daily lives together. Via our allegiance to it, whether it is the evangelical right version or the version of progressive evangelicals, "the Christian nation" detaches us from the actual lived relationships that make for true Christian reconciliation in Christ Jesus. As a result, we are strangely complicit with broken economic relationships while giving generously to the poor at a distance. We are hampered from embodying the reign of God in a living, enfleshed community that engages the world. And we are shaped for dispassion.

This dispassion can be seen in the way evangelicals often practice justice. "The Christian nation" focuses the energies we have for the poor onto a program/agenda/voting program external to the church: either the government accomplishing a Christian agenda or, more subtly, the "justice project" at the local church that always seeks to administer justice somewhere far away. Of course these programs can indeed be integrated into the very relationships of our daily lives. They should then be applauded whenever such a social manifestation of Christ's righteousness bursts forth. Too often, however, participating in government or church programs becomes the means to work at a distance for agendas built on "the Christian nation."

The belief in "the Christian nation" as wedded to "evangelical capitalism" enables us to baptize the economic structures of capitalism as Christian, which shapes us to be economically independent. Justice then is always done as one who has money and owns it. Charity is giving out of my bounty, willing to undergo loss. It is not given out of God's abundance that can never run dry. The result is a justice done at a distance. In this way, then, "the Christian Nation" shapes us corporately into a posture of dispassion toward the poor, the hurting, and the lost. As a result, we are a politic incompatible with the gospel. We are an "empty" politic in need of another political formation.

This, then, has become our fate as evangelicals. "The Christian nation," together with "the inerrant Bible" and "the decision," has worked to shape us as a dispassionate, exclusivist, and duplicitous people. As such, we are a politic inhospitable for God's mission. Our beliefs have become signifiers of an "empty" politic. Our only option, if we seek to be a people of mission again, is to somehow reclaim the core of our political existence—the person and work of the incarnate Son as sent by the Father and continued by the Holy Spirit. We must reshape these beliefs and practices so as to nurture our participation in this life of the triune God in the world. This is the "politic of fullness" that overcomes our worst ways of political formation. It is to this task that we now turn in the following chapter.

CHAPTER 6

Recovering the Core of Our Politics for Mission:
Towards an Evangelical Missional Political Theology

*". . . until we all reach the unity in the faith and in the knowledge
of the Son of God and become mature, attaining to the whole
measure of the fullness of Christ."*
—Ephesians 4:13 NIV

*"For it was the Father's good pleasure for all the fullness
to dwell in Him."*
—Colossians 1:19 NASB

Is evangelicalism coming to an "end"? Probably not any time soon.
Nonetheless, it is at a crossroads of sorts. Evangelicalism's political
presence in North America—rife with exposed contradictions, perverse "enjoyments," incredulous episodes, and antagonistic impulses—
behaves like an ideology in crisis. Its credibility looks to be unraveling
among broad sectors of North American society. Its political life and
culture appears, for all intents and purposes, to be "empty" at its core.
Where should evangelicalism go from here? If this is not an "end" for
evangelicalism, has a space been cleared for a new faithfulness within
evangelicalism?

Žižek's "Empty Politic" Versus a "Politic of Fullness"

Žižek offers us little to help answer these questions. His program of political analysis has certainly helped us see how evangelicalism acts like an ideology. In applying many of his concepts to evangelicalism (in ways he would never embrace) he has helped us see how evangelicalism operates as a politic "empty" at its core. Yet, for Žižek, this is just the way things are.

For Žižek, there is no true way out of this ongoing conflictual swirl of social forces (otherwise known as dialectical materialism[1]). This is the reality of the conscious social world. It is a finite incompleteness that is ever seeking an impossible resolution. Žižek would therefore be quite happy with the revealing of evangelicalism that has taken place in this book. He would cheer the dissipation of any evangelical illusions that our beliefs might actually refer to something true and real (in the way we evangelicals talk about truth and reality). He would applaud the opportunities to detach ourselves from our fantasies in the hopes of living more honestly.[2] He would even see this revealing as the necessary first step towards that goal. But Žižek rarely suggests we could escape the empty nature of our politics. For Žižek, evangelicalism should respond by learning to live within the lack, the split that is inside every politic that enables us to exist as our "selves." We must simply stay within it and struggle with a brutal honesty that refuses to cover things over in fantasies. This is what love looks like. Only by staying within the materialist struggle can we love.[3] For Žižek, then, one might say "evangelicalism has seen the truth about itself. Now go figure out how to live with it without all this fundamentalist reactionary stupidity!"

But is this enough? Is this the way forward for evangelicalism? Can Žižek's construal of the world provide a sufficient basis for a truly

---

1. For a more recent statement by Žižek of his unique articulation of the dialectical materialism that draws not only on Marx and Hegel but on Lacan as well, see Žižek, *Parallax View*, ch. 2.

2. This is what Žižek calls "traversing the fantasy." The sense of this can be caught, for example, when Žižek suggests: "What this means is that in order effectively to liberate oneself from the grip of existing social reality, one should first renounce the transgressive fantasmatic supplement that attaches us to it." *Fragile Absolute*, 149.

3. Ironically, Žižek, because of the way he interprets the Pauline epistles in his later writings, sees Christianity as the example par excellence of how to live honestly in this way. Living honestly within the struggle is what it means to truly love for Žižek.

Christian political existence in the world? We can only assume not—because the Christian life in community is driven by reconciliation, not conflict. This reconciliation has already been inaugurated by God in the incarnate work of the Son sent into the world. He is our peace (Rom 5:1–10). As opposed to Žižek's conflictual politic, the Christian politic is constituted here in the reconciliation founded in Christ.

As already discussed in chapter 2, Milbank argues that Žižek's construal of politics is caught forever in an agonistic social existence formed around "an empty fetish."[4] It is founded in a never-ending struggle. Its core is "empty," driven by antagonism, and therefore cannot sustain peace and/or justice. Certainly Žižek has claimed Christianity (through the apostle Paul) as the founding event for the authentic materialist struggle that is love. According to Milbank, however, this is a pathological love that survives on struggle without purpose, that can only turn in on itself. The Christian politic, however, is constituted in the over-flowing love of "the gift" where in and through Christ God is at work reconciling the whole world to Himself (2 Cor 5:19). If we affirm this, then the Christian politic is incompatible with Žižek's void-driven conflictual politics. His political vision cannot measure up to "the politic of fullness" birthed in the triune God having come into the world in the incarnate Christ.

From this point of view, Žižek's "ideology" describes what a fallen politic looks like. It is necessarily a false politic, a secular parody of the true politic of God at work in Christ through the Spirit in the world. His political and cultural theory therefore works as the means of diagnosing a politic as fallen. This diagnosis, however, should not lead us to merely endure this fallen politic in a better way, as Žižek perhaps would have it. Instead, we seek a redeemed politic. The space that Žižek opens with his work must take us somewhere beyond his work. Within this framework, Žižek helps evangelicals to see how our politic has become "empty." In response, we must now seek "a politic of fullness," i.e., the politic that is founded in the triune God's work in the world—the politic of reconciliation and peace offered in and through the Incarnate Son.

---

4. As John Milbank characterizes Žižek in "Materialism and Transcendence," 395.

Such "a politic of fullness" will be constituted via something other than the antagonisms that are generated from within our life together.[5] It will be a politic flowing forth out of an abundance at its core.[6] It will be capable of extending a generosity that comes from beyond itself. Only then can we escape the exclusionary, duplicitous, and dispassionate politics that has come to define evangelicalism as a presence in society. Only then can we escape the playing off of our own conflictual motivations that lead to an ever re-doubling back on ourselves.[7] As opposed to the politics of lack, the church must inhabit a "politic of fullness" that can move us past the endless repetition of the same.

In metaphysical terms, and in opposition to Žižek, our politics must appeal to a reality that transcends the material. The church's political life must have its source from beyond itself. Yet we cannot merely appeal as isolated selves to a transcendent source of knowledge, for this again ends up being no politic at all. Instead this politic must be a participation of a people together in the gift of God the Father that enters the world in the incarnate Christ as the Sent One and is extended into the world via the Holy Spirit. Only here, as we participate together in the work of the fully triune God, can we overcome the trap within our immanence. Here, at the Incarnation, the gift is full, and we are invited as a people into participating in the fullness of God's love flowing forth within the endless plentitude of the Father, the Son, and the Holy Spirit.

The politic of the church, then, must be founded at the very point of the Incarnation itself—where Christ is received into this world by the people of Israel via Mary.[8] Here the transcendent enters the material, the universal enters the particular, the concrete enters into time

5. I'm playing off of Žižek's rejection of any such "fullness" as possible within the structure of the Symbolic. See for example Žižek "Da Capo," 215–16.

6. My contrasting a politic of fullness with the empty politic of Žižek may run parallel to Tonder and Thomassen, "Introduction." Yet I am defining "politic of fullness" in the completely different terms of my own theological program that I am proposing in this chapter.

7. To say a politic "doubles back on itself" is to say that we as participants are ever reflexively working off one another as the source of our drives, movements, and motivations. There is no transcendent source exterior to itself that can fund a politic's full non-antagonistic immanent presence.

8. Of course, I am playing off Milbank and his trinitarian metaphysic found in his "Can a Gift be Given?" and elsewhere. I am also influenced here by Long, *Speaking of God*, 298–326; Smith, *Speech and Theology*; and of course by Balthasar's many contributions to this line of thinking.

and space to be the core of God's politic in the world. Here is the core from which the fullness flows that reveals that the void has already been overcome. Here, as the universal becomes concrete in this one incarnational figure in history, a politic is birthed out of participation in the life of the triune God. The void, which Žižek says cannot be surmounted, has been overcome.[9] Here, as we come together as a people participating in the work of God in the Incarnation, extended through the Spirit, we avoid the trap of enclosed immanence or the ever-prohibited transcendence so prominent in the apophatic theologies of post-structuralism. As Milbank and others have shown, both forms of politics lead us nowhere.[10] But here, grounded inextricably in the life of the triune God via the incarnate Christ and extended by the Spirit, a politic of fullness is birthed—the church. Only a politic of fullness like this can provide the basis for a political evangelical theology that is truly missional: full of the presence of the hospitable, faithful, and compassionate Christ "sent into the world" in socially embodied form.

We should see immediate differences between this Christian "politic of fullness" and what we have named the "empty politic." Obviously, the empty politic is empty at its core, while the Christian politic is full as its corporeality is constituted via the gift of Christ ever flowing into its body politic by the Spirit and then into the world. The empty politic is built around a void driven by the antagonistic split that constitutes its "Real"-ity. Individuals are initiated into this ideological politic by believing (insincerely) in Master-Signifiers and participating in rituals that cynically reinforce the ongoing ideology. In contrast, the Christian "politic of fullness" (the church) is constituted differently. Here the members are formed by their beliefs and practices into a mutual participation whose core is Christ. The resulting politic will not be antagonistic towards objects/people outside of itself. Instead, out of its fullness in the Godhead, this Christian politic engages the world as the presence of the Sent One himself into the world. This politic proceeds

9. Of course, we must not forget that Žižek ironically makes the case that Christianity is the profound example of a politic that in fact embodies the honest politic he seeks, the coming to terms with the lack.

10. Milbank of course critiques Žižek on the internal imploding nature of his politics. Yet both Milbank and Žižek often critique deconstructionist apophaticism that glorifies "the never to be reached" and sucks us in to a "bad infinity." See, for instance, Milbank, "Double Glory," 118. Žižek, *Sublime Object*, 155; Žižek, *Puppet and the Dwarf*, 139–41.

from its source, the ever-flowing plentitude of the gift of the Father in the Sent One as extended by the Spirit. It produces a politic of humble presence, faithfulness, and compassion in the world that comes from this ontological participation in Christ. This politic of fullness is not built in autonomy from God but from participation in his triune life. This politic of fullness is the true politic of the church. This is what faithfulness looks like for the church in the world.

The way forward, then, for an evangelical missional politic is to ground our belief and practice in the incarnate reality of the triune God in Christ. In doing so, we recover Jesus as the ontological core of our corporate existence. As evangelicals, we must undo the ways our beliefs and practices have become separated from the ongoing work of God in Christ for the world. For when they are separated from the incarnate Christ at the core, they most surely revert to becoming Master-Signifiers all over again, supported by practices that simply reinforce behavior for ideological survival. When, however, we articulate our belief and shape our practice so as to participate in the triune life in Christ, as sent by the Father, extended into the world by the Spirit, we in essence ground our politic in God's never-ending, unfurling mission in the world. Our presence as a political community extends the incarnation of Christ into the world until the consummation. As I will explain, this is what brings the church as mission into being so that indeed our presence as church in the world becomes, in the words of the apostle Paul, "the fullness of Christ" (Eph 4:13).

RECOVERING THE CORE TO BECOME EVANGELICAL AGAIN

None of this requires that evangelicals compromise the three commitments so central to our history—a high view of Scripture, a conversionist soteriology, and a church active in society for its salvation. The task is not to reject these beliefs but to overcome their detachment (along with their concomitant practices) from Jesus Christ the incarnate Son—the core of our political existence as Christians. Re-grounding these three commitments politically in the triune work of God through Christ by the Spirit will not only establish their substance in God but also shape evangelicals into a participation in his mission in the world.

Such a re-grounding will reverse the effects of the modernist-fundamentalist controversies of the 1920s and 30s. We showed above how the modernist-fundamentalist crisis birthed the unique evangelical version of these three commitments. Prior to the modernist-fundamentalist controversies, evangelicals carried these three beliefs in different form—less defensively and with a more active stance in society than appeared afterward.[11] Faced, however, with the post-Enlightenment sundering of the Christian cultural unity that had been handed down via European Christendom churches and the Magisterial Reformation, the fundamentalists/evangelicals scurried to build their faith in Christ upon another foundation—the modernist foundations of science/historiography and the appeal to individual experience. With good intentions, they articulated their founding beliefs and practices in these terms. The inerrant Bible, the personal "decision" of faith in Christ's work on the cross, and an activist church for world evangelism before Christ's imminent return all emerged to become dominant beliefs and practices of American evangelical fundamentalism. Yet in defending the church in the midst of modernist impulses, evangelicalism eventually abandoned the core of her social existence to form what became its political presence in North America today. The way was cleared for the eventual loss of the grounding of our political life in the person and work of the incarnate Christ as sent by the Father and extended by the Spirit. It began the course towards becoming an ideology, a false politic in light of the politic of fullness in Jesus Christ. Along the way, subtly, evangelicalism as an ideology "de-missionalized" the church, setting its drives, desires, and political existence at odds with the mission of God. We took on an exclusivist, duplicitous and dispassionate posture in the world. Re-grounding these three doctrinal commitments as described above should reverse these effects.

In Žižek's terms, we might label the modernist-fundamentalist controversies of the 1920s and 30s "the primordial traumatic event" of evangelicalism's present-day ideology. In essence this event is where the evolving evangelical constituency gave up its existing implicit grounding of political existence in the triune living God who has come in Jesus Christ.[12] This grounding in Christ was exchanged for a grounding

11. The prime examples here are the aforementioned Dayton, *Discovering an Evangelical Heritage* and Moberg, *Great Reversal.*

12. Put another way, if for Milbank and Radical Orthodoxy it is Duns Scotus

that was defended and articulated in the terms set down by the modernist threats to that previous, unquestioned political existence. The source of our politics turned antagonistic. This set the stage for each of these three beliefs/practices (Scripture, salvation, and the church in the world) to later become Master-Signifiers promoting the survival of evangelicalism many years later. Looking back, in Žižekian terms, the fundamentalist-modernist controversies were the traumatic event in which we evangelical Christians were forced to give up "something" in order to consolidate our politic for its ongoing survival amidst the modernist intellectual crisis of the 1920s, 30s, and beyond. As a result, evangelicalism today is a fallen politic, and its fall took place here in the modernist-fundamentalist controversies.

Many years later, our political presence is more defined by what we are against—"the liberals," "the gay/lesbian," "those who would steal our country from us"—than by the redemptive life we are called to live in and be before the world. Faced with the "empty politic" that evangelicalism has become, our task is to recover the grounding of our beliefs in the core of our life together: Jesus the incarnate Christ, as sent from the Father, extended in the Spirit. The three hard-won commitments of the 1920s and 30s are worth building upon for our time. In doing so, however, we do not seek to return nostalgically to a prior time, for the confident sweep of Enlightenment modernism with all its accoutrements has been chastened and replaced already with the sweeping creep of a new post-Christendom and its varying forms of postmodern intellectualism. We do not need another accommodation. We need a politic that embodies the integrity of our existence "in Christ" incarnationally for God's mission in the world. We need a restoring of the ontological core of our political existence in the life of the triune God that carries its own integrity. This is the path towards our political life in the world becoming evangelical again.

Each one of our three belief/practices, therefore, must be restored to a belief and practice that shapes us into our participation corporately

---

and Ockhamist nominalism that precipitated the fall for modernity, which led to the nihilist outcome of modern metaphysics and Protestant theology, for me the fall of evangelicalism can best be read in terms of the modernist-fundamentalist controversies, where evangelicalism decidedly aligned itself with modernity and its autonomous structures of epistemology and politics. Here began the loves that sealed the fate of a politic that was to lose its core.

in Christ as his very body extended into the world by the Spirit, as sent by God the Father. This is the singular goal of what follows. For if this is what takes shape among us, we evangelicals will not only hold onto the heritage of orthodoxy that we claim, we will also be shaped politically into Christ and what God is doing for his mission in the world.

In what follows, then, I offer some initial directives for the reshaping of evangelical beliefs and practices in a way that restores the incarnate Christ to the core of our political life together. These are only initial directives. A fuller exposition must wait for another time. Nonetheless, in a limited way, I hope to show the promise that evangelicalism's three doctrines hold for shaping a politic of mission. I hope to display how our practice of these doctrines can change and, as a result, our communal disposition in the world can shift towards a missional stance, a posture that embodies socially the incarnate presence of God in Christ that participates in his mission in the world.

How Does God Reveal Himself? Recovering the Core of Our Belief and Practice of Scripture

Regarding the first of the three evangelical doctrinal commitments, how can evangelicals speak about Scripture's authority and practice so that our political existence is bound into the very being of the Incarnation as the work of the triune God and his mission in the world? How do we center our belief and practice of Scripture in the incarnate, living Christ so as to overcome the ways of arrogance and exclusion attached to "the inerrant Bible" and instead have our political existence itself constituted by Christ in God's mission? How do we understand the way God reveals himself so that it does not sequester us from the world but rather shapes us as a politic in the world? For answers to these questions, let us look briefly to Karl Barth, Hans Urs von Balthasar, Kevin Vanhoozer, and Christopher Wright.

Karl Barth, like few others, sets the stage for grounding the authority of Scripture in our participation in the incarnate Son. He famously locates all revelation of God in Christ as part of the eternal work of the trinitarian God. For Barth there is no knowledge of God or about God apart from God's revelation in the Incarnation. He therefore derives the authority of Scripture from its connection to this revelation of God in the incarnate Christ.

For Barth, Scripture is inextricably a part of being in relationship with the triune God. To know God is to already be within the sphere of relationship within the trinitarian God via the incarnate Son of God.[13] As a result, to know God via the Scriptures is a direct extension of God's coming to us in the mission of the Incarnation. The authority of the Scriptures is derived from our relationship to the incarnate Christ. Here is where God is revealed first before any other realm.

We cannot therefore assess an authority that is outside of His work in the world in Christ Jesus. We cannot pretend to know God apart from Him. The order of knowing cannot be separated from this order of being. God's being cannot be known apart from Immanuel—"God with us"—the incarnation of God in the Son and then, after the ascension, in His continuing presence with us by the Holy Spirit in the proclaimed Word.[14] There is therefore no knowledge of God apart from being in this faith relationship with God through Jesus Christ.[15] Within this relationship lies the authority of Scripture for the believer.

This relationship to the Scriptures, however, *is not* an individualist one—isolated into the individual's relationship to God through Scripture. For Barth, the Scriptures are in effect an extension of the incarnation of Christ into the world through the existence of the church. As Barth states, "There is but one place where all this is known and acknowledged. That is the congregation founded upon the biblical witness, the witness of the prophets of the Old Testament and the apostles of the New Testament."[16] The revelation of God in Christ, the written Word (the Scriptures), and the ongoing proclamation of the Word are all part of the one and same revelation as extended through the church and cannot be separated.[17] To know the authority of Scripture,

---

13. Here I am following Alan Torrance's exposition of Barth's understanding of Revelation in "Trinity."

14. This theme of any knowledge of God being the product of "God with us" is expounded on by Barth in *CD* I/1, 107–24. See also Torrance, "Trinity," 74.

15. The mistake according to Karl Barth is "when Christian histories of dogmatics and theology separated *gnosis* and *pistis*. *Pistis* rightly understood is *gnosis*; rightly understood, the act of faith is also an act of knowledge." *Dogmatics in Outline*, 23.

16. Barth, *God: Here and Now*, 57.

17. Although Barth does say in *CD* I/1 in the section on "The Unity of the Word of

therefore, is to participate in this ongoing presence of the incarnate Christ in the church by the Holy Spirit. Thus Barth can talk about the Scriptures as "the visible form of the presence and Lordship of Jesus Christ Himself, which makes the congregation the first fruits of the whole of humanity . . ."[18] God has entered history in the Incarnation. His presence in Christ is carried on in history and witnessed to the world via the ongoing corporate witness of His people. Although Barth wishes to maintain the Scripture's authority over the church, it is from within the corporate relationship of faith to God in Christ via the proclamation of the Word that God reveals himself. God cannot be an object of our knowing (our possession). Rather as we enter into a place where we become known by God, then, out of this relationship, we can know God. The Scriptures are part and parcel of this dynamic. Here in the dynamics of the Incarnation, lies the authority of God's Word as the Scriptures are proclaimed and known in the church. The Scripture's authority is an extension of the "sentness" into the world of the Son by the Holy Spirit

In these ways, Barth shows evangelicals how both to maintain our high view of the authority of Scripture and, at the same time, to recover Christ at the core of what we believe about Scripture. In following Barth, evangelicals can move away from an individually self-encapsulated understanding of authority grounded in the "inerrant divinely inspired words of Scripture" to an understanding of authority derived in and from Jesus Christ Himself as sent from the Father. This very authority of Christ is extended in the Scriptures into history via the church, its prophets and the apostles, and the ongoing development of orthodoxy in the church, all overseen by the Holy Spirit. This authority is received only through our ongoing participation in this relationship with Christ as his people through faith in submission to the Holy Spirit in the proclamation of the Word.

In this process, our formation as a people changes. Far from being possessors of authority unto ourselves (with the potential arrogance that instills), we become participants via Christ in the life of the triune God's mission in the world. In our participation "in Christ" we are ever humbly receiving from God His revelation and then witnessing to it. As

18. Barth, *God: Here and Now*, 58.

theologian Stanley Hauerwas argues along with Anabaptist theologian John Howard Yoder, "the church must abandon all attempts to secure the gospel through foundational epistemological strategies," for these are Constantinian strategies. They are attempts "to make the church safe by joining its strategies to worldly powers."[19] Evangelicals of the past, by joining their articulation of Scripture's authority to "inerrancy" as defined by modern science, historiography, and the modern academy, aligned themselves with the forces in power, seeking to secure position within the wider world. Arrogance resulted as we practiced the spiritual formation of building arguments and nailing down interpretative details, all in an attempt to be right in the eyes of the world. In contrast, when we understand that the authority inherent in Scripture is as we are "in Christ," we are able to embody witnessing to what we know in and through Him as extended from Him via the apostles, the church, all by the Holy Spirit. This embodiment by definition incarnates the Savior, the spirit of vulnerability and humility, always inviting those we engage into dialogue and to receive the gift of God in the gospel. The posture of arrogance that has so inhibited evangelicalism's participation in God's mission is overturned. Living under the secure Lordship of Jesus Christ as the core of our political existence, we can be humble and vulnerable.

Of course, Barth presents a problem for a missional political theology. Most obviously, if all knowledge of God comes exclusively in and through the incarnate Christ alone, those who are outside this revelation in Christ can become closed off from the community who believes. The community can view itself as singularly in control of the truth of God. This would be a community closed off from the mission of God, incapable of translating our beliefs beyond our own language.[20]

In this regard, Barth's friend in Basel, Catholic theologian Hans Urs von Balthasar, provides a helpful corrective. Balthasar, like Barth, understands all knowledge as Christologically-centered. Yet, for Balthasar, the Incarnation of God in Christ is the explicit revelation that makes possible the manifestation of God to all humanity in all the various forms of human experience and knowledge in creation. Christ is the pure "form" in which we see God. This pure form is where we

19. Hauerwas and Coles, *Christianity, Democracy, and the Radical Ordinary*, 21.

20. See Long, *Speaking of God*, 93–110, for a treatment of this accusation against Barth and a partial refutation.

most assuredly see and know God, yet by this same form God manifests Himself in all of creation. Christ as pure form becomes "the center of all revelation" in, by, and with whom we see the world as it is.[21] We, therefore, are able to see Christ in all the world by our participating in this pure form of Christ—Scripture—in and through the church and tradition.[22] Scripture is inextricably part of this pure form of Christ. In Balthasar's words, "Scripture does not stand over against this form of revelation (the pure form of Christ) by way of imitation as a second autonomous form, complete in itself: for Scripture itself belongs to the sphere of revelation and, being the normative testimony, it is itself part of that revelation."[23] In other words, Scripture is part of Christ himself.

In following Balthasar, evangelicals can restore Christ to the core of our doctrine of Scripture in a way that calls us into an openness and hospitality for God's work in the whole world by the Spirit. We go from possessing Scripture's authority as our own to embodying it as the source by which we are ever seeking God revealed in the world. This does not diminish the authority or truth of Scripture in a correlational sense (as Barth might have feared).[24] Neither does this diminish the uncompromising truth of God for the whole world as evangelicals have feared.[25] Christ, the Sent One, remains the core of our life together. Yet in and through Christ, we see God in the world in and through all things. We see God at work, by the Holy Spirit, through the Son, bringing people into the completion of grace in their lives while recognizing there will be those who sadly reject Him anyways (2 Cor 2:14–17). By participating in this very life in Christ via Scripture we see the world

21. The title of one of Balthasar's key headings in *Glory of the Lord*, therefore is "Christ the Center of the Form of Revelation." *Glory of the Lord*, 541.

22. Long therefore rightly describes Balthasar's form as his Christological reinterpretation of the analogy of being in his *Speaking of God*.

23. Balthasar, *Glory of the Lord*, 541. The words in brackets are mine for purposes of clarification.

24. Following Long's reading of Balthasar: "worldly truth . . . is never neutral because the world is always either related positively or negatively to God. Thus grace perfects or contradicts the world, but can never be indifferent to it." *Speaking of God*, 312.

25. Evangelicals have had a troubled history with Barth. In our history, figures like Cornelius Van Til and Carl F Henry interpreted Barth via the modernist epistemologies interpreting Barth to be making truth somehow more subjective. See Morrison, "Barth, Barthians," Presumably the time has come for evangelicals to reassess Barth in light of the post-modern chastening of modernist epistemologies as well as the political malformation that such epistemologies have bred in our politics as evangelicals.

differently. We are able to see God's work revealed in the world and become actively engaged in the world to point others towards Christ.

Barth and Balthasar push evangelicals to re-think the authority of Scripture and how God reveals himself in terms of our participation in Christ, the Incarnation of God, and his mission in the world. Our belief and practice of Scripture bonds us politically into Christ for the world. God is active in the world, bringing about His purposes in history as revealed in the triune God (what some have called the economic Trinity). The center of this history is the incarnate Christ. By speaking about the authority of Scripture à la Barth and Balthasar, our belief of Scripture grounds us into a corporate participation in this same Christ and the trinitarian history of God's mission into the world.

Still, even with all that Barth and Balthasar bring, one might be misled to think that Scripture brings us into a purely mystical relation to Christ that does not call us into the *missio* of what God is actually doing in the world (even if this relation is corporate). The talk of Scripture as participation in Christ, even on the terms set down by Balthasar, might be misconstrued in individualist terms or, even worse, static terms. In this regard, it is helpful to speak more explicitly of Scripture and our participation in Christ in terms of the trinitarian history. In other words, to participate in Christ via Scripture is also to participate in God's ongoing presence and work in history for the salvation of the whole world.

In this regard, evangelical theologian Kevin Vanhoozer's *The Drama of Doctrine* adds something essential to the reshaping of the evangelical doctrine of Scripture's authority. He proposes that we understand Scripture as the authoritative "script" for "the Drama of God" in history of which Jesus is the center.[26] Salvation history is a "theo-drama" in which God is protagonist and Jesus is the center and pivotal climax. The drama has five acts: Creation, Israel, Jesus, Church, and Eschaton, and the Bible is the authoritative script for this drama. The goal of both script and direction is to serve God's drama. In Vanhoozer's words, "script and performance are equally necessary, though not equally authoritative. Biblical script without ecclesial performance is empty; ecclesial performance without biblical script is

---

26. Vanhoozer, *Drama of Doctrine*, 1–75.

blind."[27] The authority lies with the script (Bible); the teleology with performance (praxis); the mediation with direction (theology). God is both the script(ure) writer and player in the drama. Humans are actors following a script. Like the audience at a dinner theater, the church is invited to enter in and become part of the drama. Our participation in the drama shapes us into the continuing drama. In this grand drama, as the church plays out her part before the surrounding world, the world itself shall be drawn into the drama and all God is doing to reconcile the world to himself.

In speaking about the Bible in this way, Vanhoozer follows people like Balthasar, Hauerwas, Hans Frei, and the Yale School's earlier theologians, all of whom have proposed we understand doctrine and Scripture within the context of theo-drama, narrative, or story. Scripture is more than the means for correct knowledge about God[28] or a relationship with God; it is the authoritative script by which we participate in (perform) the ongoing work of God in Christ extended by the Spirit for the redemption of all creation. Scripture's authority is constituted among a people in the very shaping of a people as actors in this drama of God—God's mission in the world.[29]

Old Testament scholar Christopher Wright, in his *The Mission of God*, argues along similar lines. For Wright, the entirety of Scripture is a document produced as a part of God's ongoing mission. Missional activity gave rise to each of its writings. God's communication itself is always in mission. Wright, therefore, proposes that we cannot know the authority of Scripture apart from our own participation in God's mission in Christ by the Spirit. Instead of attempting to define the authority of Scripture externally to Scripture, we should only hope to know Scripture's authority in our lives as it is revealed within our inhabitation

---

27. Ibid., 362.

28. Vanhoozer's work in *Drama of Doctrine* and elsewhere uses speech-act theory to show the multitude of ways speech functions within the Bible that go beyond modernist propositional modes of understanding language.

29. Of course, Vanhoozer would not subscribe to understanding Scripture's authority in this communally dependent way. His proposal puts forth a "canonical linguistic" approach that extols the authority of the canon over the church. He remains an advocate for the continued role of authorial intent as central to the church's interpretation of Scripture, thereby isolating Scripture's authority over the church. For a critique of Vanhoozer on this score, see Byasee, *Praise Seeking Understanding*, 255–56.

of God's mission in the world. Scripture's authority is itself part of the *missio Dei.*

Together, Barth, Balthasar, Vanhoozer, and Wright push evangelicals to see Scripture's authority as derived directly from the incarnate Christ via participation in his mission in the world. There can be no higher authority for we who confess Jesus as Lord. The Sent One became incarnate. He was born of a virgin, died, rose again, ascended into heaven and sits at the right hand of the Father. He reigns and remains present and active via the Holy Spirit for the redemption of the world. He shall return. Upon completion He shall deliver the kingdom to the Father. This is God's drama. This is God's mission. Scripture's authority is made manifest in our participation in this mission, indeed in our participation in the incarnate Christ. These theologians prod us to leave behind the Bible as "inerrant according to the original autographs" to instead understand it as *"our one and true story of God for the whole world—infallible in and through Jesus Christ our Lord."* Scripture is authoritative in and outside the church in terms of its solidarity with the Sent One, the incarnate Son, and with God's mission in the world. Its authority is birthed in the concrete interpretation of Scripture that happens in each context of mission. This way of speaking about Scripture breeds a people for mission and leads to a profound refashioning of how we practice Scripture, both corporately and personally as a people in the world.

Our preaching, for instance, moves away from the traditional evangelical expository techniques where the goal is correct exposition—word for word—so as to dispense accurate doctrinal information and practical guidelines for how to live the Christian life.[30] In this way of preaching, the person in the pew takes notes, learns some principles and, in cognitive fashion, applies these principles in the hopes of an improved Christian life. Taking good notes can lead us further along in our sanctification. When, however, this approach emphasizes individualized control of truth—three points and an application to take home and use according to my own personalized, Spirit-guided prompting—it promotes distance and control. It acts like a Žižekian "behavior reinforcement" of an ideology, reminding us that the Bible is inerrant

---

30. The prime example of this kind of preaching is MacArthur's *Rediscovering Expository Preaching.* See also Robinson, *Biblical Preaching.*

truth we can all possess if we just learn it well enough.[31] Within the politic of the Master-Signifier "the inerrant Bible" (consciously or subconsciously), expository preaching of this kind breeds a stunting in our personal discipleship and arrogance in our corporate disposition in the world.

On the other hand, preaching—where Scripture is the drama of God's mission in Christ—proclaims the grand reality of God's work among us and then invites God's people into it. It demands a concrete hermeneutic as part and parcel of the authority that the Scriptures bear in Christ by the Spirit. Such preaching unfurls God's mission before us, funding the imagination of all who would hear and inviting everyone to join in. It always leads to a response of the people into Christ in the liturgical moment. At its very best it culminates in the Eucharist celebration of God's gift of Christ in the bread and wine and then the sending out into the world. In such preaching, we grow into our relationship with the living Christ and His presence both in the church and in the world. This kind of preaching is always a) a proclamation of God's reality out of Scripture; b) a gesture of inviting all who would hear into it; and c) a call for a response. Herein, the authority of Christ in his Scriptures is participated in. The response always shapes us deeper into God's mission.[32] As opposed to possessing the Scriptures as a Master-Signifier for ourselves, this kind of preaching enables us to participate in Scripture so as to be shaped for hospitality and the inviting of the world into God's mission.

Likewise, the practice of Bible reading—both personal and corporate—changes from common evangelical habits of inductive Bible study and personal Bible study. There will always be a time and place for the explanatory study of the Bible academically, factually, and historically. Christians will always need to understand Scripture in its historical development. But if we seek to become a politic derived from the fullness of Christ within the triune history, this alone is insufficient. We need practices that draw us individually and corporately into the presence of Christ and the manifestation of Christ by the Spirit in the world. The church's discipleship, then, must include some of the ancient ways of reading Scripture, such as reading the lectionary in church gather-

31. I have written more extensively on this subject in *Great Giveaway*, ch. 5.

32. On this, see for example J. Wright, *Telling God's Story.* I have expounded further on this kind of preaching in my *Great Giveaway.* ch. 6.

ings and using the *lectio divina* approach to reading Scripture. Here the disciple reads Scripture, prays with Scripture, is silent before Scripture, is careful to listen, meditate, and even sing from within God's word in the Scriptures. This kind of immersion promotes communion in Christ through the Scriptures that leads us into being with Him in the world.

As evangelicals, if we would participate in the incarnate Christ, we must also learn to read Scripture communally within our churches. This is especially true of evangelicals in times of conflict. When times of conflict occur among a local people of God, as they inevitably do, we must practice intentionally gathering those concerned to practice humility, charity, and mutual submission, praying and listening to each other and the Holy Spirit over Scripture while discerning God's will together. We must ask, "What is God saying to us in this situation?" Out of these times, we break the divisive "inerrantist" habits of reading Scripture and learn to listen to the Spirit, through each other, recognizing the gifts (including the gifts of learned exegetes and teachers in our midst) and submitting to each other's gifts in the reading of Scripture communally.[33] We inhabit Scripture together towards the manifestation of Christ in a unity where we say corporately, with James in Acts 15, "It seems good to us and the Holy Spirit." Studying Scripture in this way, we become a community called out of our individual arrogances into submission to Christ and his mission for the world.

These are just some of the ways of speaking about and practicing the authority of Scripture that shape us into "a politic of fullness" in the world. As opposed to the previous ways that shaped us for arrogance and an exclusionary disposition towards others, these ways shape us corporately for hospitality, humility, and vulnerability in the world. As opposed to holding the Scriptures over people in both a defensive and coercive posture, we inhabit Scripture and its authority in our contexts. We do not grasp onto the Bible as a repository for all truth to wield it as a weapon. Instead, as a people we ourselves become participants via the Scriptures "in Christ" and his mission, taking on the posture of ever inviting the world into what God is doing.

We avoid the divinizing of the Bible as a divine object while refusing to make it only a muse for our own personal mystical experiences. The Scriptures and its language take on what James K. A. Smith calls

33. In this regard read Fowl, *Engaging Scripture*, ch. 3.

"an incarnational logic." The words speak of/embody Christ yet always point to a reality that is bigger than can be contained.[34] We are always in reception of God's revelation in Christ via the Scriptures. We are never grasping it for our own possession. We live as witnesses extending, by Scripture in the Holy Spirit, Christ's humble, non-violent, and even vulnerable presence in the world. These ways of articulating and practicing our belief in Scripture shape our political posture so as to embody Christ in his mission in the world. This is an incarnational politic. This is a politic of fullness.

Missional theologian David Bosch famously argued that the church must be understood in terms of the classic Christian doctrine of *missio Dei* and the Trinity. He said "God the Father and the Son sending the Spirit [is] expanded to include yet another 'movement': Father, Son, and Holy Spirit sending the church into the world."[35] The church, then, becomes an extension of the Trinity into the world as a participant in this sending, the *missio Dei*. By articulating the evangelical belief in Scripture in the terms set forth above—*our one true story of God for the whole world, infallible in and through Jesus Christ our Lord*—we in essence have the basis for becoming the church Bosch speaks about. The full political ramifications of Bosch's statement are realized as Christians ground themselves via Scripture as a people in Christ—the Sent One—and in the participation in the drama of God's mission where He is the center. Speaking about and practicing Scripture by the Holy Spirit in the ways articulated above makes such a politic possible. The politic of the church is shaped by Scripture as the very real incarnational presence of Christ extended by the Spirit into the world—a politic of fullness in the world.

---

34. This guards us from not only divinizing the Scriptures as an object but also from reducing its significance to anything more than personal mysticism. James K. A. Smith argues for a third way between the violence of kataphatics and the silence of apophatics. This third way is what Smith describes as the "incarnational logic" of language. In using this term here, I am drawing heavily from Smith, *Speech and Theology*, ch. 5.

35. Bosch, *Transforming Mission*, 390.

WHAT IS THE GOSPEL? RECOVERING THE CORE OF OUR BELIEF AND PRACTICE OF SALVATION

Moving to the second of the three evangelical beliefs, how can evangelicals speak about our belief and practice of salvation so that our political existence is bound into the very being of the Incarnation as the work of the triune God and his mission in the world? The way we have proclaimed the gospel via "the decision" has in essence separated us from this life "in Christ." It has bypassed the ordering of desire in our bodies, thus shaping us for a duplicitous politic in the world. How can we evangelicals speak about salvation and conversion (the gospel) so as to overcome this "empty politic" so that we are shaped for a politic of authentic witness in the world? Here, I contend we should look for direction to N. T. Wright, Michael Gorman, John Milbank, and Dallas Willard.

Biblical theologian N. T. Wright lays the groundwork for such a politic in the way he challenges the traditional evangelical/Protestant understanding of justification. He asks that we place justification squarely within the greater context of the entire covenantal promise of God with Israel "to set the world right."[36] He rejects a narrowly forensic view of "justification by faith." Justification, he argues, is less about one's pardon from personal guilt and more about entering into membership in the covenantal people of God in whom God is at work to fulfill his promises "to set the world right."[37] Righteousness is not so much a status of character imputed by God upon those who believe.[38] Rather it concerns God's faithfulness to his covenant with Israel to make all things right in the world.[39] To be justified, therefore, means to be set right with God in terms of the righteousness God is working out for the whole world. It is to participate in the bringing about of

---

36. In what follows, I am drawing on N. T. Wright's arguments found in simple form in *Justification*. Of his numerous other publications on the subject, see *Paul in Fresh Perspective*, *What Saint Paul Really Said*, and his commentary on *Letter to the Romans*.

37. In regard to justification, Paul "always had in mind God's declaration of membership, and that this always referred specifically to the coming together of Jews and Gentiles in faithful membership of the Christian family." N. T. Wright, *Justification*, 116.

38. N. T. Wright, *Justification*, 150. See also 63.

39. Ibid., 99.

this righteousness. It is not so much about putting our personal faith in God but rather about personally participating in God's faithfulness in what He is doing in and through Jesus Christ to make the world right (which of course requires personal faith).[40] God has inaugurated his Kingdom, the making of all things right, in and through the death, resurrection, and now reign of Christ. The gospel is that God is at work already in Christ making the world right, and we are invited personally to participate in this transformation.

Yet none of what Wright advocates negates the necessity for conversion. Indeed, none of what Wright advocates negates the (traditionally Reformed) substitutionary aspects of the atonement. There still must be a point when each believer enters God's work in Christ through faith. Likewise, for Wright, Christ certainly died as the representative lamb for the whole world within God's covenant with Israel. Jesus Christ in his obedience fulfilled God's covenant with Israel. Out of this great act of God in Christ, He has now begun to fulfill the purposes of his covenant with Israel: to make *all* things right, i.e., the establishment of the Kingdom of God. As a result, all who put their trust in him have their sins atoned for within the covenant promises of God. Yet this is only a part of God's overarching plan to "make the world right" through God's covenant. Our sins being atoned for in Christ is part of the larger whole of God reconciling the whole world to Himself in Christ Jesus (2 Cor 5:19). Conversion is still necessary. The whole goal here, however, is not singularly my own forensic pardon as an individual, although that is part of it. It is the reconciling of all things unto Himself, the Kingdom of God. This is God's mission in the world (the *missio Dei*).

---

40. N. T. Wright, as well as other "New Perspective" authors, point out the shift that takes place when we translate justified "by faith in Christ" in Gal 2:16 with the subjective genitive translation—the "faithfulness of Jesus Christ." In simple terms, it changes the nature of how we are justified, for we are now justified not (only) by personal faith alone in Christ but by joining in the faithfulness of Christ in the covenantal work of God in the world. We immediately move from a faith that is my own in Christ to the focus upon Christ's faithfulness to complete the covenant in obedience to the Father and our participation in that. See *Justification*, 117. Jesus becomes the fountainhead of a new corporate covenantal people who have been saved—put right with God and each other—as part of the first fruits of the covenantal promise of God to make the world right.

Wright's reformulation in essence makes justification impossible for the believer apart from his/her wider participation in the work of God in Christ by the Spirit to set the world right. I cannot possess this salvation as my own. I am justified only as I am a participant "in Christ," in the righteousness God is working in the world. There can be no distancing of myself from Christ in accepting God's pardon from sin made possible in Christ. In Christ, I find my status as one declared righteous only as part of the first fruits of the righteousness God is working for the whole world.[41] Individual salvation is a by-product of God's entire plan to restore the world. We enter into salvation in Christ by entering into the entire work of God in Christ by the Spirit for the mission of God in the world. "The decision," therefore, cannot be made complete in itself, to be possessed and promulgated all by itself. I do this not so much "that he may be my personal Savior," but "that I may be found in him (Phil 3:9a) . . . incorporated into the-Messiah-and-his-people," the people in which God has chosen to work for the redemption of the world.[42] This makes it impossible to turn anyone's conversion into the Master-Signifier of "the decision." Yet it retains the significance of one's conversion nonetheless.

Understanding justification in this way connects personal conversion ontologically to the Sent One's work to bring righteousness to the world. In Christ, we are invited to enter a salvation already in motion, of which we must become a part. We are joining in the Kingdom of God under Christ's Lordship. Following Wright, it would be impossible for one to be saved by faith in Christ without also being "in Christ." The order of salvation cannot be separated from the order of being. We are saved only as we *are* "in Christ," part of an ongoing participation in Christ, as God's mission in the world. We are grafted into a new politic, the people of God, that makes Christ the core from which God is working to make the whole world right. The gospel, framed in these terms, provides the basis for a "politic of fullness" in Christ.

Yet Wright lacks explicit attention to how this participation might transform the individual (sanctification) into an integrity with Christ and God's work in and through Him for the world. The historic later-

---

41. Wright, *Justification*, 150.
42. Ibid.

Reformed[43] evangelical separation of justification from sanctification in the *ordo salutis* made possible an individual's justification without entering into sanctification via "the decision" of evangelicalism. In other words, a person can "be saved" (within American evangelicalism) yet remain untouched in body and in concrete everyday life. Is it not still possible to continue this split with Wright as well? [44] Is it not also possible that believers can participate in "the justice of the world" without being transformed personally into "the making of all things right"? Is it not just as possible that "Christ's justice for the world" becomes a Master-Signifier as "the decision for Christ" has become? Could not "social justice" become another rallying cry (a master-signifier) accompanied by some token practices that reinforce the ideology serving to make us all feel better? As a result, we might still live untransformed, duplicitous lives that do not display the justice we preach (some may argue this already typifies evangelicalism as well as other Christians churches in the West). Are we then susceptible to another form of duplicitous social formation? Our belief and practice of salvation, therefore, must go one step further to describe how participation "in Christ" transforms one's body and one's desires into what God is doing in the world "to make all things right."

In this regard, New Testament scholar Michael Gorman offers additional directives. Gorman proposes that Pauline "justification by faith" must be understood in terms of participating in co-crucifixion with Christ. It is through "justification by co-crucifixion" that the individual participates in the covenant-fulfilling act of Christ that sets all things right.[45] Similar to Wright, Gorman sees no bifurcation between forensic and participatory models of justification in Paul. He contends that the forensic aspect of God's justification must be understood within the wider covenantal, relational, participatory, and transformative framework of the triune God's salvation in the world.[46] This transformative salvation-work in the world, however, must be understood in terms of the cruciform character of God as manifested in Christ. Salvation is, in

43. Again, we must take special care to distance Luther and Calvin from this problem. See n. 24, ch. 4.

44. At the time of this writing, Wright is coming out with a book *After You Believe* where I am sure he addresses directly this concern.

45. Gorman, *Inhabiting*, 45.

46. Ibid., 55.

essence, the transformation of our body-souls into the cruciform shape of Christ himself, which is the very character of God and how he works righteousness throughout the world.[47] In a certain sense, for Gorman, salvation is theosis. By participating in the continual crucifixion and rebirth in Christ, the believer embodies "the image of the kenotic, cruciform God revealed in the faithful and loving cross of Christ" (Phil 2:6–11). We are transformed into a "Spirit-enabled theosis" wherein justification and sanctification cannot be separated.[48]

Following Gorman eliminates the bypassing of desire in salvation. Justification by co-crucifixion is that daily putting to death of idolatry and injustice through crucifixion and the giving of oneself over to resurrection—the birthing of a new righteousness in Christ. Disordered desire in body and soul occurs when we worship something other than God.[49] Its outworking is idolatry ("impiety") and injustice. The justified are those who have begun the process of replacing idolatry ("impiety") and injustice with faith and righteousness (as well as love).[50] This righteousness is not a mere individual status before God. This is the birthing, through death and resurrection, of a new political righteousness in the world. There is a linking here between the transformation of our bodies and the transformation that God is working in the whole world, the *missio Dei.*

In this regard, Gorman melds together a more unified *ordo salutis* with the politic it produces in the world. He unites the believer's salvation (justification and sanctification) to a corporate participation in Christ—his death and resurrection—which reorders all desire, thereby birthing the new political justice/righteousness that God is bringing about in the world.[51] As believers participate in this *ordo*, argues Gorman, Christ births a cruciform politic that is always "kinetic" (nev-

---

47. "Theosis is transformative participation in the kenotic, cruciform character of God through Spirit-enabled conformity to the incarnate, cruciform, and resurrected/ glorified Christ." Gorman, *Inhabiting*, 162.

48. Ibid., 161.

49. Ibid., 50.

50. Ibid., 51.

51. ". . . justification is not a private experience, but a public and corporate one." *Inhabiting*, 70. See also his further expounding of the politic that is birthed out of the "justification by co-crucifixion" in *Inhabiting*, 94–99.

er static) ever engaging the world via the cross.[52] A politic of fullness is shaped that is active in the world for the reconciliation and restoration of all things "in Christ."

Putting Gorman together with Wright provides a basis for re-articulating the gospel for a politic of fullness. Wright helps us see how our salvation in Christ cannot be possessed—only corporately participated in as a matter of necessity. Entering into this salvation in Christ ontologically connects us to the work of the triune God and his continuing work in a people for the world. Gorman meanwhile adds the submission of our very bodies to this way of salvation in Christ for the world—his death and resurrection. Desire cannot be bypassed. And so, in the preaching of the gospel, a new politic is birthed that is ever shaping our bodies and souls into God's mission in the world.

This gospel of salvation "in Christ" disposes us as a people towards faithfulness as opposed to duplicity. As believers, we are bound together in the sacrificing of our bodies for the crucifixion of all idolatries (Rom 12:1-2). We are ever called to die. We are ever seeking the renewal and transformation of all things, personally as well as corporately. We do not hide behind "a decision" in search of a security in our salvation. There is no need. We are "in" Christ. Exposure of sin/idolatry is never a surprise, only an opportunity for further faithfulness through dying to it and being restored. We are never seeking to be confident in our own holiness. Instead, we are living before the world the politic of death and resurrection in Christ for the renewal of the whole world. Our witness is to the death and resurrection, the renewal and the healing that is always ongoing and available in Christ and His reign in the whole world.

Gorman and Wright together, therefore, overcome the evangelical split between justification and sanctification that made space for the evangelical Master-Signifier of "the decision." We cannot receive justification separate from daily participation "in Christ." We cannot rally around this gift as something already attained over against someone else. The question "Have you entered into the salvation already begun in Jesus Christ that God is working for the sake of the whole world?" trumps the question "have you made the decision to receive Christ as your personal Savior?" We proclaim this gospel only as we practice it

52. Ibid., 94–99.

daily by submitting to the reconciliation of all things in Him. We can only receive salvation as we participate in it for the world.

One of the founders of the Radical Orthodoxy movement, theologian John Milbank, helps us see how a trinitarian understanding of salvation works to refuse the duplicity inherent in "the decision." His "theology of the gift" illumines "the fullness" inherent in this articulation of salvation and the politic that springs forth from it.

For Milbank, the created world is determined by the category of "gift." Gift here is not the "gift" as determined by capitalist exchange wherein the only gift is one made unilaterally and with no expectation of return. By contrast, Milbank defines "gift" as that given by God the creator, "inexorably" in and through creation and ultimately in the gift of the incarnate Christ.[53] As opposed to a unilateral gift that asks for no return, this gift elicits an ongoing response, a reciprocity—the continual giving of a different gift in return.[54] This is the true ("purified") gift of the incarnate Christ that draws us into a reciprocity: a relationship with God based on the cycles of gratitude and obligation that gift giving perpetuates. Here, God gives out of plentitude and draws humanity into a never-ending gift exchange.

As with Wright and Gorman, Milbank shifts the focus of the gospel away from (the Reformed tendency to empower) the isolated Christian's "decision to receive" salvation by faith. He rejects the receiving of salvation as a unilateral gift that leaves us passive unto ourselves. For Milbank, when one receives the gift of salvation, one is caught up in the never-ending, reciprocal relation within the triune God as determined by the political ontology of the gift. The isolated self is called out of "self government" (and sin management) into a self that is determined by the reciprocal nature of God.[55] Salvation is received

53. Milbank, "Can a Gift be Given?" 135. The following summary of Milbank's "theology of gift" is drawn from "Can a Gift be Given?" Milbank later fleshed out this theology in additional articles and chapters of books including Milbank, *The Word Made Strange*, ch. 2; Milbank, "Soul Part One"; Milbank, "The Soul Part Two"; Milbank, *Being Reconciled*.

54. Milbank, "Can a Gift be Given?" 136.

55. See Milbank's "Can Morality Be Christian?" Here Milbank argues against the Barthian notion of command as the basis of a morality in relation with God. For Milbank, this morality cannot escape the ontology of violence inherent in the Cartesian self. He states, "In [this kind of] morality there is no love for the other nor opening to the other, but always and everywhere a principle of self-government, whether of the

via a corporate participation in the gift of Christ that shapes all desire towards God. As opposed to being distanced from Christ as a Cartesian self—making an individual decision to receive the gift of pardon and righteousness from God in Christ—the self actually receives a self as part of its corporate solidarity in Christ. Out of the plenitude of God, the gift of Christ draws all humanity into a trinitarian gift exchange. Here, there can be no self against other selves seeking personal assurance of grace and transformed life, for we are all caught up together in the fullness of God's gift giving and exchange. This is truly a "politic of fullness"—the church being caught up into an abundant participation in Christ as the core of our life together in God.

By placing the gospel of salvation in this framework, Milbank makes it impossible for one to separate our personal justification from the sanctification of our entire lives. Milbank takes aim at rectifying the later Reformed forensic accounts of salvation that leave the receiver lying passive with ones' desires untouched.[56] Evangelical understandings of the gospel often fall into this rut. As we have stated before, within this split between justification and sanctification lies the space for the Master Signifier: "the Decision."

In following Milbank, the one receiving salvation cannot avoid the reshaping of all desire into Christ's love. Receiving the gift is always an "active reception" that breeds the giving and return of love both vertically and horizontally.[57] Within this reciprocity—the give and take, call and response of the trinitarian gift exchange—all desire is shaped towards God. Our love is shaped towards union with the Godhead and His purposes. We grow in love—body and soul—towards God. There is no space for the duplicity that the split between justification and sanc-

---

soul or the city. In order that the totality may be . . . it must rule itself, divide itself from itself . . ." "Can Morality be Christian?" 223.

56. Milbank is more explicitly taking aim at Reformed Protestant accounts of forensic salvation in his *Being Reconciled*, ch. 8. In "Can a Gift be Given?" Milbank appears only implicitly to aim at Reformation theologies without naming them. J. Todd Billings contests whether Milbank has got it right in regards to Calvin and Reformed understandings of justification/sanctification in his "John Milbank's Theology of the 'Gift.'" Billings may be right on Milbank's critique holding no water for Calvin and Reformed theology; Milbank's arguments, however, certainly apply to the American evangelicalism that has developed in the wake of the Reformation several hundred years later.

57. Milbank talks about active reception in "Gregory of Nyssa."

tification in the *ordo salutis* breeds. As Milbank puts it, in God "One receives gift as the gift of an always preceding gift exchange. Only such a perspective makes sense of why agape arrives as an interpersonal event and not simply as a new command 'Thou shalt love . . .'." Instead of a new command to be obeyed, we are given the possibility of love because we are given the true shape of love in Christ. To be a Christian for Milbank, then, is *not* to spontaneously and freely love "of one's own originality."[58] It is rather to repeat and return in a never-ending series of returned (but never the same) gifts. Out of this movement, our desire is shaped, not out of a (Kantian) *agape* that loves in a detached, unconditional way (out of no obligation to return the gift), but into an *eros* that shapes our being into God, becoming part of the divine life itself in the Trinity.

Milbank illumines the fullness at the core of a politic shaped by a salvation centered in the triune God. Our lives as a politic become determined by the love and grace that flow abundantly into the world from our corporate reception and return of the gift in the incarnate Jesus Christ. Out of the trinitarian Godhead, we are formed as a people with no need to possess or hold onto our own righteousness over against others. We no longer need to make some "other" the object of resentment (such as "the gay/lesbian" who steals our enjoyment of our salvation) to make us feel good about what we don't have. We are always being filled. This way of believing and practicing the gospel, therefore, shapes a corporeality into both faithfulness to Christ and integrity in Christ.

Wright, Gorman, and Milbank then lead us to a gospel that births a politic of fullness in Christ for God's mission in the world. We do not need to compromise the evangelical call for conversion. The call for conversion, however is no longer, "Have you made the decision to receive Christ as your personal Savior?" It is, *"Have you entered into the salvation begun in Jesus Christ that God is working for the sake of the whole world?"* A decision will still eventually happen in the believer, but the focus has changed. This salvation is only salvation "for me" after I have submitted to, entered into, and been immersed in the righteousness God is working for the whole world—"the making of all things right." In this respect, it truly is a conversion that rejects any duplicity.

58. Milbank, "Can a Gift be Given?" 150.

It is a conversion that demands the daily dying to idolatries and daily renewal in the Spirit for the new world coming. It is a decision to enter a life that never ends.

This gospel requires a renewal of our practices of salvation in the evangelical church. At the very least, evangelicals must reinvigorate the initiatory process of adult baptism as the site for true conversion. The famous altar call for "a decision" should not be easily ridiculed. The church ever needs to be calling people into repentance and conversion. Yet to call the new believer into true conversion requires an entrance into a whole new realm of life in Christ together for God's mission in the world. Historically, this has been the process of catechesis, centered around either confirmation or adult baptism. This is not the place to debate the merits of infant versus adult baptism. In a decidedly more post-Christendom context, however, adult baptism/re-consecration of baptism becomes essential as a place of intentional spiritual formation. These processes of baptism must be deepened beyond the singular act of obedience/public confession of faith that is so prominent in evangelical churches still today. [59] It must become a process of turning that leads into the life of ever dying and rising with Christ for the sake of God's mission.

Likewise, our practice of evangelism must be shaped differently. Within the once-massive Protestant consensus of North America, evangelicals assumed they could train Christians to present a gospel message based in the post-Reformed understandings once attached to the substitutionary atonement.[60] This led to "the decision" where one prayed the "sinners' prayer" and accepted (received) the gift of salvation in Christ—pardon for sin and eternal life with God. Years later, this practice opened a space for the development of the Master-Signifier "the decision." Today we can no longer assume that the presentation of four "laws" and an isolated "sinner's prayer" is a sufficient initiation for the new believer. Instead of training people in methods that are susceptible to making salvation a transaction (a gift exchange of the kind Milbank eschews), we must teach Christians themselves to become "onramps" who through their lives offer non-Christians an avenue upon which people can enter the work God is doing in Christ

59. A good example of such a project is Webber, *Journey to Jesus.*

60. The Four Spiritual Laws, the Bridge Illustration, the Romans Road are all approaches like this with accompanying publications.

to reconcile the world to Himself (2 Cor 5:19). This of course requires a re-orientation of evangelistic practice. It requires Christians themselves to be of the disposition described above—living the politic of death and resurrection in Christ for the renewal of the whole world. It requires Christians to themselves be part of a politic that embodies the transformative reconciliation God is working in our midst and reflect that to the world-at-large.

Such a re-articulation of the gospel results in a new communal disposition towards the world. From the pretentious "Do you know where you are going when you die?," we come to the world offering a welcome: *"to enter the salvation begun in Jesus Christ that God is working for the sake of the whole world."* We do not characterize salvation in terms of "you receive this and this" if by faith you believe. Instead, salvation is a joining in with God in "the setting of all things right." It is an invitation to extend the reign of God in Christ over your life and into the world wherever sin, death, and evil still linger. The offer of salvation becomes, "Come and put your entire life under the reign of Christ for the transformation God is working to make the world right," "come and live under his Lordship over the world." In this way, no new Christian can miss that "in Christ" you are going from living for yourself, out of yourself, in yourself with all the things that you have become entangled in, to living "in Christ" where the entirety of our lives is transformed into the Kingdom politic God is bringing via the Holy Spirit for the whole world. In a practice like this, a politic of fullness is born to engage the world for the salvation of the world.

Such a gospel calls for a renewal of discipleship practices in evangelicalism. Discipleship is the shaping of desires, vision, and character into Christ, his Kingdom, and his mission for the world. This demands practices of spiritual formation. In this regard, the spiritual formation movement led by Dallas Willard and Richard Foster is already calling evangelicalism towards practices of immersion as the means to grow our people into followers of Christ into his mission. Beyond traditional, individualist evangelical discipleship that concentrates on personal Bible study, prayer, and service to the local church, Willard and others articulate spiritual disciplines as a natural extension of one's life in Christ. These disciplines include individual practices of solitude, centering prayer, *lectio divina*, confession and praying the hours, as well as other types of prayer. These disciplines also include corporate practices such as regular Eucharist, worship, communal meals and fellowship, and external practices such as service to the poor and the hurting. These disciplines, properly modeled, apprentice old and new believers alike to step into the reign of God. We coach new believers in how to "step into this by faith," "depend upon the Holy Spirit for this in your life," "discern this evil among the poor and exert the authority of Christ over evil." In the words of Dallas Willard, we invite people to "be put into motion in the Kingdom of God" by which they are saved.[61] In these practices the disciple learns how to ask "What is God doing, what is God saying?" in the situations of everyday life. The same disciples then learn to respond. These "disciplines" are not secluded away from the community so that they devolve into individualist legalism and behavior reinforcement therapy. They become a part of our every day life together. They breed a new politic of fullness.

Together, these ways of speaking about and practicing the gospel shape us as evangelicals into a new politic of faithfulness. As opposed to the previous ways that shaped us for duplicity, these ways shape us for living in Christ for God's mission in the world. As opposed to grasping hold of our secure status before God via Christ, we "own" our salvation in another way: by participating together with others in the fullness of Christ, ever inviting others into his Kingdom at work in the world. We are connected to Christ at the core of our politic.

Our witness to the gay and lesbian peoples among us takes a different shape politically. Instead of posturing ourselves into a morally superior position, we humbly and vulnerably invite all into the politic of the incarnate One, the cruciform community. We are a community involved in a "mutually transforming" politic in Christ. We offer this way of transformation to all people by first dying ourselves in order to be resurrected to a new life. We make no pre-judgments. Yet there is no entry into transformation apart from all desire being discerned via the death and resurrection of Christ for the renewal of the world. We listen, we show the way to transformation, and we invite all to join in with us as we confess our sins together and receive the Spirit and are transformed.

---

61. These words "put into motion in the Kingdom of God" I first heard from Dallas Willard at the Ecclesia National Gathering in Washington DC in 2010.

We need not hide our sin in a false duplicity, for we are ever participating before the world in dying and being born again. We no longer hold onto our status of being saved while concealing our lack in holiness. There is an integrity to our dying as well as rising. We are participating in the healing of desire that Christ is bringing to the whole world. In this integrity of being, a corporate disposition is bred in the world: that of faithfulness to attending to God's restorative grace.

Missional theologian Darrell Guder has argued that "the people of God must have a visible, tangible, experienceable shape. This is not however, simply a sociological or organizational necessity. It is essential to the *missio Dei*."[62] In other words, in order for Christians to participate in God's mission, the local politic of the church must embody the gospel in integrity and in faithfulness in its very social constitution. This is the very nature of the missional "witness" of the church. The Greek word for witness in the New Testament is *marturia*, the root for martyr. Guder states that *marturia* refers to one's entire life as a sign testifying to the good news of the gospel.[63] For Guder, this is the kind of witness that makes possible the church's participation in the mission. If Guder is right, then the politic of salvation pointed to by Wright, Gorman, and Milbank becomes all the more essential for the missional evangelical church. Only such a politic of fullness can overcome the politic of duplicity of which we evangelicals have been guilty. Only within such a politic grafted into the ongoing Incarnation itself can we witness corporately in our own bodies the salvation God is bringing to the whole world.

Where Is the Kingdom? Recovering the Core of Our Belief and Practice of the Church in Society

Moving to the last of evangelicalism's three doctrinal commitments, how can evangelicals speak about our belief and practice of the church in society so that our political existence is bound into the very being of the Incarnation as the work of the triune God and his mission in the world? "The Christian Nation" made God's work in the world into a

---

62. Guder, *Continuing Conversion*, 146.

63. Guder refers to a footnote in Selwyn's commentary on 1 Peter where he tabulates that the number of times the New Testament uses *marturia* to describe the dissemination of the gospel outnumbers *kerygma* six to one. Ibid., 53.

concept (Master-Signifier) that we can fight for "out there." It made us prone to practicing a righteousness over against those who would steal our moral society from us. In the process, we became detached from God's justice in and among our everyday lives. "The Christian nation," therefore shaped us into a dispassion for the world. Yet to center the church's politic in the incarnate Christ and his reconciliation *among us* risks turning "the church" inward. How do we live together, seeking his concrete Reign in our midst, without in turn acting as if the Kingdom is only here in this place? If God's righteousness and justice is an outworking of Christ's Reign, how does our political existence extend His Reign into the world without making "the Kingdom" itself a Master-Signifier, repeating the same mistake of "the Christian Nation." For help on these questions, I propose we look to Henri de Lubac, William Cavanaugh, and John Howard Yoder.

We look first to Catholic theologian Henri de Lubac, because his *ressourcement* of the patristic doctrine of "the threefold body" of Christ gives us the wherewithal to speak about the church in ways that ground its very being in the incarnate Christ.[64] De Lubac, a French Jesuit theologian, sought to retrieve the historical threefold distinction of Christ's body. There was a) the physical historical body of Jesus of Nazareth; b) the body of Christ present in the sacramental elements of the Eucharist, and then; c) the church itself—the ecclesial body of Christ.[65] Together, these three aspects compose the *one* Body of Christ. The ecclesial body is the visible body (the true body) of Christ in the world as it is brought into being at the celebration of the Eucharist.[66] According to de Lubac, however, this reality was lost in church history. From Patristic times via "the threefold body," the visible church was originally the focus of the real body—the true body. In the later stages of Medieval Christendom, however, the Eucharist became the focus of the real body, and the church became marginalized as the "mystical body."[67] De Lubac traces

64. De Lubac's work has stirred a new interest in "the threefold body" via the works of John Milbank, Graham Ward, and William Cavanaugh.

65. De Lubac cites William of Saint Thierry on *The Threefold Body of Our Lord*. De Lubac, *Catholicism*, 388. Cavanaugh's summary of this can be found in *Torture and Eucharist*, 212.

66. As de Lubac states, "Literally speaking, therefore, the Eucharist makes the church." De Lubac *Corpus Mysticum*, 88.

67. Ibid., 41, 107. Thanks to Jonathan Foiles for these insights into de Lubac's

how, during these times, the doctrine of "the mystical body," which taught how Christ as "the head" incorporated the church by the Spirit into his very body, became the means to marginalize the social reality of the church as the real body of Christ. The church became mystical in the sense of invisible. The Eucharist became the focus. It became a spectacle. The church as social body was rendered passive and invisible in the world, thereby losing its wherewithal to be a political reality. It became a society of individuals bound together by the regular spectating of the Eucharist.

From this account of "the threefold body," de Lubac asks a question to Catholics that can just as easily be asked of evangelicals regarding their belief and practice of the church: Have we become a society of individuals bound together by a form of spectating? Whether it be an evangelical megachurch gospel presentation or a large evangelical gathering to hear the preacher, it could be argued that evangelicals have been caught up in the same spectating of which de Lubac speaks. We too thereby become invisible in the world. In these large events, enhanced with video and "podcast" technologies, the church becomes defined as the meeting of the invisible, which then defines our engagement with society in the same manner. We are forced to engage society by rallying the individuals who gather together on Sunday around a Christian ideal for society. They then are sent out as a voluntarist work force for this Christian ideal in the world. This makes possible the making of a Master-Signifier out of our engagement with society ("the Christian nation"). For de Lubac, it is at the Eucharistic table where such an invisible church can (and should) be resisted. Here believers are conjoined into the visible body of Christ under the Lordship of the Risen Christ. Here the social reality of His body takes shape as we practice the forgiveness, reconciliation, and mutual sharing of a new justice in Christ's reign. Here we become the justice of God as opposed to individuals who campaign for it as a slogan in the world. It becomes more difficult to make a Master-Signifier out of God's work in the world because this work is "us." But does this visible body engage society? In terms of Christ's Kingdom, does de Lubac's threefold body domesticate God's

---

Corpus Mysticum. De Lubac's argument is highlighted by Cavanaugh in *Torture and Eucharist*, 212.

work in the Eucharist so that the Kingdom can only happen here via the Eucharistic community?

In this regard, Catholic theologian William Cavanaugh takes de Lubac further. In his book *Torture and Eucharist*, he shows how the Eucharist births a political presence that engages society for redemption and renewal. This is a social presence that neither recoils into sectarian withdrawal nor becomes territorial and imperialistic in its engagements with society. We discern "the body" around the Eucharistic table through the practices of reconciliation, excommunication, and the mutual participation in receiving of Christ's body. A politic is thus born. Christ's reign becomes visible as we embody the infinite gifting of forgiveness, faithfulness, and love.[68] Yet this way of being together births the Kingdom not only among "us." It enables us to resist alternative politics of violence and isolation, to subvert them, and indeed to draw the world into the restoration of all things, i.e., the Kingdom of God.

Cavanaugh illustrates all of this with the example of the base communities of Chile in the 1980s. Here, in everyday Eucharistic political formation, Cavanaugh shows how these communities subverted the ways of isolation, separation, division, and antagonism that characterized the politics of torture in Pinochet's Chilean regime. He asserts that the Eucharistic community makes possible the same type of engagement within the political structures of Western liberal democracy and capitalism. De Lubac's "threefold body," therefore, is hardly ingrown and hardly territorial. It is a subversive political presence against the unjust powers of this world and for the extension of Christ's rule.

De Lubac and Cavanaugh display how the church's enfleshment of Christ impacts society. Nonetheless, despite Cavanaugh's best efforts, one still wonders whether such a concentric view of the church can do anything more than be subversive. Beyond the subversive tactic, can such a church envision that God's Reign is already at work in the world outside the church for his mission and join in beyond its own boundaries? If it cannot, will such a church inevitably become territorial and closed off to mission? Representing some of these challenges is Nathan Kerr's book *Christ, History and Apocalyptic*.

---

68. I am summarizing Cavanaugh, *Torture and Eucharist*, 234–36.

For Kerr, any primordial identity of the church prior to engagement with the world assumes a territorial posture towards the world.[69] Any politically "concentric" understanding of the church's relation to the "wider world" implies the church's "intensified concern for its own interior identity" so much so that its engagement with the world becomes a subsidiary of its own existence.[70] Jesus by default becomes domesticated by the church and becomes part of its own ideology. It therefore becomes imperialistic in its engagements with the world. Consequently, for Kerr, a church politic such as de Lubac's is unsuitable for mission.

Kerr criticizes Stanley Hauerwas's ecclesiology, and derivatively de Lubac's as well, when he states "the ontologization of the church's political worship risks conceiving the church's liturgy as an 'interior volume, a prior preparatory space (separated from the world) that is the most elemental space-time of the formation of peoplehood.'" Kerr's worry is that such an understanding of the church means that everything that is real, that is of God in Christ, must happen here in this space! It "effects an ecclesiological domestication of the work of the Spirit."[71] This defeats mission, for it says that we cannot go out into the world and participate in the Spirit working there. He only works here in our church!

Kerr challenges not only de Lubac and Cavanaugh's notions of the church but the very notion of a "politic of fullness" as put forth in this book. If anything, for Kerr, a "politic of fullness" with a defined core in the incarnate Christ is something to be overcome for mission, not the very foundation of it. Much like the popular missional authors Alan Hirsch and Michael Frost, Kerr essentially advocates that missiology must precede ecclesiology in the formation of the church (and Christology must precede both).[72] For Kerr, "mission makes the church," as opposed to

---

69. Kerr, *Christ, History and Apocalyptic*, 171–73.

70. Ibid., 171.

71. Ibid., 169–70. Kerr is quoting Roman Coles here and playing off Coles' statements in Hauerwas and Coles, *Christianity, Democracy*, 210–11.

72. See for instance Hirsch, *Forgotten Ways*, 142, 144–45, where he says, "Christology determines missiology, and missiology determines ecclesiology." A little further down Hirsch says, "We first engage in incarnational mission, and the church, so to speak, comes out of the back of it." These are classic expressions of the popular notion of what Kerr is arguing for.

de Lubac where "the Eucharist makes the church." Kerr pushes, therefore, for a church that is dispossessed—without place or center—always diasporic, scattered into the world.[73] Here, in the encounter with the world, is "the very 'non-site' of the church's gathering."[74] The church is always coming into being in the event of mission—the encounter with the other as the outpouring of God's love in Christ into the world.

The question, however, remains: How does Christ arrive at this missional encounter post-ascension? If not via the church—its continuous social embodiment of Christ via the Spirit through its ongoing practices in the world—are we not dependent upon individual, mystical relationships with Christ that somehow seek to inhabit missional contexts?[75] Is not Kerr relying on Spirit-led individuals to discern the Spirit in the world, a means so prominent already in evangelical church practice? There is no coming together, no political presence in this. Surely Kerr is advocating more. Yet Kerr seeks to avoid the materialization of the church in ways that recall the evangelical Protestant antipathy towards the visible church.[76] He sees the church as a sign or a "sacrament" which always points forward to the gathering that is to come. It is an ever-provisional new recurrence of Christ's love coming into being in the encounter with "the other" in mission. The church comes into being in its "continual conversion to the living Lord Jesus Christ in the world."[77] The church, then, according to Kerr, is the ever open, non-territorial enactment of Jesus love in the world.

73. Kerr, *Christ, History, and Apocalyptic*, 181.

74. Ibid., 192.

75. This seems to be the criticism most appropriate to missional authors Alan Hirsch and Michael Frost who seem to imply an "evangelical-like" immediate access to the "wild Messiah" version of Jesus for all individuals who read the gospels as the basis for Missional contextualization. See Frost and Hirsch together, *ReJesus*.

76. Long has traced this as the "protestant principle." See Long, *Divine Economy*, 136. See Tillich, *Systematic Theology*, I:37; and *Systematic Theology*, II:243–45. According to the "Protestant principle," anything that is temporal and historical is too impure to ultimately be Christian. Christ therefore is always removed from concrete politics. We cannot expect that Christ actually affects real concrete politics in an ultimate way among a people that indeed choose to follow Him.

77. I am quoting Kerr's words here from his comments made in a blog post on his book. See http://churchandpomo.typepad.com/conversation/2009/03/christ-history -and-apocalyptic-nate-kerrs-response.html. Although there are significant differences between Kerr and Guder, Kerr echoes Darrell Guder's title of his classic missional text *Continuing Conversion*.

Many of Kerr's themes resonate with the current missional church movement. Kerr provides foundations for many of its central themes including a) "missiology precedes ecclesiology"[78]; b) "the continual conversion of the church,"[79] and; c) "the dispersed nature of the church."[80] The enduring question, however, remains from our study: does Kerr's "non-sited-church" provide for the "subjectivizing" of Christians into yet another Master-Signifier, thereby defeating mission as opposed to making it possible? Or, perhaps worse, do Kerr's proposals leave Christians susceptible to some other form of ideology when they are left devoid of political formation in the church, thereby undercutting mission as well?

If we follow Žižek, the answer to both questions must be "yes." For if we are left with no material church in the world constituted by the Eucharist, "the church in the world" is then at least open to becoming a concept/signifier we pursue in the world as individuals. Our allegiance to it becomes susceptible to an ideologization of an "empty" kind. Having rejected any "politic of fullness," we are prone once again (just as evangelicals were the first time) to being shaped around a lack— aligning ourselves with a cause for the identity and protection it provides us. Such an "empty" politics is incompatible with mission, for it inevitably shapes us for complicity and/or antagonism with those who are "not us." The challenge, then, is that if we reject all "politics of fullness" for the church, how can the authentic Christian avoid being put at the mercy of one more empty politic driven by antagonisms formed by ideology? For we are all subjects of political formation according to Žižek.[81] Every believer (or any one else for that matter) who has no politic from which to live will find one. We can only assume, then, that every believer will eventually become the subject of yet another ide-

---

78. See again Hirsch, *Forgotten Ways*, 142–45.

79. Guder, *Continuing Conversion*.

80. The "dispersing of the church" is a theme, for example, in Frost, *Exiles*, as well as what lies behind the whole argument against attractional models of church in Christendom. This anti-attractional argument circulates among many of "the missional church" authors. See for example Hirsch and Frost, *Shaping of Things to Come*, ch. 2.

81. In other words, there can be no subject apart from one's subjectivization into a political ideology. We are all subjects in this way.

ology, one where Christ is not at the core, and by default a politic of emptiness is birthed all over again.

In essence then, Kerr's individualist de-ecclesiologized cultural engagement is prone to the same mistakes as evangelicalism. Over against Kerr, however, these problems dissolve once we embrace the church as a "politic of fullness." We need not worry with Kerr that such a politic is inevitably territorial and/or closed off from the world because if the church indeed becomes the very body of Christ in the world à la de Lubac, then it should necessarily embody the very disposition of incarnation in the world in its politic. Such a political presence takes on the humble, open, vulnerable, and hospitable position of Christ in the world as it is formed "in Christ," the Sent One of the Father extended in life and being by the Holy Spirit. Its very politic inhabits the posture of a servant to the world. It incarnates compassion by living along and among the struggles of those cultures we inhabit as Christ. Only in the church's participation in the triune work of God in Christ by the Spirit for the whole world can our attempts to "live together" as church in the world avoid becoming the antagonistic, territorial, and violent politic that Kerr fears.

De Lubac's "threefold body," therefore, should not be seen as a politic devoid of mission. De Lubac himself sought to resist these tendencies in Catholicism. He sought a political presence that participated in the Incarnation as part and parcel of the triune God's work in the whole world.[82] More than de Lubac, however,[83] it is Anabaptist theologian John Howard Yoder who makes explicit how a "politic of fullness" can not only answer the problem of an "empty politic" but can also address Kerr's warning that any such concentric politic is one that is shut off from mission. Yoder shows us more explicitly than de Lubac how

---

82. To quote Balthasar's characterization of de Lubac referring to his *Catholicism*— one of the places where de Lubac outlines "the threefold body": "His major work, *Catholicisme*, which sets the style and orientation for all that will follow, reveals the fundamental decision as a decision for fullness, totality, and the widest possible horizon—it is precisely the power of inclusion that becomes the chief criterion of truth— so that, negatively, it becomes a major concern of his to point out where the entire tradition, and in particular the ecclesial and theological tradition, has become narrow or rigid . . ." Balthasar, *Theology of Karl Barth*, 28–29.

83. De Lubac's first concern was the theology of the Eucharist itself, less with the socio-political dimensions of the Eucharist and the church. For this reason, the open and "catholic" posture of the body of Christ in the world is less prominent in his work.

the church, by its members participating directly in Christ's Lordship, constitutes the open incarnational presence of Christ as participant in the triune God's mission for the whole world. He helps us see how centering our politics in Christ and his Reign necessarily participates in his Kingdom at work beyond the church.

For Yoder, more than any other theological figure of the twentieth century, the incarnate Jesus could not be separated from a concrete, on-the-ground politic in the world. Jesus could not be sequestered from the world as a purely personal Savior for the individual who is lost in sin. Neither could he be reduced to an ahistorical exemplar for Christian moral principles to be followed in personal and social life. For Yoder, Jesus, in his life, death, resurrection, and exaltation, ushered in the Reign of God. In his authority as exalted Lord a new social order had begun.[84] God has begun a new political "Kingdom" to be lived in and witnessed to ahead of its final consummation in the age to come.

For Yoder, this new political order takes shape when the authority of Jesus inhabits the practices of Christian community. In contrast with de Lubac where the social "body of Christ" is brought into being at the Eucharist, or Barth, where "the church" is brought into being at the proclamation of the Word, for Yoder, this "politics of Jesus" is brought into being via the Lord of the church inhabiting its sociality via "the gifts" and what Yoder called the practices of "body politics."[85] In his book *Body Politics*, he describes five practices—binding and losing, breaking bread together, baptism, the universal ministry of the gifts, and the rule of conversation (Paul)—which bind individuals together under a living social relationship to Jesus as Lord. The very authority and presence of Jesus Christ—the Lord of the church and the world— inhabits the universal ministry of the gifts in the community. This is "the fullness of Christ." For Yoder, this fullness of Christ describes a new mode of political existence.[86] The distribution of the gifts and their inhabitation by the Spirit are all "part of the victory of Christ."[87] By participating in these five practices, Christ's Reign is present in the church community by the Spirit, birthing a politic in and for the world.

---

84. This is all most famously presented in Yoder's magnus opus, *Politics of Jesus*.

85. Yoder, *Body Politics*. Yoder also treats these practices in his *Priestly Kingdom*, 22–34, 93–94.

86. Yoder, *Body Politics*, 47.

87. Ibid., 48.

Yoder even suggests that these five practices should be designated sacraments: human action in which God acts definitively in the flesh-and-blood world of daily living.[88] And so here in the dynamic processes of Christian community, Christians are united into a politic of Jesus, with the Incarnate Christ at its core in the form of an actual participation (through the "body practices") in the Lordship of Christ in the world.

This politic, however, though concentric in nature, hardly creates the territorial church that Kerr is worried about.[89] Instead, for Yoder the church and world are "two levels of the pertinence of the same Lordship of Christ."[90] There is no dividing line between the church and the world. The church may precede the world today, yet it is only living today what the world itself is ultimately called to in the future.[91] The Kingdom is breaking in among us as a foretaste of the final victory of the King. The church in essence bleeds into the world, ever calling it to its true destiny.[92] As a foretaste of the renewal of all creation, the church cannot be discontinuous with creation. Neither can it be discontinuous with the world, because the church is in the process of becoming that very world renewed in Christ. The church cannot merely blend into the world, for then all mission and renewal is lost. Its presence will be in, among, and for the world, even as it will be distinct from the world. This is what it means to take on the incarnational nature of Christ. It is this very incarnational nature that requires the church to be a discerning community that at times both refuses conformity with the world while at other times joins in with what God is already at work doing in the world via the Holy Spirit. As Yoder puts it, loving the world as well as refusing conformity to it are "two sides of the same coin" of the church's incarnational presence in the world.[93]

88. Ibid., 71, See also for example *Priestly Kingdom*, 93–94.

89. Yoder has long battled the Niebuhrian prejudice that any Anabaptist form of ecclesiology necessarily implies a tribalistic sectarian withdrawal or even a coercive posture towards the world. See Yoder, "How H. Richard Niebuhr Reasoned" for a rebuttal of this prejudice.

90. Yoder, *Body Politics*, ix

91. Ibid., ix

92. In fact, Yoder presents these five practices as offering a pattern for the life of the larger society. Ibid., x.

93. Ibid., 79. In Yoder's words elsewhere, "When we then speak of Incarnation it must not mean God sanctifying our society and our vocations as they are, but rather His reaching into human reality to say what we must do and what we must leave be-

What makes such a social presence incarnational is the very social embodiment of the vulnerability and servanthood that characterizes God's sending of the Son. For Yoder, the church is formed around an obedience to Christ that follows the way of the cross into the world. This is the ultimate renouncing of worldly power. Over against territorialism or coercion, by following him who "emptied himself," taking the form of a servant who humbled himself, becoming "obedient to the point of death," we participate in Christ's being in the world (Phil 2:3–11 RSV). We take on the very disposition of Christ in all its particularity, including "the love of the adversary, the dignity of the lowly, repentance, servanthood and the renunciation of coercion."[94] We are shaped into the disposition of Christ's body in and for the world. "Identifying with the incarnation . . . as the motivation and the power of Christian obedience . . ." changes our very posture in the world so that we are always identifying ourselves "with the 'other,' the enemy."[95] This vulnerability and openness defines the very posture of church in the world. In this posture the church is enabled to participate in the triune work of God in the world. It makes possible a joining in with his coming Kingdom. It makes possible a participation in his mission. It is a politic that joins in with God "when he works among us, aligned with the ultimate triumph of the Lamb."[96]

For Yoder, such a community of openness depends upon our common assent to the words "Jesus is Lord." God reigns in Christ, and His Kingdom is manifesting itself over our lives. Yet He reigns over the whole world, "for he must reign until he has put all his enemies under his feet" (1 Cor 15:25 NIV). It is the sovereignty of God over the world that allows us to resist controlling the world, for we can only participate in God's work by submitting ourselves to it. To say "Jesus is Lord" assents to an authority that "is not coercive" and never "imposed, only offered."[97] This is because true power, the authority of the Lamb, is manifest in vulnerability and weakness. The person who is secure, who knows he/she possesses truth, who is grounded and not afraid can be vulner-

---

hind." Yoder, *Original Revolution*, 112.

94. Yoder, *Royal Priesthood*, 258

95. Yoder, *For the Nations*.

96. Yoder, *Politics of Jesus*, 238.

97. Yoder, *For the Nations*, 25.

able, completely non-violent, for he/she knows where history is going. For Yoder, the affirmation that "Jesus is Lord" binds us into dialogical vulnerability and relationality with the world. Similar to Kerr, for Yoder the church's centering in Christ happens in the becoming vulnerable to encounter with the otherness of history. Any separation from being "in Christ," any ceasing in the practice of encountering outsiders in peace, love, and caritas, and the church loses its distinctiveness and becomes assimilated into the violence of the world.[98]

For Yoder, then, the church is an "open community of witness" in the world. Pluralism is not a cause for fear. The event of Babel in Genesis 11, the dividing of the world into languages and cultures, is not the result of sin or a fall. Rather, it was God's designed plan to prevent people from taking God's will into their hands. Humanity is now dependent upon each other by design in order to learn in submission to His Lordship in mutual vulnerability.[99] By constant dialogue and openness we are ever able to grow beyond our own finite points of history. Still, many will see the affirmation "Jesus is Lord" and the stance of vulnerability to be mutually incompatible.[100] Yoder shows us that indeed the two are inseparable and one can only be carried with the other.

All of this amounts to a "politic of fullness" that makes mission possible. Christ is the ontological core of this politic brought into being by the mutual participation in the practices and gifts of the Spirit in the Christian community. Rather than inhibiting mission, however, this politic makes it possible in three ways. It makes possible the church's incarnational inhabitation of the world as the very extension of the Sent One by the Father through the work of the Holy Spirit. The church takes on the very vulnerability and servanthood of Christ himself. This is the basis of witness in the world. Second, it makes possible the community's participation and discernment of the Kingdom

---

98. In other words, for Yoder, any other approach is Constantinian in posture, which assumes we are in control of the world.

99. Outlined by Yoder in his "Meaning After Babel"

100. According to Romand Coles, "Could it be that the jealousy of Jesus as Lord— not just the concept, but as stories, dispositions, habits, practices—is entwined with and works in spite of itself toward the closure of the church's generous and receptive participation in historical generativity?" Coles, *Beyond Gated Politics*, 135.

by neither blending in nor remaining separate from the world.[101] We know God's reign is manifesting itself in our midst as a foretaste of what is to come. By seeing his manifest kingdom take shape socially among us by the Spirit, we can then better discern God by the Spirit working in the world so as to join in the bringing of it to fulfillment in our midst. Mission cannot be a program of the church. Rather we, as His sent people, are a participant in God's *missio* in the world. Lastly, it provides a porous boundary between the church and the world because the church is living already where God is taking the world. The church is an open, vulnerable, and ever moving social presence centered in Christ's reign. It is a centered set as opposed to a bounded set, as missiologist Paul Hiebert once famously described. There is a center within the social space by which the multitudes surrounding it are moving either towards it or away from it, but there is no firm boundary that is maintained to keep people in or out.[102] In this way, we participate in God's mission in the world.

Yoder, de Lubac, and Cavanaugh, therefore, lead us in a way of speaking about and practicing "the church in the world" that breeds "a politic of fullness." Evangelicals have put forth the church as *Christ's voluntarist army dispersing individuals into the world to do the work of Christ and his mission.* This is insufficient because such a dispersion would surely repeat the making of another Master-Signifier. It makes the church's work in the world something abstract that we fight for outside of "us." Yoder, de Lubac, and Cavanaugh point us to the church as *the social body of His Lordship (His Reign) incarnating Christ in the world for God's mission.* They help us see that much more than a democracy,[103] the church is the constitution of a new way of being

101. As Yoder is fond of saying, the church "precedes the world epistemologically." Yoder, *Priestly Kingdom*, 11. Instead of hindering mission, however, Yoder sees this precedence making it possible.

102. Hiebert's "bounded set-centered set" missiological theory is described most accessibly in his "Category 'Christian.'" It is used profusely among missional authors. See for example Allan Roxburgh's "Missional Leadership"; Hirsch and Frost, *Shaping of Things to Come*, 47–49. For a summary of the idea, see also Volf, *Exclusion and Embrace*, 71, n.3.

103. The danger with Yoder is that the church becomes a form of democracy where the sacraments become merely the servants of a form of social-economic organization. This is why it is important that de Lubac and Cavanaugh provide a balancing corrective.

together in the world. It is the social incarnation of the Sent One, by the Spirit, the foretaste of His Kingdom, which inhabits the world for mission. Under these terms, we cannot make a Master-Signifier of God's work in the world because this work is "us." Neither can we as individual Christians become subject to another ideology. Here, in our participation in Christ's social body, we participate in his inbreaking Rule as a politic together. We are shaped to join in with the Kingdom God is bringing forth in the world.

This way of speaking about the church changes the way evangelicals practice being the church. For instance, on Sundays, we gather not to attract people into church, whether they be wandering Christians or those outside the faith. Gathering as spectators keeps us as individuals looking for a cause to justify our existence in the world. It shapes us to seek for "a cause" in the world instead of living "out there" what God is already doing among us. It sets us up to serve another empty signifier.

Instead, we gather on Sundays to be shaped together into his body for the world. We practice the Eucharist, thereby becoming a reconciled people carrying the forgiveness and new life of God's salvific work "in Christ" into the world. We gather here before the proclaimed Word from which we are formed into the reality that Jesus is Lord. We then enter the world with the eyes to see God at work in the world. The preaching of the Word, therefore, is not a slick presentation to distribute information for personal Christian self-improvement. It is the gathering of Christians to submit to the "reality of his Lordship" in the Spirit as manifested among us and from which we can respond in obedience into his mission. We also gather to practice the mutual sharing of the gifts of God's people for the building up of the body as "His fullness" in the world (Eph 4:13). From this gathering every Sunday, we are "sent out" at the benediction into mission. We leave formed by the encounter to enter our world, our neighborhoods, and our workplaces as the very extension of Christ. Surely there will be times "outsiders" come in and recognize that "God is surely among you" (1 Cor 14:25), but this place of the gathering is primarily a place of formative encounter for the shaping of God's people for participation in his mission.

The Sunday gathering gives us the wherewithal to see God at work in the world and to thereby participate in his mission. Around the table we recognize what forgiveness, reconciliation, and the renewal of all life looks like. We can then recognize God at work in the world, for He is already at work in Christ by the Spirit "reconciling the world to Himself (2 Cor 5:19). The recognition of Christ at the Eucharist in Matthew 26 makes possible the mission of Matthew 25 where we recognize Christ in the sick, the thirsty, the hungry, and those in prison.[104] As we practice forgiveness, reconciliation, mutual sharing, and the recognition of Christ's presence among ourselves, we become the distinctive righteousness/justice of God through Christ (2 Cor 5:21). We can then go and recognize where this is already beginning in the world. We should therefore work to keep the purpose of the Sunday gathering focused in the liturgies of life with God. The entire congregation should be involved. We must resist any organizational efforts to make it a production separated from daily life. It should be a seamless part of the rhythm of our lives in the world. The Sunday gathering, however, should never be diminished for it is essential to God's mission. Missionally oriented people do not "grow on trees." They are shaped for mission by the Holy Spirit into the Story of God we have been invited into.

However, having said that, the Sunday gathering is limited. If the church is *the social body of His Lordship (His in-breaking Reign) incarnating Christ in the world for God's mission* it must not be segregated into a gathering on Sunday morning. The church must be present as Christ in the neighborhoods. It must gather to be present among the hungry and hurting, however that might look. This means the practice of the church must be decentralized in its organization away from one central place to being present in the everyday lives of the people. This may mean that the church's house gatherings take on the look of "missional orders": groupings of twelve to twenty to even forty people gathered in a home to pray for and serve a neighborhood. These gatherings find their common life together in the ministry to the neighborhood where they live. They meet to eat, read Scripture, submit to the Spirit, pray, and discern where God is working in order to be available for the smallest act of mercy and reconciliation. They live this life rhythmically as part of their daily lives. They become the laborer in a harvest that is "full" (Luke 10:2) and waiting to be brought into life with God through Jesus Christ.

---

104. I owe this insight from Matthew 25–26 to Geoff Holsclaw with whom I co-pastor Life on the Vine Christian Community in the Northwest Suburbs of Chicago.

This notion of the church as Christ's social body should be evident in times of disagreement within the church. Under the voluntarist assumptions of evangelicalism, conflict within the church signals that one or the other has diverted from "the Truth." It becomes a contest of individuals to set forth the best defense of what the Truth might be for this occasion of conflict. Seeing the church as Christ's social body inhabiting the mission of God in the world reverses this. We realize that engaging the world means we should expect differences in the community. In other words, we as a community are engaging new territory where God is already at work. There will be issues we have not seen before. There will be differences and courses of action to be discerned. Mission therefore breeds conflict, and this conflict is always a place where God is working. It is the sacred occasion for Christ to be incarnated further into the world. We, therefore, engage together in discerning conflict, recognizing that Christ himself incarnates his presence among us as we mutually submit to the Holy Spirit and one another, praying, studying, and discerning the Spirit. Here Christ says "wherever two or more gather in my name and agree on anything, there am I in the midst" (Matt 18:19). In a process of mutual submission modeled on Matt 18:15–20, we model Christ's "revolutionary subordination" before the world,[105] and the discernment of conflict becomes an essential practice that makes possible Christ's social body inhabiting the world for God's mission.

Likewise, if the church is *the social body of His Lordship (His inbreaking Reign) incarnating Christ in the world for God's mission*, the practice of justice will take on a distinctly local and incarnational operation—a new form of local economics will be born among us. Justice can no longer be a concept extracted as a principle to be enforced by individuals in and outside the church, for this too will lead us to making a Master-Signifier of justice. Instead, the righteousness of God[106] must take concrete form among us, incarnating Christ among us by the Holy Spirit. Justice will start locally among us. We cannot minister to those who are hungry as the living body of Christ in the world if there are those hungry within the body itself (1 Cor 11:21). We need

105. Of course "revolutionary subordination" is Yoder's famous phrase first introduced in Yoder, *Politics of Jesus*, ch. 9.

106. Of course I aim to follow N. T. Wright in affirming that righteousness in Pauline and Christian usage is synonymous with justice in its OT and NT derivatives.

to know what justice looks like here in order to know what it might look like elsewhere. The justice of Christ must take shape as a way of being his body, a form of sharing and caring for each other that results in another form of economics that breaks down the isolation and well defended personal financial security that capitalism requires of us all in North America. A new way of relating to each other economically is birthed that is "in but not of" capitalism.[107] In becoming the justice of God in the world, then, we have the ability to do so much more than subvert the social injustices of our day. We in fact offer a new way of being together. We have the ability to not only show the world its injustices but to participate where God is already at work for the justice of the world because we can see it, recognize it, and even complete it by joining in with God for the "setting of all things right." In this way, local justice makes possible the participation in the justice of *missio Dei* in the whole world. Justice cannot then be just another program at the local church. It must be our way of life together as we live "in Christ" for God's mission in the world.

Such a practice of the church in the world blurs the lines between church and world, between sacred and secular, yet there is a social integrity to this space called Christ's body. There can be no division between what justice looks like here around the table versus what we seek in the world. There can be no hard division between the life we lead together as His body, and the life we live in and among the world. One world bleeds over into the other. Yet as theologian Stanley Hauerwas is right to say, "I have no doubt that Jesus is present by his Spirit at work in the world outside the church, yet the church, in gathering around the Eucharist, is the one place where we know he is present. And so it is here where we learn to recognize Jesus and his work and from whence we can move in the world and see him clearly there as well."[108] The church as Christ's social body always lives among the world, inhabiting the world as one of the world. It is the extension of the incarnate Christ,

---

107. I discuss this at more length in my *Great Giveaway*, ch. 6, entitled "Practicing Redeemed Economics."

108. This is my best recollection of a quote I once heard him make but cannot recollect where. Rowan Williams argues in similar fashion when he states ". . . human history is the story of the discovery or realization of Jesus Christ in the faces of all women and men. The fullness of Christ is always *to be* discovered, never there already in a conceptual pattern that explains and predicts everything; it is the fullness of Christ that is to be discovered . . ." Williams, *On Christian Theology*, 173.

sent by the Father to join in with what he is already doing by the Spirit. As such it is inextricably part of the triune mission already ongoing in the world. This "of-ness," however, is distinctive. We always carry the tension of incarnational witness, of being "in but not of" the world.

Together, these ways of speaking about and practicing the church in society shape us for a "politic of fullness" in the world. As we speak and practice being the church in this way, we are shaped into a compassion for and with the world. No longer separated by a distance offered to us by the Master-Signifier, we take up residence among the broken as Christ's body. Our passion for those who hurt is as one alongside and with—com-passion—as opposed to one at a distance, who gives resources out of a position of safety and security—dis-passion. We do not sit protected on Sunday morning next to someone who goes hungry without knowing it. Rather, because "Jesus is Lord," we leave behind the fear of our security that is bred in us by capitalist markets and our need to protect what is ours. We minister one to another out of who we are "in Christ": His forgiveness, renewal, and never-ending provision. The practices of the body around the table and in fellowship shape us towards walking alongside those among us, first in "the body" and then among those who have not yet found Him. We open ourselves jointly to the world God is making anew in Christ. This breeds a corporate disposition of compassion in the world as opposed to the dispassion of the voluntarist church we have known in America. This shapes us for participation in God's mission.

All of the above makes possible what Lesslie Newbigin called "the logic of mission."[109] Newbigin taught that the church could no longer ground its existence via the universal foundations of reason and/or cultural power. The church is in a missionary situation in the post-Christendom cultures of the West. The church then must itself become the foundation for mission in the world by socially embodying the Reign of Christ in visible communities. Here in this political body, the reign of God is breaking in before the watching eyes of the world. Here, we embody the humility of the cross as the means to engage the powers of evil and injustice in our world. "The church represents the presence of the reign of God in the life of the world, not in the triumphalist sense (as the "successful" cause) and not in the moralistic sense

---

109. "The Logic of Mission" is the title of ch. 10 of Newbigin's *Gospel in a Pluralist Society.*

(as the righteous cause), but in the sense that it is the place where the mystery of the kingdom is present in the dying and rising of Jesus made present here and now . . ."[110] Here, the incarnate community of Christ's presence embodies his compassion, vulnerability, and servanthood to the world. The birthing of such communities of His reign, Newbigin argues, makes possible the means by which God's mission goes forth into all the world.[111]

This, then, is the politic of fullness named "church." Such a politic makes possible the witness of the gospel in all the ways evangelicals once hoped for. It is active and engaging the world for God's righteousness and his mission in the world.

RESTORING THE CHARACTER OF EVANGELICALISM'S WITNESS IN THE WORLD

Where then have we arrived after six chapters? Hopefully, a new direction has been set forth in these pages for evangelicalism. Of course, it can be nothing more than an initial direction. There is much more work yet to be done. Nonetheless, out of the upheaval of present-day evangelicalism, out of the exposure of its emptiness as a politic via Slavoj Žižek, I have offered a theological direction for evangelicals to pursue.

This direction, I believe, points us towards a theology and practice that shapes a people for God's mission. For as we gather around (to participate in) Scripture as *our one true story of God for the whole world* we are shaped into the *missio dei*. We know *this story* infallibly as we live our lives together in and through the Sent One, the incarnate Christ, Our Lord, by the Spirit. We the church now become participants in God's story. We do not possess the truth of God in Scripture over against those who do not, or "those who would steal it from us." We are not the primary actors here. We in essence participate in what the triune God is doing through the Son extended by the Spirit. Through our submission to and living out of God's ongoing work in the world as revealed in Scripture we become the very extension of Christ's words:

110. Newbigin, *Open Secret*, 54. See also Newbigin, *Foolishness to the Greeks*, 124–28.

111. Newbigin, *Gospel in a Pluralist Society*, 120–21.

"As the Father has sent me, so send I you" (John 20:23). We are able to embody an understanding of the church as participant in the *missio Dei* or, again, as Jürgen Moltmann once described it, "the mission of the Son and the Spirit through the Father that includes the church."[112] There is a direction here that leaves behind the arrogance and exclusion of "the inerrant Bible" and forges in us a new kind of hospitality in the world, one that invites the world into the Story we are living, yet does not deny the place of Scripture's authority in our lives.

Likewise, as we gather around (to participate in) God's salvation for the world "to set all things right" in Christ Jesus, we are able to live an authentic witness to the work of God before the world. We are not proclaiming a salvation of morally superior status over against those who are "not us," which always leads to duplicity. Instead we are participating in the salvation that God is bringing into the entire world "in Christ," ever dying and rising so that we are always in the process of becoming this salvation. We are therefore able to invite others to join with us in *entering the salvation begun in Jesus Christ that God is working for the sake of the whole world*. We ourselves enter into the death and resurrection of Christ by which our own lives are set right. Yet this "setting right" is part of what God is doing in the whole world. We are converted into a salvation that is bigger than us. We become worshipers of God and his glory, forgivers, sharers of mercy, and provokers for justice: in other words, we become participants in God's work of reconciling the whole world to Himself (2 Cor 5:17–21). This is the gospel. There is an integrity to this salvation at work in us and in the world. As Guder says, "This witness takes place in the relationships of Christians to one another as a community called and shaped by Gods' Spirit."[113] Its inner workings are, as Newbigin says (along with Yoder), "the hermeneutic of the gospel" for us and the world.[114] The community is a foretaste of God's Kingdom for the whole world that the world can see, test, and participate in. There is a direction here that leaves behind the duplicity of our past for a new faithfulness. It shapes us into a genuine integrity with the triune God's life in the sending of his Son incarnationally to live, die, defeat death, and sit at the right hand wherein he is "making all things right." And yet, this disposition also upholds the necessity of

---

112. Moltmann, *Church in the Power of the Spirit*, 64.

113. Guder, *Continuing Conversion*, 137.

114. Newbigin, *Gospel in a Pluralist Society*, 222. Yoder, *Priestly Kingdom*, 15.

conversion eventually in the life of the participant. Everyone eventually must make a decision as to whether to join in.

Likewise, as we gather around (to participate in) the being of the church in the world, we become the extension of His presence, the in-breaking of His reign into the world. We do not practice a social reality over against those "who would steal our moral society from us." In Newbigin's terms we become the "society . . . in which the presence of the kingdom . . . is carried through history and revealed in the life of that community."[115] The communal nature of this reality does not separate us from the world. Rather, by becoming the very righteousness of God (2 Cor 5:21), we can humbly, vulnerably incarnate justice and reconciliation in the world. The line between church and the world is blurred. Activist communities of Christ therefore are birthed (or renewed) into living life together as *the social body of his Lordship (his inbreaking Reign) incarnating Christ in the world for God's mission.* We in essence become a politic formed into the very participation of the Sent One of the Father by the Holy Spirit into the world. There is a direction here that shapes us for compassion in the world, an embodying of the hope in Christ in and among the world. And yet we give up nothing of evangelicalism's activism in the world for individuals being welcomed into Christ's Kingdom. Reconciliation with God is inseparable from the reconciliation God is working among all people and creation.

In each case, this theological direction preserves the three core commitments of evangelicalism. Yet, in each case, a way of speaking about our beliefs and practicing them is provided that shapes evangelicals as a people into the ongoing work of God in Christ for the world (*missio Dei*). We do not practice these beliefs only in terms of personal piety. Rather these beliefs and practices ground us into the very life of God through the incarnate Christ thereby generating a concrete politic in the world. This politic extends the sending of the Son by the Father concretely into the world by the Spirit. It is a politic of "Christ's fullness" (Eph 4:13). This is the politic the world longs for. This politic of fullness is the politic of God's mission.

Likewise, in each case, the practice of these three core commitments, which previously had become the means for our malformation, now shape us into the character of God's people shaped for his mission.

---

115. Newbigin, *Open Secret*, 52.

These three beliefs, which had produced in us an arrogant, duplicitous, and dispassionate disposition—now shape us for an inclusive, hospitable, authentic, faithful, compassionate, and vulnerable incarnational engagement in the world. It is the political demonstration of the character of Christ and his gospel that will, in the end, argue so strongly for articulating evangelical belief and practice in the terms laid down in this book.

Judging the Merits of an Evangelical Political Theology: His Mission

We began this book by asserting that there is a crisis in evangelicalism and this crisis is the character of our politic in North America. Through Žižek, and a host of theologians, we have now come full circle. The character of evangelicalism's political presence in North America was revealed as lacking, thereby debilitating evangelicalism from participating in God's work. The merits of the current proposal must pass the same challenge: will this belief and practice shape the character of our political existence in such a way that it is capable of entering God's work in the world, his mission?

I have argued in this book that a belief and practice rightly centered in the incarnate Christ should shape its people's politic into the character of "the Sent One" and the mission of God in the world. Such a political community participates in the life of the Son as sent by the Father and extended by the Spirit into the world. The resulting character of our political existence should take on the Son's disposition in the world: one of inclusive hospitality, integrity (faithfulness) with the gospel, and compassion in and alongside the world. This then should be the test of a political theology rightly ordered "in Christ." This belief and practice should shape churches that embody the character of the Son. This is the true strength, I suggest, of the political missional evangelical theology proposed in this book.

It is theologian Stanley Hauerwas who has argued most notoriously for this kind of test. For Hauerwas, the test of the truthfulness of our theology is the kinds of people formed (by God) in the world. We evangelicals are not used to doing theology in this way. It is political in a way we are not used to thinking about. We are used to examining the

Scriptures for what is right or wrong and then addressing our churches with the demands of Scripture.[116] We address the relation between theology and practice in terms of how theology informs practice and then "tell people what to do." There is nothing immediately wrong with this. Yet, in the process we miss the notion that belief, together with how it is practiced, shapes a community's political witness in the world. As a result, this way of political theology has rarely been on evangelicalism's radar.

Stanley Hauerwas turns our evangelical theological habits upside down. He asks evangelicals to consider what kinds of people we need to be in order to make sense of the things we say Scripture demands of us.[117] He forces us to realize that it is only from within our commu-

116. Evangelicals have traditionally thought about the moral life in terms of how the Scriptures direct each "saved" individual Christian to choose right versus wrong. The question of spiritual formation of Christian character (especially its political dimensions) has for the most part not been on the map of evangelical church practice. When it comes to the moral life, evangelicalism teaches the individual what to do, then leaves him or her to battle against sin cognitively and piously with the tools given. This is what Dallas Willard calls the gospel of sin management. Willard, *Divine Conspiracy*, ch. 2. In the words of Stanley Grenz, for evangelicals "the basis of ethics lies in the objective character of divine revelation found in the Bible. . . ." He describes evangelical patriarch Carl F. Henry's ethical project as "nothing less than to bring all of life under the divine will as revealed in Scripture." Grenz, *Moral Quest*, 197–98. The program of moral theology for Evangelicals has largely followed Henry. John Jefferson Davis attests to this theological program in the opening salvo of his book *Evangelical Ethics*. He says, "The teachings of Scripture are the final court of appeal for ethics. Human reason, church tradition, and the natural and social sciences may aid moral reflection, but divine revelation, found in the canonical Scriptures of the Old and New Testaments, constitutes the 'bottom line' of *the decision making process* (emphasis mine)" Davis, *Evangelical Ethics*, 3. Evangelical icon Norman Geisler carries out similar sentiments in his *Christian Ethics*, 17. All of the above reinforces that for evangelicals, the moral life is about the individual discerning the right decisions from the Bible augmented by science and reason and enabled by the Holy Spirit's activity in the individual. The character of our life together in the world is simply not on the radar for most evangelicals. Even the progressive and socially engaged work of evangelical ethicist Stephen Mott of early 1980s reflects these same assumptions in the title to his noted work, *Biblical Ethics and Social Change*. Many evangelicals, including Stanley Grenz, have certainly nuanced this theological method in their works on Christian moral living. Yet by and large, evangelicals possess a blindspot regarding the questions of moral formation and the politics of Christian discipleship.

117. In this regard, see again Hauerwas, *Community of Character*, 195–224; *Suffering Presence*, 100–181; *Truthfulness and Tragedy*, 163. See particularly the many places Hauerwas poses the question "What kinds of people should we be in order to . . . ?" (i.e., *Community of Character*, 199) or the question "what kinds of people ought

nity's life that we can make sense of what we believe thereby enabling us to navigate what is right and true. If we are not a community whose life can make sense of what we assert as true, we should stop trying to figure out what is true. We should instead stop everything and figure out what went wrong in the disparity. This is more than a cute methodological device aimed at corporate self-introspection. Hauerwas is telling us that if the character of our political existence does not emulate the gospel we preach, we should examine our belief and practice for the ways it has made such a social condition possible.

This book is a call for us evangelicals to do just that. Let us test what has happened with our belief and practice such that our corporate witness is so poorly received in North America. Let us take a look at the "kinds of people we have become" and the theology and practice that has produced us. The path of this book points us beyond the exercise of being right in our theology. Instead, it invites us to examine our core beliefs and practices for the ways they shape us socially into the very extension of "the Sent One." Let us pursue this route together and in so doing let the goal of our theology be the becoming of his very "fullness" (Eph 4:13) in the world, a politic that carries the disposition necessary to participate in his mission. May this book contribute in a small way to making such an exercise possible. May it create an opening for evangelicals to pursue a new faithfulness as his people amidst the malaise we find ourselves in in the twenty-first century.

---

we to be so . . . ?" (i.e., *Suffering Presence*, 167).

The Emerging and Missional Church Movements:
Possibilities for a New Faithfulness

". . . even the religion we are committed to and in which we found God and purpose and meaning and truth, can become . . . the religious public relations department for an inadequate and destructive ideology."

—Brian McLaren[1]

Several vibrant church-like movements have emerged from within (and around) evangelicalism in the last ten to fifteen years. The "emerging church," "missional church," "neo-monasticism," and the organic house-church movement are just a few of them. In most of these cases, the leaders, pastors, authors, and followers of these groups come from evangelicalism in some way. They form the contours of the post-evangelical landscape in North America.

Each of these movements, in their own way, has been birthed from the discontent towards evangelicalism in North America. They are the evidence that this current crisis is not necessarily the "end" of evangelicalism but rather the place for the birthing of a renewed Christian political presence for our time. Yet these movements are in the embryonic stages of their development. They face the same question set forth in the sixth chapter of this book: Can we carry on a belief and practice sufficient to shape a politic of fullness "in Christ"

---

1. McLaren, *Everything must Change*, 29.

in the world? How this question is resolved will determine whether these movements can avoid repeating the failed mode of evangelical politics. Will they in other words, engender a politic of faithfulness or, after evangelicalism's failure, merely "go on and fail better."[2]

Of course these questions presuppose this book's assumptions about the shape of any new political faithfulness. For instance, it goes without saying that it will not be enough for these movements to get their beliefs "right" concerning Jesus, God, salvation, and Scripture. In order for a new faithfulness to emerge among these post-evangelicals, these beliefs must be sufficiently practiced so as to nurture a faithful politic in the world. Nor will it suffice for these movements to get Christ's call to "social justice" right. For as the above project has taught, this means nothing if there is not a Christian political presence embodying such a "justice" out of its source, the incarnate Christ, the Sent One, our Savior and Lord. These movements must carry a belief and practice sufficient to shape "a politic of fullness" out of the shambles of evangelicalism. They must have the wherewithal to inhabit what James Davison Hunter has described as a "faithful presence" in North America.[3]

There's an Anabaptist impulse at work here. I am refusing the impulse of the church to tell society what they need to do or be because of Jesus.[4] Rather, we ourselves need to inhabit His very life as a politic of His fullness out of which we can engage the world. This book therefore does not offer a new model for evangelicalism's engagement of culture. It offers a way to diagnose the state of our current political presence as evangelicals in light of the gospel and a direction to pursue a new faithfulness in the midst of that diagnosis. I see evangelicalism's current upheaval as an opportunity for evangelicals to forge such a new faithfulness. In the midst of our crisis, we have the opportunity to be

2. Žižek, *In Defense of Lost Causes*, 7. Žižek is actually quoting Samuel Beckett here in an approving manner, believing this is how a politic progresses "in fidelity to the Event," which is Alain Badiou's way of putting things.

3. See Hunter, *To Change The World*.

4. Ironically, I see Hunter's proposal for a "faithful presence" in the closing chapters of *To Change the World* as very Neo-Anabaptist. It is ironic because he spends large parts of the book arguing why the present Neo-Anabaptist leaders'/theologians' proposals for cultural engagement are wrong, too defined by the negative.

shaped (by God) as a politic "in Christ" capable of participating in what God is already doing in the world for his mission.

Žižek's ally and sparring partner, philosopher Alain Badiou,[5] famously argues that Truth erupts from within given structures of knowledge (what he calls "situations"). Any true transformation requires an invasion of something radically new because the existing structure of knowledge is so complete and dominating. Badiou calls this invasion "the Event." He sees political systems as structures of knowledge. For Badiou, then, when such political systems implode, there is an opening for an Event, the possibility of a radically new beginning, the unexpected, the heretofore unknown.[6] The Event clears the site for a subject—a "militant"—to emerge to be faithful to the truth of the Event.[7] Badiou says this subject—either a person, or a group of followers—is defined by his/her "fidelity to the Event."[8] This new subject of faithfulness is the place from which truth can materialize and even coalesce around a new political order.

I suggest that evangelicalism can be seen as such a political system and the current crisis as an Event from which several potential militants have emerged. There is an opening here for a new faithfulness to emerge out of evangelicalism's disarray. I think it's helpful to examine the various emerging movements and their leaders as potential "militants." Is there a faithfulness here that God can use to shape a new "fidelity" amidst the current post-evangelical confusion? Of course Badiou would find such an analysis curious to say the least. He views the truth as knowable only afterwards by its political affects. I also do not subscribe to the radical discontinuity Badiou prescribes as the ba-

---

5. Žižek summarizes Badiou and offers an analysis of his theories in *Ticklish Subject*, ch. 3.

6. For example, "No available generality can account for it, nor structure the subject who claims to follow in its wake." Badiou, *St. Paul*, 14. "A truth is, first of all, something new. What transmits, what repeats, we shall call knowledge. Distinguishing truth from knowledge is essential." Badiou, *Infinite Thought*, 45.

7. Badiou's best exposition of the structure of knowledge and his notion of (the post-Cartesian) subject is found in Part VIII of *Being and Event*.

8. "Grasped in its being, the subject is solely the finitude of the generic procedure, the local effects of an eventual fidelity. What it 'produces' is the truth itself, an indiscernible part of the situation . . . It is abusive to say that truth is a subjective production. A subject is much rather taken up in fidelity to the event . . . from which it is forever separated by chance." *Being and Event*, 406.

sis for the Truth-Event. The politic that must be birthed here in this space must be one that is necessarily extending from the work of God in Christ already begun in history via the Incarnation.[9] Only in this way, by reconnecting to the mission of the triune God centered in the Incarnation and extended by the Spirit, can a community be birthed that avoids repeating the traps of the "empty" ideology that evangelicalism has become. Such a politic must carry a belief and practice capable of shaping this "politic of fullness" founded in Christ. So the question regarding the current emerging movements is, Do they have a sufficient belief and practice (to be used of God) to give shape to the new political faithfulness to come after evangelicalism? Do they have the wherewithal in their belief and practice to center a politic "in Christ" so as to birth a viable "politic of fullness" for God's mission in the world?

In this regard, one must surely answer that these movements and their leaders show enormous promise. The kind of energy surrounding these leaders recalls the early days of evangelicalism's formation out of the modernist-fundamentalist crisis in the previous century. They have addressed directly, and with vigor, the three doctrinal commitments of evangelicalism just as I have in this book. They have spoken to the lacks in evangelicalism's political witness just as I have. Several of the authors of this movement have the potential to emerge as "militants" capable of articulating and gathering a new faithfulness for our time. There is a vibrant possibility here for a new faithfulness.

Yet there are vulnerabilities in these movements and their theologies. The potential weaknesses within these theologies/movements could leave them as non-starters incapable of sustaining a lived politic on the ground. These weaknesses could leave those gathered around them susceptible to the same ideological trap of evangelicalism's demise, the lure of becoming yet another politic driven by antagonisms

9. Douglas Harink comments on this same issue regarding Badiou in a paper presented in 2004 at the American Academy of Religion. Here he says that the "weakness" of servanthood and grace, founded in the crucifixion of Jesus, "is nevertheless in reality the power of the one God of all . . . making its way to the 'ends of the earth' through the concrete, local, militant, peaceable, life together and mission of the cruciform community, in the power of the Spirit. This is the theo-political vision of Paul. This, and not Badiou's severing of a truth from the truth-procedure, is a proper Pauline response" to the dangers of a violent universalism of a particular truth taking shape in a particular community. Quoted from his unpublished paper "False Universal?: Badiou's Paul sans Jesus, Israel and the Church."

and suspect enjoyments. If fallen into, these traps have the potential to separate the emerging politic from the triune life of God in mission as founded in the incarnate Christ. The politic of faithfulness is then aborted.

In what follows, I offer only a brief examination of three ideological traps as they relate to the emerging/missional church's re-configuration of the three doctrinal commitments of evangelicalism we have studied in this book. I focus on three "militants" in the emerging/missional church as the spokespersons for these new articulations of belief and practice. This is not a thorough examination. Rather, these are initial observations meant to spur on conversation for a new faithfulness in the days that lie ahead.

The Emerging View of Scripture: Peter Rollins and Avoiding the Trap of De-Incarnationalizing the Word

Emerging church writers have spilt much ink on evangelicalism's modernist assumptions on Scripture. They have criticized evangelicalism's excessive propositionalism, interpretive hubris (confident of one true interpretation tied to the author's original intent), and its resulting exclusionary arrogance.[10] Theologian and artist Peter Rollins, a former evangelical Pentecostal, addressed these issues on behalf of the emerging church with his books *How (Not) To Speak of God* and his follow-up book *The Fidelity of Betrayal*.[11] His deconstructive approach has proved popular among the emerging church leaders in North America.

According to Rollins, the established church, which often means evangelicalism, is too certain about what we know about God and too hyper-cognitive towards Scripture, thereby taking the mystery out of our encounter with the living God. We evangelicals, so Rollins suggests, tend to colonize the text. We equate our interpretation of the text with the truth of the text. We therefore make Scripture our own possession and in effect make the words of Scripture an idolatry.[12] We know Scripture, yet we are untouched by it and so we insulate ourselves from

---

10. See for instance two popular texts representing the emerging movement: McLaren, *New Kind of Christian*, ch. 6.; Jones, *New Christians*,140–48.

11. Rollins, *How (Not) To Speak*; *Fidelity of Betrayal*.

12. Among the places this can be found in Rollins, *How (Not) To Speak*, 11--16, and Rollins, *Fidelity of Betrayal*, ch. 3.

the God who seeks to reveal Himself in and through Scripture. As a result, we have become a controlling, uninviting, exclusionary people, losing the ability to encounter the living God and the opportunity to invite others into such an encounter.[13] In short, Rollins agrees with everything I have written in this book concerning the evangelical practice of "the inerrant Bible." Rollins solution is to move us from "right believing" to "believing in the right way."[14]

To get us to the right way, Rollins provides a diet of pre-Medieval mystics, apophatic theology and the post-structuralist ideas of Derrida, Jean Luc Marion, and John Caputo. Rollins says we must approach revelation with a sense that God can never be fully revealed in words, even the words of Scripture. True to his apophatic leanings, there is always more of God concealed than is revealed in any human words. We therefore always fall short of knowing what we mean when we talk about God. The evangelical tendency to concentrate on the known content of Scripture, therefore, misses the point. God is made known in the unknown. We must approach all revelation with a humility and openness appropriate to this reality. In true deconstructionist terms, we must acknowledge "that our various interpretations of revelation will always be provisional, fragile and fragmentary."[15] Context, culture, and language both limit the extent of our understanding of God as well as make it possible. Truth is not so much about what we can conceptually grasp. It is about the living encounter with God that transforms our very selves in what Rollins labels the "soteriological event."[16]

To those of us who have suffered the modernist habits of the evangelical practice of Scripture, Rollins comes as a breath of fresh air. He helps shape a humility in us towards Scripture that can breed the hospitality and conversation we need for a politic of mission.

Rollins' proposal, however, poses a danger. His version of truth risks suggesting that the gospel never hits the ground sufficiently to shape a political reality. After all, Rollins is serious about his apophatic views on religious language. God can never be contained in language. All interpretations of revelation must be provisional. The resulting

13. See for example Rollins, *How (Not) to Speak*, 5–8, 17 and throughout this book.

14. On the Hebrew way versus the Greek way, see ibid., 2–3.

15. Ibid., 18.

16. Ibid., 55

danger is that we could end up always postponing judgment as to what God is saying such that we end up never testing, engaging, or allowing it to shape our everyday lives together as a people. Because God is revealed in what we cannot know, we may get lost in contemplation and/or conversation that never provides the determinacy to actually participate in the mission God in concrete ways as a people. There is a danger that Rollins has not provided for a sufficient enough confidence in what God has revealed to order a politic of truth, justice, and reconciliation in the world. The gospel might never be "incarnated" politically in the world.

This is what I call the danger of *de-incarnationizing the Word of God*: the danger of the Word of God never "landing" in the concrete circumstances of our life together. It is the same critique of deconstructionism already mentioned in this book by Milbank, Žižek, and others. They suggest that deconstruction glorifies "the never to be reached" and sucks us into a "bad infinity." Our life together begins to look like a "pseudo activism indistinguishable from a Buddhist quietism."[17] Rollins certainly intends to foster the incarnation of the gospel in people's lives.[18] Nonetheless, *de-incarnationalizing* is a danger that lies close at hand. It happens whenever Rollins undercuts the conviction that Jesus by the Spirit is present in the Scriptures and has given us words to discern the truth in the concrete circumstances of our every life together.

To expand on this more, *de-incarnationalizing* happens when we separate the Scriptures from their ongoing source in Jesus Christ, the incarnate Son, the Sent One from the Father, whose incarnational presence is extended via the Holy Spirit into the world. In essence, to de-incarnationalize the Word of God is to also *de-Trinitize* it (to invent another clumsy word). The Scriptures and the Word of God spoken in and through them is extracted from its connection to the Trinity's economy. It becomes disconnected from the historical work of God in the incarnation and the extension of that into history and the world by the Holy Spirit. Devoid of God's continuing work via the prophets and the apostles and the church, Scripture must now stand alone on its own

17. On these sources see n. 10, ch. 6 above.

18. For instance, Rollins states "Truth is God and having knowledge of the Truth is evidenced, not in a doctrinal system, but in allowing that Truth to be incarnated in one's life." Rollins, *How (Not) To*, 56.

merits as a container for God's truth. We now come to it as an isolated document devoid of its connection to the triune life of God as having entered humanity in Christ. The Scripture is not something we participate in as an extension of Christ's life via the Spirit but something we approach within the limits of representative language and Cartesian doubt. When this happens, then of course we are in need of Rollins' deconstructive apophatic theory to avoid the imperialist impulses typical of *de-incarnationalizing*.

But God has condescended to reveal Himself in Christ via human culture, including the language of Scripture itself. God was born in human flesh and lived among us speaking our language. He died, rose, and ascended, gifting the church with apostles, teachers, and the ongoing proclamation of the Word all by the purview of the Holy Spirit. Because his Holy Spirit is among us, the very presence of Christ continues and inhabits the ongoing language of his people. As we situate ourselves in this language, we are able to encounter God in it and discern him here and elsewhere.[19] The Incarnation of Christ, sent by the Father, extends historically through the Holy Spirit into the world via the preaching, the table, and the community of his people. The Scriptures are part and parcel of this extension. Through this incarnational way of language we avoid the kataphatic habits (capturing God in the representational control of language) of modernist notions of language.[20] We learn to listen and discern humbly "in Christ."

19. Louis-Marie Chauvet fleshes this out on in his book *Symbol and Sacrament*. He embraces the potential abuse of placing God under our control via language (onto-theology). This "representational" function of language must be closely guarded according to Chauvet as well as Rollins. Nonetheless, there is another function to language, what he calls "recognition" (versus "cognition") where the function of language is intersubjective. Here, language assigns "a place to the subject in relation to others." *Symbol and Sacrament*, 119. Within this world of language, its gestures and practices, where God has invested Himself, God becomes known and we become known as His subject. The primary example of this is Jesus' presence revealed in the Eucharist. Language becomes the medium by which we live in relation to God. Although the focus here is on the Eucharist, I would contend that Chauvet is eminently applicable to preaching, community, and other forms of language so inhabited by God through Jesus Christ. I thank Geoff Holsclaw for pointing this out to me. Holsclaw's writing on this in relation to Rollins can be found online: http://churchandpomo.typepad.com/conversation/2006/10/if_the_lord_is_.html.

20. In the words of Lesslie Newbigin, "it is only by 'indwelling' the Scripture that one remains faithful to the tradition. By this indwelling (abiding) we take our place and play our part in the story that is the true story of the whole human race and of the cosmos." *Truth and Authority*, 49.

As we situate ourselves in this way, through the Scriptures, we are able to discern justice, righteousness, reconciliation, and the ways of God in our lives together for the world. The Incarnation extends into his people and from there into the world. Truth takes up shape in the discernments of our daily lives together because the church is defined as more than a conversation. It is a discerning politic of Christ by the Spirit, and from here we can see, test, and prove God at work in the world by that same Spirit. To separate the Scriptures from the incarnate continuity of the Son, extended by the Spirit, renders them impotent to shape us politically as the reconciliation of God at work in the world.[21] We are in danger of receiving a truth that can never land in the social realities of our everyday lives. We are left with endless conversation and individual, private revelatory acts of justice.

That Rollins is at least vulnerable to this trap is evident in some of the liturgical services of his Ikon community as outlined in the second half of *How (Not) to Speak of God*. These well-crafted performances are meant to be "soteriological events." They invite the participant to engage in Scriptural stories in ways that deconstruct the most commonly held interpretations of Scripture. Their operating mode is to clear some space for a fresh encounter once it has been determined "what God is Not." Often this means turning the received interpretation "on its head." The events are inventive and engaging to say the least. There is no doubt they foster an encounter with God. Yet these liturgies can also have the affect of deconstructing the participant—pulling him/her out from our history in Christ. Yet the very purpose and profundity of Christian liturgy, as I understand it, is the opposite: to draw us into the participation in our history of God in Christ. These Ikon services, then, can have the effect of removing the participants from the very context or language that we need to locate ourselves within *the story*.

The *modus operandi* here illustrates what happens in the *de-incarnationalization* of the Word. In an effort to avoid the "creedalizing" of doctrine, we are left devoid of (disconnected from) the history

---

21. This critique is indebted, of course, to Jamie K. A. Smith's treatment of language and the logic of incarnation in *Speech and Theology*. Smith gives an account of language that suggests that once we remove the Bible from the Incarnation, one of two errors must eventuate: either kataphatics, the violence of positivism thereby reducing God to immanence, or apophatism, reducing God to transcendence thereby disabling the ability to say anything of God in the world.

of what God has done and is doing, whereby we can see God in the world and participate in mission. As a result, these "Ikon services" can come off almost as performance art. They can leave the participant with no place to go and no context from which to move into the world to locate God's mission. When this happens, these liturgies are incapacitated from incarnating a people into a life together in Christ for his mission in the world.

In some ways, then, Rollins' truth as "soteriological events" opens the way for the same ideological mistakes of "the inerrant Bible." These events are indeterminate enough to allow people to import into them whatever each one deems important. In the name of "encounter" or "event," they lure us into believing we can be serious about God without being serious about the way we lead our lives together as a people of God in the world. As with "the inerrant Bible," after the encounter is over we can go on being complicit with the politics we are most comfortable in. We are left with a self-engrossing experience of the ineffable that cannot shape a politic in the world. We have lost the wherewithal to be shaped for participation in *our one and true story of God for the whole world* (where "right believing" and "believing in the right way" are one and the same). Herein is the potential ideological trap that lies with the emerging view of Scripture as exemplified by Rollins.

I nonetheless applaud Rollins' work because he and many other emerging leaders are teaching us how to approach the Scriptures with humility and submission in all the ways it is practiced. They remind us that the language God has given to his people always points beyond itself to the fuller reality, which it cannot contain. These are the beginnings of a politic of faithfulness. If there is to be such a politic in our future, however, we must avoid the trap of *de-incarnationalizing* our belief and practice of Scripture.

The Emerging Belief in Salvation: Brian McLaren and the Trap of De-Eschatologizing Salvation

Emerging church writers have also spilt much ink criticizing evangelicalism's narrow understanding of salvation. Author/pastor Brian McLaren has led the charge in this regard. For McLaren, truly the father of the emerging movement,[22] evangelicalism has over-personalized salvation, making it into a transaction and has generally been preoccupied with the afterlife and escaping hell. As a result, evangelicalism's gospel has distanced the believer from the salvation that God is doing to transform the unjust world. As a result, evangelicals have become dispassionate and even duplicitous in the way we lead our lives in the world. Again, in short, McLaren agrees with everything I have written in this book concerning evangelicals and our practice of "the decision."

McLaren responds to these complaints by admonishing evangelicals that they have forgotten (or ignored) the singular message of Jesus in the gospels: the Kingdom of God has begun. We have focused instead on the Pauline/Lutheran doctrine of justification by faith in Christ through his atoning work on the cross.[23] As a result, he argues, evangelicalism's salvation has become a personalized middle-class gospel accommodated to the comforts of American prosperity. It is a message hardly recognizable as what Jesus preached when He announced that the Kingdom of God has broken in—a new way of life in God has begun. McLaren, true to the evangelist he is, invites his readers to identify with the Kingdom of God and join in living the way of Jesus in this new Kingdom. As opposed to an evangelical conversion that emphasizes the afterlife, McLaren urges his readers to join in with God's Kingdom now and become part of what God is doing to transform the world.

In his *The Secret Message of Jesus*, McLaren takes this theme and refashions it for evangelism. McLaren makes accessible the century-old "Jesus versus Paul" debate in New Testament scholarship. He invites his readers to follow Jesus into the socio inter-personal and political dynamics of the Kingdom. In Anabaptist fashion, McLaren describes how God is working not through coercion or power but in the daily (even mundane) lives of committed followers of Christ willing to participate in what He is doing through love and reconciliation. To those of us

22. McLaren was prominent especially among the original Emergent Village (http://emergentvillage.org), which played so prominent a role in the emerging church's rise to prominence at the turn of the millennium. His influence of course has extended well beyond this founding group.

23. McLaren denies the need to bifurcate Paul from the Jesus of the gospels. See, for instance, *Secret Message of Jesus*, 91ff.

weary of the individualist-consumerist habits of evangelical salvation, Brian McLaren is a welcome breath of fresh air. He offers a salvation that includes repentance and a decision, but is grandly holistic. It is a belief and practice that shapes us out of the duplicity and dispassion that has seemed so much a part of evangelicalism's practice of evangelism.

In McLaren's next book, *Everything Must Change (EMC)*, he expands on this vision. He describes the message of Jesus as a new way of life founded upon "a counter story." This story is of course the Kingdom of God, "a framing story" offered by Jesus that truly helps us see what God is working in the world. Over against the stories of domination in our world, which are destroying the earth, inflicting suffering and exploitation, and perpetrating gross injustice, McLaren calls for an awakening to this new framing story, the "creative and transforming story" of Jesus,[24] where God's love, reconciliation, sacred beauty, restoration, justice, and renewal take shape among us and in the world. This is a story "that changes everything."[25] McLaren calls his readers to become true believers and participants in this "framing story," the Kingdom of God. His work in these books has been a galvanizing force for the reshaping of a politic of faithfulness in the aftermath of evangelicalism.

It is in *EMC*, however, that we see McLaren's temptation to *de-eschatologize* the Kingdom. *De-eschatologizing* the Kingdom happens when one separates the Kingdom of God from its fulfillment in the historical (i.e., incarnate) triune work of God in Jesus Christ. It is in *EMC* that we notice that McLaren is comfortable differentiating "the message of Jesus" (the Kingdom of God) from "the message about Jesus" (that Jesus Christ, in His life, death, resurrection and as Reigning Lord, has Himself come to bring in the Kingdom).[26] It is therefore possible to read him in this book as advocating that we must put our faith and trust in God and His framing story—the message of the Kingdom—as opposed to submitting ourselves to the one who has been exalted as Reigning Lord and is actually bringing in this new in-breaking Kingdom. Jesus becomes, if McLaren is not careful, the guide, the exemplar in helping us do this as opposed to very means. This move *de-eschatologizes* the Kingdom, separating it from the ongoing work of God in the world

24. McLaren, *Everything Must Change*, 274.

25. Ibid., ch.3.

26. Ibid., 22, 98.

through the Reigning Christ by the Holy Spirit. It risks thwarting the formation of a politic for mission in three ways.

First, *de-eschatologizing* sets the stage for "the Kingdom" to become another nebulous Master-Signifier which can mean anything. When we separate the Kingdom from the ongoing in-breaking work of Jesus as reigning Lord, the Kingdom is set free from its moorings in the Triune God's eschatological work. No longer grounded in the history of the nation of Israel and the fulfillment of this history in Christ, and the extension of that history in the Holy Spirit's work in His people and the world, the Kingdom can be applied as a concept to any number of activities that one thinks qualifies as God's "ethic" for bringing justice into the world. It can become the means of another form of ideological complicity as now we casually associate "the Kingdom" with various causes without discerning whether this is of Christ and His Kingdom. "The Kingdom" becomes an ideological badge we use to justify any number of causes much like "the Christian nation" has become for American evangelicalism.

The Kingdom has, of course, become a Master-Signifier before. Some might even suggest that president George W. Bush used evangelicalism's amalgamation of democracy and the Kingdom to justify the Iraq War as the bringer of God's "freedom" to the world. There is a long history in North America of such Kingdom abuse.[27] I have no question that some government initiatives qualify as God's Kingdom, especially when Christians get involved. Yet we can discern such things only from within the church's participation in God's eschatological activity to bring this Kingdom to fulfillment "in Christ." Separated from the eschatological fulfillment of this Kingdom in Jesus Christ, the Kingdom can become just another signifier that distracts us from God's

---

27. To rehearse this theological history, Ritschl, Harnack, and other leaders of nineteenth-century Protestant theology preached that the Kingdom of God was the primary message of Jesus. In the aftermath of the sweeping acceptance of the "Quest for the Historical Jesus" (Schweitzer et al.), they accepted that Jesus was a failed apocalyptic prophet, yet the message of Jesus, the Kingdom of God, was the real truth of the matter. This "Kingdom of God" was interpreted to refer to what God was doing in the world as understood in the surging progress of democracy (most notably by Rauschenbusch) and all things liberating the individual from economic and social oppression. Democracy became the stand-in for "the kingdom of God." Ironically, it is today's evangelical right that best represents this vision.

justice as opposed to building a politic of God's justice/mission in and among our everyday lives.

Second, *de-eschatologizing* the Kingdom strips us of our ability to inhabit the gospel in peace and hospitability. When the Kingdom is *de-eschatologized*, we are tempted to make it into a cause, which we then advocate over against those who disagree with us. We are tempted to take control of history when the Kingdom is separated from the certainty that God is working to bring it to completion in history in Christ (1 Cor 15:25–28). Ironically, we become set apart from the world into which God has called us for His mission. As a result, the onus to bring in the Kingdom is shifted more onto what we do than what God the Father is doing, in sending the Son as extended into the world by the Spirit. In the process, we lose the wherewithal to participate in God's work as patient and non-coercive participants of the Kingdom which is what McLaren wants. It is only as we are confident of what God has in store for the world that we can participate daily as His subjects, not as agents who need to control the world.[28] McLaren's own words in his title, "Everything must change," belie the stress of such a *de-eschatologizing*. Instead, against the imperative that "Everything must change," we believe "Everything has changed" already in Christ and we must now participate in what God has already begun and is bringing to completion in the world. Only in practicing such a belief can Christians avoid taking on "the Kingdom" as another cause we must fight for over against those who disagree with us. This patience and hospitality is essential for a political presence that can participate in God's Mission in the world.

Lastly, *de-eschatologizing* the Kingdom loses the very dynamic that gives us hope for something different coming into the world. One of the first things I learned about the Kingdom in seminary is what we used to call "the already, but not yet" character of it. From Oscar Cullman, George Ladd, and other NT theologians we learned there is a tension in the NT that acknowledges the Kingdom has "already" begun but is "not yet" completed. We then are a people baptized into the new

---

28. It is curious and a serious mistake in my estimation for McLaren to give up on the second coming of Christ in *New Kind of Christianity*, 197, because the very participation he wants in a nonviolent mode of witness is only made possible by the surety that God ultimately guarantees the coming of the Kingdom. On this subject I recommend Yoder, "If Christ is Truly Lord."

age all the while continuing to live among the old. We are called to live under and bear witness to the new realities of the Kingdom, Christ's Lordship, his defeat of the powers, his victory over death, sin, and evil. This takes seriously the fact that something actually happened cosmically to the world in Jesus Christ, yet it has not been fully manifested (it comes as a mustard seed). If we separate the Kingdom from the Reign of the living, resurrected Christ, we lose this tension.[29] We lose the dynamic that makes credible our invitation for all *to enter into the salvation begun in Jesus Christ that God is working for the sake of the whole world?* In essence, we lose the wherewithal to engage the world for the transformation God is bringing to the world through the Son in His Mission (1 Cor 15:25).

De-eschatologizing the Kingdom therefore opens an avenue for "ideologizing" the Kingdom. It allows for making the Kingdom a Master-Signifier that means nothing, plays on antagonisms, and indeed offers little to truly transform the world. One's decision to join in with this kingdom then can be another form of the same evangelical salvation known via "the Christian nation" and "the decision for Christ." It is an ideological trap with the potential to neuter the Kingdom and its righteousness for the sake of preserving the status quo.

Nevertheless, I applaud Brian McLaren's work for leading post-evangelicalism into a new faithfulness for mission. He teaches us evangelicals a salvation of the Kingdom that breeds hospitality and authentic witness to what God is bringing to the whole world. He takes the foundational teachings of Jesus and expounds them for a new evangelism in our time. He has set in motion the beginnings for a politic of faithfulness. If there is to be such a politic in our future, however, we must avoid the trap of *de-eschatologizing* our belief and practice of salvation.

29. McLaren sometimes reads like a man who wants to maintain the tension, but hasn't got the Christology to do so.

The Emerging Belief in the Church in Society: Alan Hirsch and Michael Frost and the Trap of De-Ecclesiologizing the Church in Mission

Emerging/missional church leaders have also challenged evangelicalism's practice of the church in the world as too defensive and inward looking. The evangelical church, they say, has become an organization set off over against society as opposed to being a people in and among society in God's mission. Missiologists Alan Hirsch and Michael Frost, two of the main leaders of the missional church movement in North America, have challenged evangelicals in this regard to embrace a "missional ecclesiology" in North America.

Early on in their writing, Frost and Hirsch chided the North American church for its obsession with attracting people to come to its services and programs. In *The Shaping of Things to Come*, they labeled the North American church as fundamentally "attractional." It is structured primarily around a building that is to be the center of all its various services and programs. This "attractional" *modus operandi* has engulfed all of the church's functions including evangelism. According to Hirsch and Frost, we even seek to reach the hurting and those seeking faith by inviting them to church to a program we built to meet their needs. For Frost and Hirsch, this notion of the church is fundamentally flawed. It depends upon the social orbit of Christendom society where the societal expectation is that the church would be the center for all things having to do with God. This Christendom world, however, is slowly passing away. Today, this attractional "indrag" works to close off the church from the hurting, the poor, and the ever-increasing world of non-Christians.

For Frost and Hirsch, the North American church is carrying on the bad habits of Christendom. We still believe we possess power and influence in our culture "to compel them to come to us." We organize ourselves into hierarchical business-like structures that centralize the church's operations instead of dispersing it into the world. In order to preserve our own culture, we divide what is sacred (the church) from the secular (the world). It is a power play requiring those who believe to come to church to meet God. As a result, the church is self-enclosed, trying to defend its own view of the world. It has not only withdrawn from mission, it has become antagonistic to it. In many ways, then,

Frost and Hirsch agree with just about everything I have written in this book concerning evangelicalism's practice of the church in society and "the Christian nation."

In response to this state of affairs, Hirsch and Frost preach a dispersed notion of the church where it inhabits the neighborhoods and contexts of everyday life. Recounting some of the core themes of missional thinkers, they describe how the church is to live missionally as an extension of the mission of God in the world (not as a church that does missions as a program). We are to follow Christ and the incarnational model of God's sending the Son into the very context, rhythms, and language of everyday human life. We are to inhabit the context and witness to the Kingdom. These are "the forgotten ways" of Jesus and His disciples, which birthed the first mission of Christ into the world. It is only after we inhabit and identify with those we are with that the church can then take shape in terms of its programs and services. To do the reverse is to revert to the attractional ways of Christendom.

This brief summary does not do justice to the contributions of Hirsch and Frost to the burgeoning missional church movement in North America. They have provoked the church, especially the evangelical church, to rethink its position in society and take up the posture of Christ in the world, who came humbly, vulnerably to serve, seek, and save the lost. They offer us a practice of church that shapes us out of the dispassion and protectionism that has plagued so much of our churches. Their work is helping to shape among us a politic of faithfulness for mission in our time.

Nonetheless, there is a potential ideological trap that lies within the missiological practices of Hirsch and Frost. It is the trap of *de-ecclesiologizing* the church's relationship to society. By the word *de-ecclesiologize*, I am not referring merely to Frost/Hirsch's resistance to the institutionalizing of the church. Indeed, some of that might be warranted. I refer instead to the separating of the practice of the church from any continuous work of the incarnate Christ in history as extended in the forms of the church by the Holy Spirit. If this happens, I contend that the church is set adrift from any determination in Christ and the work of Christ in the world. It becomes *de-ecclesiologized*.

This trap is not immediately apparent in Frost and Hirsch. On the contrary, they have written extensively in sympathy with themes of this book: the restoring of the incarnate Christ to the core of the politic of the church in the world. The central task of their book *ReJesus* is to "reinstate the central role of Jesus . . . in the life and mission of God's people."[30] They do not wish to separate the practice of the church from Christ, they seek to "reinstate" it. They often summarize their approach to this issue with the formula: "mission must precede ecclesiology and Christology must precede missiology."[31] For Hirsch and Frost, this phrase requires that Christ must come first and be the source of the church's formation in the world. It is Christology that drives mission from which the church is birthed in the world.

It is this formula, however, that reveals the potential for the *de-ecclesiologizing* of the church. Implicit in this formula is that we (anyone) can know/encounter Christ determinately apart from the ongoing forms of the church. The continuous forms of the church, including Eucharist, the preaching and interpretation of the canon of Scripture, the fellowship of the gifts, are therefore dispensable for mission. Jesus forms the church directly in mission. Ecclesiology—who and what the church is in Christ—is fluid.

Hirsch and Frost, of course, are following the founding theological mantra of missional church theology, that "It is not the church that has a mission of salvation to fulfill in the world; it is the mission of the Son and the Spirit through the Father that includes the church."[32] That the church should be defined as an extension of God's mission in the sending of the Son should not be questioned. Yet for Hirsch and Frost, this doctrine means that the church carries no continuous form from context to context. According to Hirsch, first comes entering the cultural context, identifying with its people, getting to know, understand and live among the context. Only then, after one's life takes shape in the culture, after redemption has taken hold in the culture, can the church take on form. The church, as Hirsch is fond of saying, "comes out the back of mission."[33] The forms in which the church takes shape in the world are all a matter of *post facto* development after "we" have inhabited a context. The questions however remain: Who is the "we"

30. Frost and Hirsch, *ReJesus*, 15.

31. Hirsch, *Forgotten Ways* 142–44.

32. Moltmann, *Church in the Power*, 64.

33. Ibid., 143–44.

that engages the context prior to being the church?[34] Does not this mis-siological engagement assume the prior existence of the church? And how does one know Christ in this context apart from the continuous forms of the church to carry on His presence in the world?

Hirsch and Frost imply in *ReJesus* that it is through "a direct and unmediated relationship" between the individual believer and Christ that He is known in the context.[35] They go to great lengths to "debunk the many false images" of Jesus that have existed in the church down through the ages. They then seek to "go back to the daring, radical, strange, wonderful, inexplicable, unstoppable, marvelous, unsettling, disturbing, caring, powerful God-Man."[36] They deserve credit for refo-cusing the church on the question of Jesus and the image of Jesus we follow? They give serious attention to Scripture as they call us to the "wild Messiah" Jesus of the four gospels as the basis for mission in the world. There remains the question, however, of how we seek after this Jesus without ourselves becoming victims of another encultured view of Christ, this time "the wild Messiah" of Frost and Hirsch. For Frost and Hirsch, it is a fresh encounter with the living Christ that overcomes the forms of the church instead of being made manifest in these same forms as Christ has given them to the church.[37] The danger here is that Christians are left without a basis for our very connection to the ongo-ing presence of Jesus Christ by the Holy Spirit in the triune history. We become a bunch of individuals seeking a personal mystical experi-ence of Christ via our own interpretation of the gospels. We become individual worshipers of a self-described Jesus devoid of the means to be immersed in the work of the triune God in the world. We become

34. I owe this way of putting this to Dan Hinz, a student at Northern Seminary.

35. "However difficult it is to remain open to God, it is vital that this relationship must take the form of a direct and unmediated relationship with Jesus. It must involve a constantly renewed, up to date experience with our Lord. . . ." Hirsch and Frost, *ReJesus*, 50. Frost and Hirsch affirm Kierkegaard's understanding of contemporane-ousness. They write that "contemporaneousness is a conscious effort by the believer to reach beyond the church's entire two-thousand year tradition and free of inherited presuppositions, encounter Jesus, seeing him with eyes not of the first Christians but of the first eyewitnesses . . ." Frost and Hirsch, *ReJesus*, 55.

36. Ibid., 105, 111.

37. "The more one replaces a fresh daily encounter with Jesus with religious forms, over time he is removed from his central place in the life of the church. The result of this removal (by whatever means) is the onset of dead religion in the place of living faith." Ibid., 71

individuals charged with doing God's mission instead of participants as a people in what God is already doing in the world.

The church, however, has been given the practices of the church in continuity with Christ as the Sent One from the Father to embody Christ in the world by the Spirit. Within these practices of the Eucharist, the preaching of the Word, baptism, the fellowship of the "gifts" through mutual submission, ordination, service to the poor (Matthew 25), and the presence of Christ in mutual discernment (Matt 18:15–20), the body of Christ is materialized in the world. We must be persistent in contextualizing these various practices for each place we inhabit God's mission. Yet it is here in these practices that we learn that the incarnation is more than a principle to be applied as a missiological method—it is a reality extended in and through the church. These practices should not separate us from the world, they should incarnate us as his body in the world. They enable what we have called *the social body of his Lordship (his in-breaking Reign) incarnating Christ in the world for God's mission*. To somehow separate these practices from the extended work of Christ in history into the world via the Spirit is to risk setting up on high an ideological picture of Jesus as the personal possession of each individual. Instead, through these simple ecclesial practices, we are enabled as individuals to submit to and participate in the full trinitarian mission of God in which the church has been sent and is a part. In these ways, missiology does not precede ecclesiology, missiology is ecclesiology and vice versa.

The danger in all of this is that God's people can fall into the trap of becoming ideologized. Without the ongoing forms of the church, we Christians are left without a source of political formation in the world. Without a practice to be formed "in Christ," we as individuals instead gravitate around compelling causes that have little to do with the mission of God. We find ourselves caught up in ulterior purposes, whether it be the building of a large organization or the accumulation of power for purposes devoid of Christ. If the church has no stance from which to engage the world, discern the issues, and participate in God's work in the world, it is susceptible to contextualizing itself out of existence. [38] It

38. Hirsch suggests that such contextualization happens ". . . when the surrounding culture intrudes on the lordship of Jesus and his exclusive claim overall aspects of our lives . . ." *Forgotten Ways*, 98. The question is, how might one know when this has happened? Such a broad statement might indeed promote the total withdrawal from

can then become an ideology, or worse, the instrument of an ideology. Devoid of its own purpose, its followers enlist with others. Either way, the church loses its faithfulness. "Mission" becomes an ideological banner because it too is undetermined by a concrete practice in the world. It in essence becomes a concept to be applied. We can then be lured to put the church into the service of the pragmatics of making an organization more successful in terms and for purposes that have little to do with God's mission. In all these ways, *de-ecclesiologizing* the church's place in the world makes the church susceptible to turning "mission" into another version of evangelicalism's "the Christian nation," a cause that rallies individuals to gather but accomplishes little in the world.

Hirsch and Frost rightly want to guard against the Western habit of imposing a form of imperialism on the host cultures we seek to inhabit. They want to guard against the church thinking it has got it all figured out before it lands in a culture. They want to guard against the tendency for the church to think that the Holy Spirit is only working in the church and its practices. For all of this, Hirsch and Frost are to be applauded. The practice of the church needs be contextualized although not discarded. We need to realize that God's mission is at work outside the church, that Jesus is Lord over all things, and the church exists to inhabit, discern, and be responsive to His work, not our own pre-agendas. The church has often failed at this in its history. We therefore need to listen to Hirsch and Frost. Yet we must do so while taking heed to avoid the trap of *de-ecclesiologizing* the church's stance in society.

Hirsch and Frost are leading post-evangelicalism towards a new faithfulness for mission. They teach us how to be the church, Christ's living body, in the world. They teach us the ways of compassion, of being among the poor and the needy. They teach us how to be an hospitable witness, which embodies the justice of Christ in the world. These are truly the beginnings of a politic of faithfulness. If there is to be such a politic in our future, however, we must avoid the trap of *de-eccelesiologizing* our belief and practice of the church in society.

---

cultural engagement apart from a community of discernment. My simple point is that such a statement presumes the prior existence of the church in mission.

THE POSSIBILITIES FOR A NEW FAITHFULNESS

Rollins, McLaren, Hirsch, and Frost represent only a few of the voices emerging on evangelicalism's horizon. There are myriad authors, organizations, and church movements being spawned in recent years all speaking into the malaise of evangelicalism in North America. If it is true what they say, that nature abhors a vacuum, then we should not be surprised at the intensity of new movements flowing into the empty space that has been left in the wake of evangelicalism's upheaval. In a thoroughly non-Žižekian way of interpreting the current situation, evangelicalism has become a vortex for new movements rushing in to respond to the problems of what must still be considered the dominant Christian faith in North America. In the midst of this swirl, the emerging church movements, the missional church movements, as well as the neo-monastic and house church movements all show enormous promise for nurturing a new faithfulness. There is much to look forward to here. The outcome will depend in no short measure on whether they can avoid the ideological traps outlined above. Will they avoid becoming a swirl of human activity built upon antagonisms and false enjoyments? Will they actually shape a politic of fullness in Christ capable of sustaining a social witness in the world? If they do avoid, in the words of a famous observer, "doing these things merely on their own," then in the words of that same observer, "no one will be able to stop them" (Acts 5:38–39 NLT).

Glossary of Žižek's Terms

Fantasy: Every ideology must provide a "fantasy," an imaginary situation, in which the subject can see him or herself and where his/her desires are legitimated. Each fantasy must provide a scenario wherein the citizenry can act *as if* they believe even if there are several reasons, or incursions, which might suggest otherwise. This fantasy is not about what the subject wants. It is about the *Che voui*? ("what do you want?" in French) of the Big Other, i.e., what does society want, what do they want from me which in turn tells me what I should want? In the case of "the inerrant Bible," for instance, I act as if I have the truth because this is what others also want and expect of me. "The inerrant Bible" and all the stories around it provide the imaginary for my social organization. My parents and my church friends all become part of this fantasy, which enables us all to live in desire of "the truth."

Ideological cynicism: Ideological cynicism recognizes that the political subject already knows the falsehoods of ideology. He or she is already aware that things are not what they seem and already realizes certain particular interests enforce the ongoing perceived truth of the reigning ideology, yet these subjects still choose to act like true believers. In other words, "they know it, but they are doing it anyway." We watch CNBC/Fox News and analyze why policy makers do what they do in order to make the other side look a certain way or pay off a special interest contributor. Yet we continue to go on voting and playing along. These are the new conditions for political analysis acknowledged by

Žižek. My question for this book is, In what ways does evangelicalism function as an ideology in these ways and for us Christians who are a part of the evangelical church?

Ideology: Ideology refers to the set of ideas by which a people make sense of their social world by covering over certain unwanted features of their governed social existence. A certain "false consciousness" is implied because, as Marx said, "they do not know it, but they are doing it." People believe ideology in the sense that "this is the way things really are," and this is what makes it possible for the ideology to maintain its governing hold on its subjects. It is the job of the critique of ideology to expose the various false assumptions and power interests that are interwoven in ideology's operations.

Irruption of the Real: An "irruption of the Real," as I define it, is an excessive episode within a political system that reveals the drives (the antagonism, the *jouissance*, and/or the basic lack) that lie beneath its ideology. While not a Žižekian term *per se*, it sums up the sense of some of his cultural observations. Such "irruptions" often happen when someone or something takes the ideology too literally—taking its implications to its excess, revealing the absurdity or false motivations that lie beneath the surface of it. Such a revealing affords the opportunity to break free from the ideology's hold. It also happens when, in an episode, an irrational enjoyment (*jouissance*) is released exposing some of the excess drives behind the beliefs. In this book, several figures within evangelicalism provide occasions for such an excess revealing that so typifies the "irruption of the Real."

Jouissance: *Jouissance* is a French term that is translated "enjoyment" referring to the various kinds of excessive and irrational enjoyments that hold the subject in the grasp of the governing ideology. There is a demand placed upon us by the ideology to enjoy an object put forth for our desire within an ideology. It keeps us locked in as subjects to the ideology. In this book I use *jouissance* often to describe the enjoyment of pursuing an object withheld from us (or "stolen" from us) that becomes more powerful than if we possessed the actual object. It is a perverse enjoyment that comes forth when an ideology displaces an immediate enjoyment onto an object (often the *objet petit a*) thereby playing off resentment. When an ideology reaches "a pressure point," the release of *jouissance* often proves excessive and irrational. Žižek uses *jouissance* in other more complex social-psychoanalytic ways, which I sometimes play off of in the book. .

Master-Signifier: A Master-Signifier is a conceptual object to which people give their allegiance thereby enabling a political group to form. It represents something to believe in. Yet it is an enigma for the members themselves because nobody really knows what it means; but each of them presupposes that all the others know. Concepts such as Obama's "Change We Can Believe In" or Bush's "Freedom" are examples of Master-Signifiers in recent history. In this book I contend that within evangelicalism "the inerrant Bible," "the decision," and "the Christian nation" function like key Master-Signifiers for our social organization.

Objet Petit A: An *objet petit a* is French for "small other." The "a" stands for "autre" in French. It is an object we order our desire towards as subjects of the ideology because this object is a desired "something" the political system/ideology could not in itself fulfill. This object then becomes that which is unobtainable, that which I want/pursue all the more. It becomes the cause of our desire. The *objet petit a* of an ideology helps us diagnose the *jouissance* which often becomes aimed at it. In the book I used "the liberals," and their confident possession of the truth, as the *objet petit a* (the confident possession of the truth being the true *objet petit a*) towards which *jouissance* is shaped via "the inerrant Bible."

Overidentification: Overidentification is a means whereby the failures of a given ideology can be exposed. In overidentification, one obeys the ideology too much, not realizing that one is not "really" supposed to take it that seriously. Overidentification thus serves to confront and embarrass those woven into a given ideology, for it represents that which we are all supposed to know that we are not to do, yet it appears to be more faithful (rather than less) to the reigning ideology. In the book, I suggest that the King James Bible Only Baptists represent such a case of overidentification with the inerrant Bible especially when they pronounce that one cannot be saved except via the words of the KJV Only.

The Real: The Real is that empty void which for Žižek lies at the heart of all social existence. It is that which can never be totally encaptured within the realm of language or the Symbolic Order. It always presents something that cannot be contained by the Symbolic Order and therefore requires "ideologization," i.e., some covering over. As a result, it is the place from which antagonisms, contradictions and false enjoyments swirl around in the formation of a political system and/or symbolic order. In Žižek's world, it is what keeps us going.

Sublime Object: The Sublime Object, for Žižek, often plays an overlapping role to the Master-Signifier in an ideology. It is the object we rally around to pursue together. Yet this term emphasizes the unattainable quality of this object, /signifier. Using Lacan's *definition*, it is "an *object* raised to the level of the (impossible-real) *Thing.*" Žižek, *Sublime Object* (1989), 202–3. Because it is always just outside our reach, it often plays on that perverse enjoyment we experience when blaming somebody or something for stealing it from us. It therefore has the allure to hold us captive as subjects within the ideology.

Symbolic Order: The "Symbolic Order" refers to the various linguistic structures which make possible a social system including its institutions, rituals, social norms, and language. With the Symbolic Order one has already entered and become a subject for and to the social system. Here we find ourselves in relation to "the big Other" of the system, that societal "group think," or "what everyone knows," that enables us to believe in something and find our "selves" within it. In this book, I explore how evangelicalism functions as a social system ordering our lives together.

Traversing the fantasy: "Traverse the fantasy" most often refers to the psychological process of breaking free from the fantasy's hold on us as subjects thereby enabling us to renounce the Symbolic Order—the Big Other. Such a traversing does not occur for Žižek as a heroic individualist act of critique that rises above the ideology thereby unmasking its lies. Instead it happens when we believe within the ideology excessively so as to force its unfounded arbitrary character to be revealed. In this book, by exposing the excessive contradictions of those who seek to believe evangelicalism's master-signifying beliefs "too much" I seek to traverse some of evangelicalism's fantasies thereby opening a space for a new faithfulness from evangelicalism.

Bibliography

Aune, David. "Recent Readings for Paul Relating to Justification by Faith." In *ReReading Paul Together: Protestant and Catholic Perspectives on Justification,* edited by David Aune, 188–245. Grand Raids: Baker, 2006.

Badiou, Alain. *Being and Event.* Translated by Oliver Feltham. London: Continuum, 2006.

————. *Infinite Thought: Truth and the Return to Philosophy.* Translated and edited by Oliver Feltham and Justin Clemens. London: Continuum, 2005.

————. *Manifesto for Philosophy.* Translated by Norman Madarasz. Albany: SUNY Press, 1999.

————. *Saint Paul: The Foundation of Universalism.* Translated by Ray Brassier. Cultural Memory in the Present. Stanford, CA: Stanford University Press, 2003.

Barber, Benjamin R. *Jihad vs. McWorld.* New York: Times, 1995.

Balmer, Randall. *Thy Kingdom Come: How the Religious Right Distorts the Faith and Threatens America.* New York: Basic, 2006.

Balthasar, Hans Urs von. *The Glory of The Lord: A Theological Aesthetics.* Vol. 1, *Seeing the Form.* Translated by Erasmo Leiva-Merikakis. Edited by Joseph Fessio SJ and John Riches. San Francisco: Ignatius, 1998.

————. *The Theology of Henri de Lubac.* Translated by Susan Clements. San Francisco: Ignatius, 1983.

Barna, George. "Surprisingly Few Adults Outside Christianity Have Positive Views of Christians." *Barna Report* (December 3, 2002). No pages. Online: http://www .barna.org/barna-update/article/5-barna-update/86-surprisingly-few-adults -outside-of-christianity-have-positive-views-of-christians.

Barna Group. "New Study Shows Trends in Tithing and Giving" No pages. Online: http://www.barna.org/barna-update/article/18-congregations/41-new-study -shows-trends-in-tithing-and-donating.

Barth, Karl. *Church Dogmatics.* I/1: *The Doctrine of God.* Translated by Geoffrey W. Bromiley. Edinburgh: T. & T. Clark, 1975.

————. *Church Dogmatics.* IV/2: *The Doctrine of Reconciliation.* Translated by Geoffrey W Bromiley. Edinburgh: T. & T. Clark, 1958.

————. *Dogmatics in Outline.* Translated by G. T. Thompson. New York: Harper & Row, 1959.

————. *God Here and Now.* Translated by Paul M. VanLondon: Routledge, 2003.

Bebbington, David. *The Dominance of Evangelicalism*. Downers Grove: InterVarsity, 2005.

Billings, J. Todd. "John Milbank's Theology of the 'Gift' and Calvin's Theology of Grace: A Critical Comparison." *Modern Theology* 21 (2005) 87–105.

Boff, Leonardo. *Holy Trinity, Perfect Community*. Maryknoll, NY: Orbis, 2000.

Bosch, David. *Transforming Mission: Paradigm Shifts in the Theology of Mission*. Maryknoll, NY: Orbis, 1991.

Boyd, Gregory A. *The Myth of a Christian Nation: How the Quest for Political Power is Destroying the Church*. Grand Rapids: Zondervan, 2005.

Byasee, Jason. *Praise Seeking Understanding: Reading the Psalms with Augustine*. Grand Rapids: Eerdmans, 2007.

Carpenter, Joel A. *Revive Us Again: The Reawakening of American Fundamentalism*. New York: Oxford University Press, 1999.

Carson, D. A. *Becoming Conversant with the Emergent Church: Understanding a Movement and Its Implications*. Grand Rapids: Zondervan 2005.

Cavanaugh, William. *Torture and Eucharist: Theology, Politics, and the Body of Christ*. Challenges in Contemporary Theology. Malden, MA: Blackwell, 1998.

Chauvet, Louis-Marie. *Symbol and Sacrament: A Sacramental Interpretation of Christian Existence*. Translated by Patrick Madigan and Madeleine Beaumont. Collegeville, MN: Liturgical, 1995.

Clark, David K. *To Know and Love God: Method for Theology*. Wheaton, IL: Good News, 2003.

Clark, Victoria. *Allies for Armageddon: The Rise of Christian Zionism*. New Haven, CT: Yale University Press, 2007.

Coles, Romand. *Beyond Gated Politics: Reflections for the Possibility of Democracy*. Minneapolis: University of Minnesota Press, 2005.

Collins, Kenneth. *The Evangelical Moment: The Promise of an American Religion*. Grand Rapids: Baker, 2005.

Comfort, Ray. *Hell's Best Kept Secret*. New Kensington, PA: Whitaker House, 1989.

Connolly, William. "The Evangelical-Capitalist Resonance Machine." *Political Theory* 33 (2005) 869–86.

Corbin, Wyndy. "The Impact of the American Dream on Evangelical Ethics." *Crosscurrents* 55:3 (2005). Online: http://www.crosscurrents.org/corbin2005.htm.

Cunningham, Conor. *A Genealogy of Nihilism: Philosophies of Nothing and the Difference of Theology*. Radical Orthodoxy. London: Routledge, 2002.

Dayton, Donald W. *Discovering an Evangelical Heritage*. New York: Harper & Row, 1976.

———. "'Evangelical': More Puzzling Than You Think." Occasional Paper no. 29. Ecumenical People, Programs, Papers. *Newsletter of the Institute for Ecumenical and Cultural Research* (May 1988) 5–8.

———. "The Search for the Historical Evangelicalism: George Marsden's History of Fuller Seminary as a Case Study." *Christian Scholar's Review* 23 (1993) 12–33.

———. *Theological Roots of Pentecostalism*. Grand Rapids: Zondervan, 1987.

Dayton, Donald W., and Robert K. Johnston, editors. *The Variety of American Evangelicalism*. Memphis: University of Tennessee Press, 2001.

Davis, John Jefferson. *Evangelical Ethics: Issues Facing the Church Today*. Phillipsburg, NJ: P. & R., 1993.

Draper, Robert. *Dead Certain: The Presidency of George W. Bush*. New York: Free, 2007.

Drummond, Lewis. *The Evangelist.* Waco, TX: Word, 1982.

Dyrness, William A. *The Earth is God's: A Theology of Culture.* Maryknoll, NY: Orbis, 1997.

Ehrich, Tom. "Not Heard From the Pulpit." *USA Today,* March 12, 2006.

Ehrman, Bart. *Jesus, Interrupted: Revealing the Hidden Contradictions in the Bible (And Why We Don't Know About Them).* San Francisco: HarperOne, 2010.

———. *Misquoting Jesus.* San Francisco: HarperOne, 2007.

Erickson, Millard J. *Christian Theology.* 2nd ed. Grand Rapids: Baker, 2009.

Falwell, Jerry. *Listen America.* New York: Doubleday, 1980.

Ferraro, Ken. "Does Religion Increase the Prevalence and Incidence of Obesity in Adulthood?" *Journal For the Scientific Study of Religion* (June 2006) 269–81.

Fitch, David. *The Great Giveaway: Reclaiming the Mission of the Church.* Grand Rapids: Baker, 2005.

Fineman, Howard. "Bush and God." *Newsweek,* March 10, 2003.

Flett, John. *The Witness of God: The Trinity, Missio Dei, Karl Barth, and the Nature of Christian Community.* Grand Rapids: Eerdmans, 2010.

Fowl, Stephen E. *Engaging Scripture: A Model for Theological Interpretation.* Challenges in Contemporary Theology. Oxford: Blackwell, 1998.

———. *Philippians.* The Two Horizons New Testament Commentary. Grand Rapids: Eerdmans, 2005.

Frost, David, and Fred Bauer. *Billy Graham: Personal Thoughts of a Public Man.* Colorado Springs: Chariot Victor, 1999.

Frost, Michael. *Exiles: Living Missionally in a Post-Christian Culture.* Peabody, MA: Hendrickson, 2006.

Frost, Michael, and Alan Hirsch. *The Shaping of Things to Come: Innovation and Mission for the 21st-Century Church.* Peabody, MA: Hendrickson, 2003.

———. *ReJesus: A Wild Messiah for a Missional Church.* Peabody, MA: Hendrickson, 2009.

Galli, Mark. "On the Lasting Evangelical Survival." *Christianity Today* (March 11, 2009) No pages. Online: http://www.christianitytoday.com/ct/2009/marchweb -only/110–31.0.html.

Geisler, Norman. *Christian Ethics.* Grand Rapids: Baker, 1990.

Gilgoff, Dan. *The Jesus Machine: How James Dobson, Focus on the Family, and Evangelical America are Winning the Culture War.* New York: St Martin's, 2007.

Goodstein, Laurie "Disowning Conservative Politics, Evangelical Pastor Rattles Flock." *New York Times,* July 27, 2006.

Gorman, Michael. *Inhabiting the Cruciform God: Kenosis, Justification, and Theosis in Paul's Narrative Soteriology.* Grand Rapids: Eerdmans, 2009.

Graham, Billy. *How to Be Born Again.* Waco TX: Word, 1977.

Greeley, Andrew, and Michael Hout. *The Truth About Conservative Christians: What They Think and What They Believe.* Chicago: University of Chicago Press, 2006.

Grenz, Stanley. *The Moral Quest: Foundations of Christian Ethics.* Downers Grove: InterVarsity, 1997.

Grudem, Wayne. *Systematic Theology: An Introduction to Biblical Doctrine.* Grand Rapids: Zondervan 2000.

Guder, Darrell. *The Continuing Conversion of the Church.* Grand Rapids: Eerdmans, 2001.

Gushee, David, and Justin Phillips. "Moral Formation and the Evangelical Voter: A Report from the Red States." *Journal of the Society of Christian Ethics* 26 (2006) 23–60.

Hansen, Colin. *Young, Restless, Reformed: A Journalist's Journey with the New Calvinists.* Wheaton, IL: Crossway, 2008.

Harris, Sam. *Letter to a Christian Nation.* New York: Knopf, 2006.

Hauerwas, Stanley. *Character and the Christian Life: A Study in Theological Ethics.* San Antonio, TX: Trinity, 1985.

———. *Community of Character: Toward a Constructive Christian Social Ethics.* Notre Dame, IN: University of Notre Dame Press, 1981.

———. *Suffering Presence: Theological Reflections on Medicine, the Mentally Handicapped, and the Church.* Notre Dame, IN: University of Notre Dame Press, 1986.

———. *Truthfulness and Tragedy: Further Investigations into Christian Ethics.* Notre Dame, IN: University of Notre Dame Press, 1977.

Hauerwas, Stanley, and Roman Coles. *Christianity, Democracy, and the Radical Ordinary: Conversations Between a Christian and a Radical Democrat.* Theopolitical Visions. Eugene, OR: Cascade, 2008.

Hedges, Chris. *American Fascists: The Christian Right and the War on America.* New York: Free, 2007.

Hiebert, Paul. "The Category 'Christian' in the Mission Task." *International Review of Mission* 72 (1983) 421–27.

Hiemstra, Rick. "Evangelical Giving and Volunteering." *Church and Faith Trends* 2:2 (2009). Online: http://files.efc-canada.net/min/rc/cft/V02I02/Evangelical_Giving_and_Volunteering.pdf.

Henry, Carl F. "Evangelicals in the Social Struggle." In *Contemporary Religious Issues*, edited by Donald Hartsock, 284–99. Belmont, CA: Wadsworth, 1968.

———. *The Uneasy Conscience of Modern Fundamentalism.* Grand Rapids: Eerdmans, 1947.

Hirsch, Alan. *The Forgotten Ways: Reactivating the Missional Church.* Grand Rapids: Brazos, 2006.

Hitchens, Christopher. *God is Not Great: How Religion Poisons Everything.* New York: Hatchette, 2007.

Hodges, Zane. *Absolutely Free! A Biblical Reply to Lordship Salvation.* Grand Rapids: Zondervan, 1989.

———. *The Gospel Under Siege.* Dallas: Redencion Viva, 1981.

Hunter, James Davison. *American Evangelicalism: Conservative Religion and the Quandary of Modernity.* New Brunswick, NJ: Rutgers University Press, 1983.

———. *Culture Wars: The Struggle to Define America.* New York: Basic Books, 1991.

———. *To Change The World: The Irony, Tragedy, and Possibility of Christianity in the Late Modern World.* New York: Oxford University Press, 2010.

Hyles, Jack. *Enemies of Soul Winning.* Hammond, IN: Hyles-Anderson, 1993.

Johnston, Adrian. *Žižek's Ontology: A Transcendental Materialist Theory of Subjectivity.* Evanston, IL: Northwestern University Press, 2008.

Jones, Tony. *The New Christians: Dispatches from the Emergent Frontier.* San Francisco: Jossey-Bass, 2008.

Kerr, Nathan R. *Christ, History and Apocalyptic: The Politics of Christian Mission.* Theopolitical Visions. Eugene, OR: Cascade, 2009.

Kinnaman, David, and Gabe Lyons. *UnChristian: What a New Generation Really Thinks about Christianity . . . and Why It Matters*. Grand Rapids: Baker, 2007.

Kirwan, Michael. *Political Theology: An Introduction*. Minneapolis: Fortress, 2009.

Kluckholn, Clyde, and William H. Kelly. "The Concept of Culture." In *The Science of Man in the World Crisis*, edited by Ralph Linton, 78–106. New York: Columbia University Press, 1945.

Kotsko, Adam. *Žižek and Theology*. London: T. & T. Clark, 2008.

Kristof, Nicholas. "Learning from the Sin of Sodom." *New York Times*, February 27, 2010.

Kurtz, Paul. "The Free Market With a Human Face. *Free Inquiry Magazine* 24 (2004). Online: http://www.secularhumanism.org/library/fi/kurtz_24_2.htm.

Kyle, Richard. *Evangelicalism and Americanized Christianity*. Newark, NJ: Transaction, 2006.

Lacan, Jacques. *Ecrits: A Selection*. New York: Norton, 1971.

Laclau, Ernesto. *Emancipation(s)*. London: Verso, 1996.

Laclau, Ernesto, and Chantal Mouffe. *Hegemony and Socialist Strategy: Towards a Radical Democratic Politics*. London: Verso, 1985.

Lanham, Robert. *The Sinner's Guide to the Evangelical Right*. New York: New American Library, 2006.

Lawton, Kim A. "Evangelism Explosion Retools its Approach." *Christianity Today* (March 3, 1997). Online: http://www.christianitytoday.com/ct/1997/march3/7t3058.html.

Lindsell, Harold. *The Battle for The Bible*. Grand Rapids: Zondervan, 1978.

Livingstone, David N. *Adam's Ancestors: Race, Religion and the Politics of Human Origins*. Baltimore: John Hopkins University Press, 2010.

Long, D. Stephen. *Divine Economy: Theology and the Market*. Radical Orthodoxy. London: Routledge, 2000.

———. *Speaking of God: Theology, Language, and Truth*. Grand Rapids: Eerdmans, 2009.

Lovelace, Richard. *Dynamics of Spiritual Life: An Evangelical Theology of Renewal*. Downers Grove: InterVarsity, 1979.

Lubac, Henri de. *Catholicism: Christ and the Common Destiny of Man*. San Francisco: Ignatius, 1988.

———. *Corpus Mysticum: The Eucharist and the Church in the Middle Ages*. Notre Dame, IN: University of Notre Dame Press, 2006.

MacArthur, John. *The Gospel According to Jesus*. Grand Rapids: Zondervan, 1988.

———. *ReDiscovering Expository Preaching*. Grand Rapids: Thomas Nelson, 1992.

———. *The Truth War: Fighting for Certainty in an Age of Deception*. Nashville: Thomas Nelson, 2007.

Mannermaa, Tuomo. *Christ Present in Faith: Luther's View of Justification*. Edited by Kirsi Stjerna. Minneapolis: Fortress, 2005.

Mansfield, Stephen. *The Faith of George Bush*. Lake Mary, FL: Charisma House, 2004.

Marsden, George. *Fundamentalism and American Culture*. New York: Oxford University Press, 1980.

———. *Reforming Fundamentalism: Fuller Seminary and the New Evangelicalism*. Grand Rapids: Eerdmans, 1987.

———. *Understanding Fundamentalism and Evangelicalism*. Grand Rapids: Eerdmans, 1991.

Martin, Waldo E. *Brown v. Board of Education*. Boston: St Martin's, 1998.

McCormack, Bruce. "Justitia Aliena: Karl Barth in Conversation with the Evangelical Doctrine of Imputed Righteousness." In *Justification in Perspective: Historical Developments and Contemporary Challenges*, edited by Bruce McCormack, 168–92. Grand Rapids: Baker Academic, 2006.

McGrath, Alister. *Iustitia Dei: A History of the Doctrine of Justification*. New York: Cambridge University Press, 1998.

McIntosh, John. "Missio Dei." In *The Evangelical Dictionary of World Missions*, edited by Scott Moreau, 631–33. Grand Rapids: Baker, 2000.

McIntyre, Patrick. *The Graham Formula*. Mammoth Spring, AR: White Harvest, 2005.

McKay, William Paul, and Ken Abraham. *Billy: The Untold Story of a Young Billy Graham and the Test of Faith that Almost Changed Everything*. Nashville: Thomas Nelson, 2008.

McKnight, Scot. "The Ironic Faith of Emergents." *Christianity Today* (September 2008). Online: http://www.christianitytoday.com/ct/2008/september/39.62.html.

McLaren, Brian D. *Everything Must Change: Jesus, Global Crises and a Revolution of Hope*. Nashville: Thomas Nelson, 2007.

———. *A New Kind of Christian: A Tale of Two Friends on a Spiritual Journey*. San Francisco: Jossey-Bass, 2001.

———. *A New Kind of Christianity: Ten Questions that are Transforming the Faith*. New York: HarperOne, 2010.

———. *The Secret Message of Jesus: Uncovering the Truth that Could Change Everything*. Nashville: Thomas Nelson, 2006.

McLean, Bethany, and Peter Elkind. *The Smartest Guys in The Room: The Amazing Rise and Scandalous Fall of Enron*. New York: Penguin, 2003.

Meacham, Jon. "The End of Christian America." *Newsweek* (April 13, 2009). Online: http://www.newsweek.com/2009/04/03/the-end-of-christian-america.html.

Milbank, John. *Being Reconciled: Ontology and Pardon*. Radical Orthodoxy. London: Routledge, 2003.

———. "Can a Gift Be Given? Prolegomena to a Future Trinitarian Metaphysic." *Modern Theology* 11 (1995) 119–61.

———. "Can Morality Be Christian?" In *The Word Made Strange: Theology, Language, Culture*, 219–32. Cambridge, MA: Blackwell, 1997.

———. "The Double Glory, or Paradox: On Not Quite Agreeing with Slavoj Žižek." In *The Monstrosity of Christ: Paradox or Dialectic*, edited by Creston Davis et al., 110–233. Cambridge: MIT Press, 2009.

———. "Gregory of Nyssa: The Force of Identity." In *Christian Origins*, edited by Lewis Ayres and L. Gregory Jones, 94–116. London: Routledge, 1998.

———. "Materialism and Transcendence." In *Theology and the Political*, edited by Creston Davis et al., 393–426. Durham, NC: Duke University Press, 2005.

———. "The Soul of Reciprocity. Part One, Reciprocity Refused." *Modern Theology* 17 (2001) 335–91.

———. "The Soul of Reciprocity. Part Two, Reciprocity Granted." *Modern Theology* 17 (2001) 485–507.

———. *The Word Made Strange: Theology, Language and Culture*. Cambridge, MA: Blackwell, 1997.

Moberg, David. *The Great Reversal*. 2nd ed. Philadelphia: Lippincott, 1972.

Mohler, R. Albert. "A Christian View of the Economic Crisis." (September 24, 2008). Online: http://www.albertmohler.com/?cat=Blog&cid=2550.

———. *The Disappearance of God: Dangerous Beliefs in the New Spiritual Openness.* Sisters, OR: Multnomah, 2009.

Moltmann, Jürgen. *The Church in the Power of the Spirit: A Contribution to Messianic Ecclesiology.* London: SCM, 1977.

———. *Theology of Hope: On the Ground and the Implications of a Christian Eschatology.* New York: Harper& Row, 1972.

———. *The Trinity and the Kingdom: The Doctrine of God.* Minneapolis: Fortress, 1993.

Moreton, Bethany. *To Serve God and Wal-Mart: The Making of Christian Free Enterprise.* Cambridge: Harvard University Press, 2009.

Morris, Henry M. *The King of Creation.* San Diego: CLP, 1980.

Morrison, John. "Barth, Barthians, and Evangelicals: Reassessing the Question of the Relation of Holy Scripture and the Word of God." *Trinity Journal* 25 (2004) 187–213.

Mott, Stephen. *Biblical Ethics and Social Change.* New York: Oxford University Press, 1982.

Myers, Tony. *Slavoj Žižek.* London: Routledge, 2003.

Neff, David. "Together in the Jesus Story." *Christianity Today* (September 2006). Online: http://www.christianitytoday.com/ct/2006/september/10.54.html.

Newbigin, Lesslie. *Foolishness to the Greeks: The Gospel and Western Culture.* Grand Rapids: Eerdmans, 1986.

———. *The Gospel in a Pluralist Society.* Grand Rapids: Eerdmans, 1989.

———. *The Open Secret: An Introduction to the Theology of Mission.* Grand Rapids: Eerdmans, 1995.

———. *Truth and Authority in Modernity.* Valley Forge, PA: Trinity, 1996.

Niebuhr, Reinhold. *Children of Light and Children of Darkness.* New York: Scribners, 1960.

———. *Moral Man and Immoral Society.* Reprint, Philadelphia: Westminster John Knox, 2002.

———. *The Nature and Destiny of Man.* 2 vols. Reprint, Philadelphia: Westminster John Knox, 1996.

Noll, Mark. *American Evangelical Christianity: An Introduction.* Oxford: Blackwell, 2001.

———. "Charles Hodge and B. B. Warfield on Science, the Bible, Evolution and Darwinism." *Modern Reformation* 7:3 (1998) 18–22.

———, editor. *The Princeton Theology, 1812–1921: Scripture, Science, Theological Method from Archibald Alexander to Benjamin Breckinridge Warfield.* Grand Rapids: Baker, 2001.

———. *The Rise of Evangelicalism: The Age of Edwards, Whitefield and the Wesleys.* Downers Grove: InterVarsity, 2003.

———. *The Scandal of the Evangelical Mind.* Grand Rapids: Eerdmans, 1995.

Osteen, Joel. *Your Best Life Now.* New York: FaithWords, 2004.

Padgett, Tim. "The Rise and Fall of Bernie Ebbers." *Time* (May 13, 2002). Online: http://www.time.com/time/magazine/article/0,9171,1002408,00.html.

Pounds, Marcus. *Žižek: A (Very) Critical Introduction.* Interventions. Grand Rapids: Eerdmans, 2008.

Pinsky, Mark."Blessed Ned of Springfield." *Christianity Today* (February, 2008). Online: http://www.christianitytoday.com/ct/2001/february5/1.28.html.

Rasmusson, Arne. *The Church as Polis: From Political Theology to Theological Politics as exemplified by Jurgen Moltmann and Stanley Hauerwas.* Notre Dame, IN: University of Notre Dame Press, 1994.

Robinson, Haddon. *Biblical Preaching: The Development and Delivery of Expository Messages.* Grand Rapids: Baker, 2001.

Rollins, Peter. *How (Not) to Speak of God.* Brewster, MA: Paraclete, 2006.

———. *The Fidelity of Betrayal: Towards a Church Beyond Belief.* Brewster, MA: Paraclete, 2008.

Roxburgh, Allan. "Missional Leadership: Equipping God's People for Mission." In *Missional Church: A Vision for the Sending of the Church in North America,* edited by Darrell L. Guder, 183–220. Grand Rapids: Eerdmans, 1998.

Sandeen, Ernest. *The Roots of Fundamentalism: British and American Millenarianism 1800–1930.* Chicago: University of Chicago Press, 1970.

Schaeffer, Francis. *A Christian Manifesto.* Wheaton, IL: Crossway, 1981.

Scott, Peter. *A Political Theology of Nature.* Cambridge: Cambridge University Press, 2003.

Sellers, Jeff M. "Deliver Us from Wal-Mart?" *Christianity Today* (April 2005).

Sheler, Jeffery. *Believers: A Journey into Evangelical America.* New York: Viking Adult, 2006.

Sharpe, Matthew. *Slavoj Žižek: A Little Piece of the Real.* Aldershot: Ashgate, 2004.

Sider, Ron. *The Scandal of the Evangelical Conscience: Why are Christians Living Just Like the Rest of the World?* Grand Rapids: Baker, 2006.

Smith, James K. A. *Speech and Theology: Language and the Logic of Incarnation.* London: Routledge, 2002.

Smith, Timothy. *Revivalism and Social Reform: Protestantism on the Eve of the Civil War.* Nashville: Abingdon, 1957.

Sparks, Kenton. *God's Word in Human Words.* Grand Rapids: Baker 2008 .

Stackhouse, John. "What Scandal? Whose Conscience?" *Books & Culture* (July/August 2007) 20–21, 40–41.

Stone, Jon R. *On the Boundaries of Evangelicalism: The Postwar Evangelical Coalition.* New York: Palgrave, 1999.

Suskind, Ron. "Without a Doubt." *The New York Times Magazine* (October 17, 2004). Online: http://query.nytimes.com/gst/fullpage.html?res=9C05EFD8113BF934A2 5753C1A9629C8B63.

Sweeney, Douglas, and Mark Rogers, "Walk the Aisle." *Christian History* (October 2008). Online: http://www.christianitytoday.com/ch/thepastinthepresent/ storybehind/walktheaisle.html.

Tanner, Kathryn. *Jesus, Humanity and the Trinity: A Brief Systematic Theology.* Minneapolis: Augsburg Fortress, 2001.

———. *Theories of Culture: A New Agenda for Theology.* Minneapolis: Augsburg Fortress, 1997.

Thompson, Michael. "Jessica Simpson: Her Most Uncensored Interview." *Allure Magazine* (October 2006).

Tillich, Paul. *Systematic Theology.* 2 vols. Chicago: University of Chicago Press, 1951–1963.

Tomlinson, Dave. *The Post=Evangelical.* Grand Rapids: Zondervan, 2003.

Tonder, Lars, and Lasse Thomassen. "Introduction: Rethinking Radical Democracy Between Abundance and Lack." In *Radical Democracy: Politics between Abundance and Lack*, edited by Lars Tonder and Lasse Thomassen. New York: Manchester University Press, 2005.

Torrance, Alan. "The Trinity." In *The Cambridge Companion to Karl Barth*, edited by John Webster, 72–91. Cambridge: Cambridge University Press, 2000.

Torrey, R. A., editor. *The Fundamentals*. Grand Rapids: Baker, 2003.

Tuyeson, Ernest Lee. *Redeemer Nation: The Idea of America's Millennial Role*. Chicago: University of Chicago Press, 1968.

Vanhoozer, Kevin. *The Drama of Doctrine: A Canonical-Linguistic Approach to Theology*. Louisville, KY: Westminster John Knox, 2005.

Volf, Miroslav. *Exclusion and Embrace: A Theological Exploration of Identity, Otherness, and Reconciliation*. Nashville: Abingdon, 1996.

Waller, Scott. "Ebbers tells Church Members He's no Crook." *Mississippi Clarion Ledger* (July 2, 2002). Online: http://orig.clarionledger.com/news/0207/02/b01b.html.

Wallis, Jim. *God's Politics: Why the Right Gets It Wrong and the Left Doesn't Get It*. San Francisco: HarperOne, 2005.

———. *The Great Awakening: Reviving Faith and Politics is a Post-Religious Right America*. San Francisco: HarperOne, 2008.

Ward, Graham. *Cities of God*. Radical Orthodoxy. London: Routledge, 2000.

Warfield, B. B. *Selected Shorter Writings*. 2 vols. Philadelphia: P. & R., 1976.

———. "The Inerrancy of the Original Autographs." In *The Princeton Theology 1812–1921*, edited by Mark A. Noll, 268–88. Grand Rapids: Baker, 1983.

Warren, Rick. *The Purpose Driven Church*. Grand Rapids: Zondervan, 1995.

Webber, Robert. *Journey to Jesus: The Worship, Evangelism, and Nurture Mission of the Church*. Nashville: Abingdon, 2001.

Wells, David. *The Courage to Be Protestant: Truth-lovers, Marketers, and Emergents in the Postmodern World*. Grand Rapids: Eerdmans, 2008.

White, Mel. *Religion Gone Bad: The Hidden Dangers of the Christian Right*. New York: Penguin, 2006.

Willard, Dallas. *The Divine Conspiracy: Discovering your Hidden Life in God*. San Francisco: Harper SanFrancisco, 1998.

Willmer, Wesley K. "Evangelicals: Linking Fervency of Faith and Generosity of Giving." *New Directions for Philanthropic Fundraising* 7 (1995) 101–15.

Williams, Rowan. *On Christian Theology*. Challenges in Contemporary Theology. Malden, MA: Blackwell, 2000.

Winner, Lauren. "Sex in the Body of Christ." *Christianity Today* (May 15, 2005). Online: http://www.christianitytoday.com/ct/2005/may/34.28.html.

Woodbridge, John. "Biblical Authority: Toward an Evaluation of the Rogers and McKim proposal." In *Biblical Authority and Conservative Perspectives*, edited by Douglas Moo, 55–76. New York: Kregel, 1997.

Woodward, Bob. *Plan of Attack*. New York: Simon & Shuster, 2004.

Wright, Bradley R. E. *Christians Are Hate-Filled Hypocrites. . . and Other Lies You've Been Told: A Sociologist Shatters Myths From the Secular and Christian Media*. Grand Rapids: Bethany, 2010.

Wright, Christopher. *The Mission of God: Unlocking the Bible's Grand Narrative*. Downers Grove: InterVarsity, 2006.

Wright, John. *Telling God's Story: Narrative Preaching for Christian Formation.* Downers Grove: InterVarsity, 2007.

Wright, N. T. *After You Believe: Why Christian Character Matters.* San Francisco: HarperOne Books, 2010.

———. *Justification: God's Plan and Paul's Vision.* Downers Grove: InterVarsity, 2009.

———. *Letter to the Romans.* The New Interpreter's Bible: A Commentary in Twelve Volumes, X. Nashville: Abingdon, 2002.

———. *Paul in Fresh Perspective.* Minneapolis: Fortress, 2005.

———. *What Saint Paul Really Said.* Grand Rapids: Eerdmans, 1997.

Wright, Steve, and Chris Graves. *Rethink: Is Student Ministry Working?* New York: InQuest Ministries, 2007.

Yoder, John Howard. *Body Politics: Five Practices of the Christian Community Before the Watching World.* Scottdale PA: Herald, 1992.

———. *For the Nations: Essays Public and Evangelical.* Grand Rapids: Eerdmans, 1997.

———. "How H. Richard Niebuhr Reasoned." In *Authentic Transformation: A New Vision of Christ and Culture,* edited by Glen Stassen et al., 31–89. Nashville: Abingdon, 1996.

———. "If Christ is Truly Lord." In *The Original Revolution,* 52–84. Scottdale, PA: Herald, 1971.

———. "Meaning After Babel: With Jeffrey Stout Beyond Relativism." *Journal of Religious Ethics* 24 (1996) 125–39.

———. *The Original Revolution: Essays on Christian Pacifism.* Scottdale, PA: Herald, 1972.

———. *The Politics of Jesus: Vicit Agnus Noster.* 2nd ed. Grand Rapids: Eerdmans, 1994.

———. *The Priestly Kingdom: Social Ethics as Gospel.* Notre Dame, IN: University of Notre Dame Press, 1984.

Young, Eric. "CCC Media records over 1 Million Decisions for Christ in a Month." *The Christian Post* (July 16, 2009). Online: http://www.christianpost.com/article/20090716/ccc-media-ministry-records-over-1m-decisions-for-christ-in-1-month.

Zakaria, Fareed. *The Post-American World.* New York: Norton, 2008.

Žižek, Slavoj. "Dialectical Clarity Versus the Mystical Conceit of Paradox." In *The Monstrosity of Christ: Paradox or Dialectic,* edited by Creston Davis et al, 235–303. Cambridge: MIT Press, 2009.

———. "Da Capo senza Fine," In *Contingency, Hegemony, Universality,* edited by Judith Butler et al., 213–62. London: Verso, 2000.

———. *Did Somebody Say Totalitarianism? Five Essays in the (Mis)Use of a Notion.* London: Verso, 2002.

———. *For They Know Not What They Do: Enjoyment as a Political Factor.* London: Verso, 1991.

———. *The Fragile Absolute: Or Why the Christian Legacy is Worth Fighting For.* London: Verso, 2000.

———. *In Defense of Lost Causes.* London: Verso, 2007.

———. *The Indivisible Remainder: An Essay on Schelling and Related Matters.* London: Verso, 1996.

———. *On Belief.* London: Routledge, 2001.

———. *The Parallax View.* Cambridge: MIT Press, 2006.

———. *Plague of the Fantasies.* New York: Verso, 1997.

———. "The Politics of Truth, or, Alain Badiou as a Reader of St. Paul." In *The Ticklish Subject: The Absent Center of Political Ontology*, 127–70. New York: Verso, 1999.

———. *The Puppet and the Dwarf: The Perverse Core of Christianity*. Cambridge: MIT Press, 2002.

———. *Tarrying With the Negative: Kant, Hegel, and the Critique of Ideology*. Durham, NC: Duke University Press, 1993.

———. *The Sublime Object of Ideology*. London: Verso, 1989.

———. *The Ticklish Subject: The Absent Center of Political Ontology*. New York: Verso, 1999.

———. *Welcome to the Desert of the Real*. London: Verso, 2001.

———. "Why are Laibach and NSK not Fascists?" *M'ARS-Casapis Moderne Galerij* 5:3.4 (1993) 1–12.

Index

abortion, 35, 66
adult baptism, 151
altar calls, 19–20, 75, 78–80, 87, 83, 151
Althusser, Louis, 23n9, 57n22
American democracy, driven by
    antagonism rather than ideals,
    25
American Evangelical Christianity
    (Noll), 14
American Family Association, 3n6, 104
American Patriots' Bible, 106
Anabaptist impulse, 180
Ancient Evangelical Call, 7
antagonism, at core of ideology, 25–26
Apostle, The (dir., Duvall), 74
arrogance, 71–72
atheists, militant, 3n8
atonement, 142–43
    emergence of, as evangelical
        emphasis, 16
    sacrificial aspects of, Protestants
        playing down, 77

Badiou, Alain, 181–82
Balthasar, Hans Urs von, 134–38
baptism, adult, 151
Barna, George, xiv n8
Barth, Karl, 63–64n35, 131–34, 136,
    138, 162
base communities, 157
Battle for the Bible, The (Lindsell), 51,
    62n32
Bebbington, David, 13, 49, 76, 101

belief plus practice, shaping communal
    life, xv
Bible. *See also* Scripture
    avoiding the divinizing of, 140–41
    infallibility of, through Jesus Christ,
        138
    reading of, 139–40
Bible Church movement, 50
Biblicism (Biblical positivism,
    Bibliolatry), 53n14
Body Politics (Yoder), 162
Borat: Cultural Learnings of America for
    Make Benefit Glorious Nation
    of Kazakhstan (dir., Charles),
    32–33, 70
Bosch, David, 141
Boyd, Greg, 100
Bridge Illustration, 78
Bright, Bill, 78
Bush, George W., 2, 14, 191
    supporting notion of a Christian
        nation, 104–5
    as symbol of evangelicalism, xi,
        66–70

Caffeine-Free Diet Coke, xxi–xxii
Calvin, John, 85–86
capitalism. *See also* evangelical
    capitalism
    Caffeine-Free Diet Coke as
        metaphor for, xxii
    evangelicals' alliance with, 113–16
    evangelicals shaped by
        Christianizing of, 119

217